Romantic Horizons

ROMANTIC HORIZONS

Aspects of the Sublime in English
Poetry and Painting, 1770–1850

James B. Twitchell

University of Missouri Press
Columbia, 1983

Library of Congress Cataloging in Publication Data

Twitchell, James B., 1943–
    Romantic Horizons.

    Bibliography: p.
    Includes index.
    1. English poetry—19th century—History and
criticism.   2. Sublime, The.   3. Romanticism—England.   4. Painting, Modern—19th century—England.
5. Painting, English.   I. Title.
PR575.S77T88   1983   759.2   83-3679
ISBN 0-8262-0411-2

For Kate and Elizabeth

Contents

Illustrations

Preface

I believe that one of the central concerns of romanticism was, and still is, in Wallace Stevens's words, "How does one stand / To behold the sublime?" I intend first to define the romantic sublime, then radically narrow my study by concentrating on only one aspect, the visual, to see if there is any correlation between what the poets envisioned and what their fellow painters beheld. To do this I will have to compress and condense a good deal: not only will I treat just the visual or "spectacular" aspect of the sublime, I will concentrate specifically on one element, how the romantic artist's eyes lift from the palpable designs of natural landscape to the gathering activity at the horizon. I hope to show that one of the major developments in the nineteenth century, as important as the Renaissance substitution of a painted sky for the eternally golden heavens of medieval art, was that when the English romantic artists set aside the Claude-glass of Augustan landscapists they saw a remarkably similar panorama. And this new panorama was both the cause and the result of the rapid establishment of an aesthetic category distinct from the beautiful, the majestic, and the picturesque—the sublime.

My other interest is in the psychological component of the subliming process, for as the "eye" goes up to the horizon, the "I" goes to the threshold of elevated consciousness. To be sublimed is not to be consumed, however; in fact, the sublime experience is not apocalyptic or mystical, as critics argued a generation ago: it does not take one permanently across the boundary; it is not transcendent. It is only to be transported to the edge of new consciousness. In other words, just as the horizon separates the natural from the "heavenly," the sublime separates, or rather mediates between, the conscious and the "mystical." Thus in this

study I hope to be able to answer the other questions posed by
Stevens:

> But how does one feel [to behold the sublime]?
> One grows used to the weather,
> The landscape and that;
> And the sublime comes down
> To the spirit itself,
>
> The spirit and space,
> The empty spirit
> In vacant space.
> What wine does one drink?
> What bread does one eat?
>
> (*The American Sublime*, 1953)

Although the sublime experience was in no way a privileged
English eucharist, I am going to neglect almost totally the philosophical and psychological contributions of the Germans, and
only briefly refer to the intriguing applications of the Americans.
For not only was the sublime a principal component of American
Transcendentalism, it was also visually central to what has, since
the 1950s, been called the Luminist Movement, the culminating
phase of Hudson River painting. To compress things still further,
I am going to pair up specific works of only five poets with five
painters. However, with the exception of Blake (whom I take to
be a severe critic of the sublime in both verbal and visual media),
I will not treat the paintings as illustrations or illuminations of
the texts, but rather as pictures in a tableau, images in a pattern,
at the best parallel texts.

Whom did I choose and why? Since my major interest is in poetry, I picked central works or, at least, ones in critical ascen-
dancy: Wordsworth's *Yew Trees*, Coleridge's *The Rime of the Ancient Mariner*, Byron's *Manfred*, Keats's *Endymion* (book 1), and
Shelley's *Prometheus Unbound* (Act 4). I consider them in this
sequence to give a sense of expanding vision. Admittedly, this order is the stuff of criticism, not art, and gives a neat, but contrived, sense of development. To counteract this, I treat the
painters out of chronological sequence. Where the usual pairing
has been between Wordsworth and Constable or Shelley and

Turner, I have paired Wordsworth with Joseph Wright of Derby, Coleridge with Turner, Byron with John Martin, Keats with Alexander Cozens, and Shelley with Constable. Clearly Shelley and Constable have the least in common, and I consider them last as an act of critical hubris; if my supposition is correct, then the least sublime landscapist should show at least some affinity with the most sublime mythographer. Or so we will see.

This has been great fun to write and I would like to thank Alistair Duckworth, Richard Harter Fogle, Karl Kroeber, and Aubrey Williams for their advice and encouragement. I am also grateful to the editors of *Criticism*, *Studies in English Literature*, and the *Keats-Shelley Journal* for permission to use parts of already published articles, to the Florida Humanities Council for a number of grants, and to the staff of the Yale Center for British Art for their help.

J.B.T.
Gainesville, Fla.
May 1983

Introduction

I. The Problem with/in the Word

Tis not the giant of unwieldy size,
Piling up hills on hills to scale the skies,
That gives an image of the true sublime,
Or the best subject for the lofty rhyme;
But nature's common works, by genius dress'd,
With art selected, and with taste express'd;
Where sympathy with terror is combin'd,
To move, to melt, and elevate the mind.

—Richard Payne Knight, *Landscape. A Poem* (1794)

If Richard Payne Knight is still remembered, it is not as a poet but as an eighteenth-century aesthetician, an arbitrator of taste. Today, thinking of the sublime as a matter of taste seems to belittle its importance, but that is because the meanings of both *taste* and *sublime* have so markedly changed. For us taste is rarely a subject for philosophical treatises, and the sublime, which has always been complicated, has become only more so thanks to its application in post-structuralist criticism. Two centuries ago, however, the sublime had something specifically to do with the last line of Knight's poem: it described an acquired taste for an experience that could "move . . . melt and elevate the mind."

Although the connection of the sublime with external forms of grandeur and internal sensations of sympathy and terror was a subject of considerable serious debate around the turn of the nineteenth century, the experience has usually been characterized by the process of melting and elevating. In fact, since the fifteenth century, *sublimation* has had currency in scientific parlance, referring essentially to a complete transformation of matter into purer forms. Thus, in alchemy *sublimation* described the process of converting matter by fire; in metallurgy it explained

1

the refinement of minerals; in geology it once detailed how matter from the core of the earth dematerialized to move toward the circumference; and in chemistry it described the direct transformation of matter from solid to gas.

But in nonscientific vocabularies *sublimation* has proved more elusive, more complex, and more powerful. Understanding, let alone experiencing, the sublime has been a privilege promised by most religions and many artistic movements and, from time to time, schools of criticism. In these aesthetic and theological applications sublimation rarely refers to complete transformation but rather to a qualitative purification of awareness, an elevation "up to a threshold." But exactly who is lifted to the edge of elevated consciousness and exactly how it happens have often been subjects of heated debate. And they still are.[1]

Although its etymology is hopelessly tangled and its uses manifold, I suspect that more can be learned from the linguistic deconstruction of the word *sublimity* than from any historical reconstruction of its use in science, theology, and aesthetics. Etymologically, this word contains all the paradox of poetic transport, all the ambiguities of ecstasy. We know the morpheme *sub* may mean either "under" or "up from underneath," but what is the meaning of the root *-līme/-līminal*? Here the source seems to be both *līmen*, which means "threshold," and *līmes*, which is a "boundary" as in a fenceline between fields. Furthermore, *līmen* is also aligned to *līmus*, which refers to a "sidelong" vision—a looking off to the side of the eye. Already there is an implosive cluster of meaning and contradictions developing, for the word means both vertically up to a threshold (or lintel) and horizontally out to the margin.

These Latin roots are descriptive of places; it is from the Greek roots that we are informed of process. *Līmus* seems akin to λέχ-ριος, which describes the process of slanting, of being diagonal, oblique, crosswise. When these two etymologies, Latin for place and Greek for process, are fused we are left with a vigorous hybrid. For as Ernout and Meillet contend in one of the fullest

1. Jan Cohn and Thomas H. Miles, "The Sublime in Alchemy, Aesthetics and Psychoanalysis."

discussions of the word (*Dictionnaire étymologique de la langue latine*), sublime/sublimation describes movement upward along a diagonal path. The word thus means not just upward, and not just outward, but both upward and outward.

Since the morpheme *sub* also means "below," things can be reversed: up and out can also in a semiotic sense "signal" the opposite, down and in. How serendipitous that the builders of the arch had one prefix to mean both "up from below" and "down under," for this contradiction gives with gnomic concision the essence of "sublimity." It describes the process of physically transcending external limits while simultaneously crossing a psychological boundary of consciousness. Expressed graphically, here is a crude description of the sublime experience with its dual directions:

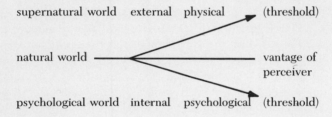

supernatural world   external   physical   (threshold)

natural world   vantage of perceiver

psychological world   internal   psychological   (threshold)

Little wonder, then, that *sublimity* became a term used in both aesthetics and psychology; a term used in the eighteenth century by Edmund Burke to describe an assemblage of physical sensations, by Immanuel Kant in the late eighteenth century to explore states of consciousness, and now by Harold Bloom to discuss the "breaking of poetic forms."

As if the word *sublime* were not sufficiently overripe, in the late nineteenth century a red herring was drawn across the etymological trail. J. A. Ward, one of those grand self-made Cambridge scholars so common two generations ago, was stymied at translating the phrase *unter der Schwelle*, as it appeared in the psychological treatises of Johann Friedrich Hebart. Ward liked the ring of the word *subliminal*, and thinking it meant "below" the threshold of consciousness (not "up to" the threshold, which would have been more appropriate), he so coined it. This was not

entirely unperspicacious because, although the usage does neglect the upward direction of the "sublime," it maintains the
sense of psychological descent. *Subliminal* thus refers to information or stimuli processed below the level of the conscious; today,
however, thanks to the use of *subliminal* in advertising jargon, its
connotations are hardly those of sublimity. It has come to mean
the sneaking of suggestion below the lintel of censorship into the
subconscious world of impulsive desire.

Sublimation, on the other hand, describes a much more dynamic psychological process. Unfortunately, no one seems to
know exactly what that is—least of all the people who use it
most. It is an inkhorn term wrenched from its place as the noun
of *sublime* to serve the exigencies of German-English translation. To Kant, or more precisely to English translators of Kant's
works, it described the anxiety produced by the Reason's inability to process certain experience.[2] Kant himself used the term
Erhaben. The translation of *Erhaben* as *sublimation* made some
sense in the aesthetics of the sublime, but then *sublimation*—
this time the actual word—was expropriated by Sigmund Freud.
He used the term *Sublimierung*, lifted from the German (al)-
chemical vocabulary where it described material transformations. It became his word; he even thought of it as a neologism, a
personal coinage, private property, and so when he first used it
he set it off with extra letter spacing to call attention to its pecu-
liarity.[3] He was clearly concerned with the alchemical context of

2. Kant explained the ironic pleasure of the sublime in *Critique of Judgment*:
"Das Gefühl des Erhabenen ist also ein Gefühl der Unlust aus der Unangemessenheit der Einbildungskraft in der ästhetischen Grössenschätzung zu der
Schätzung durch die Vernunft und eine dabei zugleich erweckte Lust aus der
Übereinstimmung eben dieses Urtheils der Unangemessenheit des grössten
sinnlichen Vermögens mit Vernunftideen sofern die Bestrebung zu denselben
doch für uns Gesetz ist." James Creed Meredith, *Kant's "Critiques of Aesthetic
Judgement,"* translated this as: "The feeling of the sublime is, therefore, at once a
feeling of displeasure, arising from the inadequacy of the imagination in the aesthetic estimation of magnitude to attain to its estimation by reason, and a simultaneously awakened pleasure, arising from this very judgment of the inadequacy
of the greatest faculty of sense being in accord with ideas of reason, in so far as the
effort to attain to these is for us a law" (p. 106).
    3. Here is Freud's definition from "'Civilized' Sexual Morality" (1908): "Man
nennt diese Fähigkeit, das ursprünglich sexuelle Ziel gegen ein anderes, nicht
mehr sexuelles, aber psychisch mit ihm verwandtes, zu vertauschen, die

"transformation to purity," because the word describes the process by which sexual energy (libido) is redirected (cathected) by the superego away from the self (narcissism) toward higher social ends. This tells us a good deal more about Freud's high Victorianism than about his talents as a wordsmith: social aims are higher, purer, than individual ones. What we call civilization is thus the result of sublimation—redirected eros creates culture. By the 1930s Freud had become so convinced of the word's applicability that he forgot the letter spacing and reduced the ever-hydrating flow of definitions. In *Civilization and Its Discontents*, he became lucidly succinct: "Die Triebsublimierung ist ein besonders hervorstechender Zug der Kulturentwicklung sie mache es möglich, dass höhere psychische Tätigkeiten, wissenschaftliche, künstlerische, ideologische, eine so bedeutsame Rolle im Kulturleben spielen." James Strachey translated this passage as, "Sublimation of instinct is an especially conspicuous feature of cultural development; it is what makes it possible for higher physical activities, scientific, artistic, or ideological, to play such an important part in civilized life."[4]

I mention the influence of Kant and Freud because some important recent interpretations of the sublime have rested on their theories, producing, I think, a fascinating ripple in the stream (flood?) of romantic criticism. Both Kant's *Erhaben* and Freud's *Sublimierung* were introduced into English via the sublime/sublimation transformation, yet the implied German meanings of perplexed reason and of sexual displacement in the service of social goals have been sloughed off. It may be time to return to the English word *sublime* as it was used in the early nineteenth century to refer to a uniquely individual experience, to describe a particular affective response to the sight of natural objects. These German theories, especially Freud's, are des-

---

Fähigkeit zur S u b l i m i e r u n g." James Strachey, *The Standard Edition of the Complete Psychological Works of Sigmund Freud*, translates this as "this capacity to exchange its original sexual aim for another one, which is no longer sexual but which is psychically related to the first aim, is called the capacity for sublimation" [Sublimierung] (9:187).

    4. Sigmund Freud, *Gesammelte Werke*, 14:457, translated by Strachey, *Standard Edition*, 21:97.

tined, I think, to create serious linguistic as well as psychological problems when applied to the aesthetics of romanticism.

Recently there have been two important works that commit this mistake of settling a German definition onto the English word: Thomas Weiskel's *The Romantic Sublime: Studies in the Structure and Psychology of Transcendence* and Stuart A. Ende's *Keats and the Sublime*. In a Freudian interpretation, Weiskel initially subdivides the sublime into "positive," in which sexual energies are successfully cathected away from the self to "other-directed" goals, and "negative," in which the erotic impulse leads inward to become acute self-consciousness. I would not contend that this kind of structure cannot produce interesting results (it can and does), but it is not really informative. It does not tell us much about the art; instead it translates one mythic situation, the experience in the poem, into another, the hermeneutics of Freud. It may be important that Wordsworth suffers from "phallic melancholy," or that romanticism is "orally fixated," or that William Collins "wishfully denies what Freud found to be the major distress of the primal scene, the perception of the female as lacking the phallus which leads normally to an acute intensification of castration anxiety" (p. 113), but those are insights into something other than the text. When the Freudian mythology runs out, Weiskel describes the sublime in semiotic terms (yet more jargon): the positive or metonymic sublime "displaces its excess of signified into a dimension of congruity which may be spatial or temporal," while the negative or metaphoric sublime "resolves the discourse by substitution." While we are still left wondering about these words, "the anxiety of poetic influence" is invoked. Now the results improve, for in describing the sublime the romantic poet must break the miltonic code and be original. *The Romantic Sublime* is still an interesting book; the spirits of Kant and Freud are very active, and the hands of Bloom and Hartman are very much in evidence (they even helped prepare the manuscript after Weiskel's untimely death), but the work never quite jells, and often the most interesting observations are suffocated in dense terminology.

Stuart Ende's *Keats and the Sublime* is easier for me to feel

uneasy about. When Ende discusses Keats in the context of sublimity from Milton to Yeats, his argument is interesting and informative, but then Ende's psychosexual interpretation almost over-
whelms the text with external apparatus. Again, I think there are
problems caused by a misunderstanding of Freud; his *sublimation* does not refer to the joys of "being sublimed in the ecstasy
that is poetic fire while retaining one's sentient being" (p. xiv),
but rather to the redirection of eros toward social ends. When
Ende writes that one of "the central elements that comprises
Keats' poetic is the apposition between identification as a mode
of internalization and the repression required by an antithetical
ideal," he risks incurring semantic aphasia in even the most sympathetic of readers. In this book we learn literary history, a little
psychology, and a good deal about Keats, but relatively little
about the sublime experience *in* poetry.

As an admittedly old-fashioned reader, I am much more at ease
with the "dated" words of Samuel Holt Monk and Marjorie Hope
Nicolson because they were more concerned with the sublime
experience as described by the poet rather than as interpreted
via some system. Monk's thorough, compendious, and a bit tiring
scholarship in *The Sublime: A Study of Critical Theories in Eighteenth Century England* has been so central to our understanding that two more recent books, David B. Morris's *The Religious
Sublime: Christian Poetry and Critical Tradition in Eighteenth
Century England* and W. P. Albrecht's *The Sublime Pleasures of
Tragedy: A Study of Critical Theory from Dennis to Keats*, often
read like a paraphrase. Yet in all the recent hubbub, Marjorie
Hope Nicolson's *Mountain Gloom and Mountain Glory: The Development of the Aesthetics of the Infinite* has been relatively neglected. This is a shame because Nicolson is wonderfully perceptive and concise. In essence she traces the relationship between
mountains and men through the eighteenth century up to the
turn of the nineteenth. However, she stops too short, as does
Monk, leaving only a brief epilogue for the romantics. Still,
working from just one thesis—the interaction of perception and
large topographic forms—she says much about the developing
relationship between man and nature, poet and the sublime. It is

here, by extending her thesis, that I should like to develop my views about the romantic vision of sublimity.

II. The Sublime in Aesthetics

sublime—derivation from *super/limas*:
"above the slime or mud of this world"—
James Beattie, *Dissertations Moral and Critical* (1783)

Sit and look out at a pleasant pastoral scene. What you can see between the middle ground and the background can be picturesque, but what you may see between the background and the beyond is the sublime.[5] As we have seen, Dr. Beattie's definition is etymologically suspect; in fact it is really quite wrong, but I like it anyway, because for all its simplification to absurdity it captures an essential aspect of romanticism. The romantic artist was very interested in nature, yes, but he was also aware that a lot of it could be mud and slime. In other words, the world "out there" may well form a landscape pleasing to the eye ("picturesque," like a picture), but without the informing mind the world can become the specter of Urthona for Blake, the "unwilling dross" for Shelley, the "sad perplexity" for Wordsworth, "darkness" for Keats, or the "dreary void" for Coleridge.

Ultimately, in romanticism, nature up too close is what confines the self, what prevents expansion. Although Blake clearly did not care about this and Wordsworth was ambivalent, nature is the boundary Shelley and Keats (and Byron, when he was not careful) attempted to transcend. Perhaps Harold Bloom said this best when he remarked that the romantic poet-hero is "a seeker not after nature but after his own mature powers, and so [he] turned away, not from society to nature, but from nature to what was more integral than nature, within himself. The widened consciousness of the poet did not give him intimations of a former union with nature or the Divine, but rather [with] his . . . self-

5. A. C. Bradley discusses the aesthetic series from "pretty" to "sublime" in "The Sublime," *Oxford Lectures on Poetry*, pp. 37–65.

less self."[6] We can see the turn to the self nowhere better than in the romantic's quest for the sublime, for the sublime is that experience both above the slush of matter and beyond the self-consciousness of the poet.

When John Ruskin in the 1850s was musing about the romantic painter's obsessions with landscapes, he imagined an intelligent contemporary entering a picture gallery for the first time. This uninitiated but perceptive viewer might well marvel, "There is something strange in the minds of these people! Nobody ever cared about blue mountains before."[7] Landscapes complete with blue mountains at the horizon had become as obsessive a subject for painters as they were for poets; they were more than subjects, they were "touchstones of taste," marks of sensibility, fit objects of sublimity. For these landscapes to be perceived as "spectacular," of course, necessitated a quite literal tilting upward of the head, as well as an extension of "depth of field." Coleridge was one of the first to understand that this was the great achievement of English landscape painters:

> in our common landscape painters . . . the foregrounds and inter-mediate distances are comparatively unattractive; while the main interest of the landscape is thrown into the background, where mountains and torrents and castles forbid the eye to proceed, and nothing tempts it to trace its way back again. But in the works of the great Italian and Flemish masters, the front and middle objects of the landscape are the most obvious and determinate, the interest gradually dies away in the background. (*Biographia Literaria*, chap. 16)

If you "look" at many of those English romantic landscapes and "read" them like a text, you will find that they are not really about "mountains and torrents and castles" at all. They are often focused on a point just where the horizontal margin of nature meets the supernatural world of the sky, where the landscape is connected with the quiet of the sky. They are about flux at the horizon; that is why the mountains are blue, that is why Mount

6. Harold Bloom, "The Internalization of the Quest Romance," in *Romanticism and Consciousness: Essays in Criticism*, ed. Harold Bloom, p. 15, and John Ower, "The Aesthetic Hero."

7. John Ruskin, *Modern Painters*, vol. 3, pt. 4, chap. 11, p. 149.

Blanc is the central image in romantic art, both pictorial and verbal; that is why Wordsworth is in the Simplon Pass, why Shelley is in the Vale of Chamonix, why Coleridge is crag-fast on Helvellyn or Byron dumbstruck at the Jungfrau. That is why low clouds and mist are all over the canvases of painters from Constable to Turner, not just as something to fill up the sky, but as the subject, the focus of our sight. The romantic attention is fixed wherever earth and sky meet because that is the break, the seam if you will, where sublimity can be achieved.

Jay Appleton, in *The Experience of Landscape*, discussed the perceptual effect of the horizon in landscape painting:

> One of the most common and effective kinds of secondary vantage-point is the *horizon*. A horizon marks the edge of an impediment to the line of vision, and such an edge invariably invites the suggestion that the impediment may not be effective, or as effective, beyond the point where it appears to end. It is a matter of common experience that the arrival at a horizon is followed by the opening up of a further field of vision, and the contemplation of a horizon therefore stimulates the expectation that such an extension of the field of vision is probable, if not certain, wherever a horizon is reached. This expectation relates particularly to that field of vision which lies beyond, that is, in the same direction as, but further than, the horizon concerned. After all, in so far as it is further vision in *this* direction which the horizon frustrates, it is the resumption of vision in this direction which is most immediately suggested by the surmounting of the obstacle. The contemplation of a horizon therefore directs the attention particularly to speculation about what lies *beyond* it, and the horizon itself seems to be the key which can provide the answer to such speculation.[8]

It is one thing to speculate on what ought to be the effect of the horizon; it is quite another to observe in various paintings that some shift has actually occurred. Clearly some changes in romantic landscapes are undeniable: triumphal arches and vegetal masses that block and channel the spectator's view became progressively less popular; gradations of color called *sfumato* became less common, with a new emphasis on bringing distance forward; vantage points were lowered and perspective collapsed; frontal

8. Jay Appleton, *The Experience of Landscape*, pp. 89–90.

planes interpenetrated each other with less emphasis on margin
and line. But were these changes the results of shifting sensibilities or simply changes in fashion?

Very often fashion and fabric are inseparable. For instance,
what the "ha-ha" was for the eighteenth century the horizon became for the early nineteenth. The "ha-ha" was an artificial
trench or dry moat dug in the middle ground of the manor house
estate: it was a sunken fence. Its practical purpose was to form a
barrier to keep the farm animals from trespassing on the lawn,
but it also provided the inhabitants of the manor a vista in which
there was no ostensible demarcation between garden and park.
It removed the fence and all that the fence implied. The "lawn"
now extended from man's domicile out into nature's pasture; all
was part of the same expanse. Horace Walpole understood the
significance of the ha-ha, for he reported of its immediate effect:
"At the moment of its creation appeared Kent, painter enough to
taste the charms of landscape, bold and opinionative enough
to dare and to dictate, and born with a genius to strike out a
great system from the twilight of imperfect essays. He leaped the
fence, and saw all nature was a garden."[9] The romantics extended this continuity to the horizon; now there was no limit between man and nature and no limit between nature and the supernatural. Just as Walpole could claim the ha-ha was the great
advance in perspective, so a generation later Byron's Childe
Harold could say, "To me, high mountains are a feeling," a continuation, an extension of the self.

To the romantic artist the sublime was a way to span the abyss
between inner and outer, and outer and "the Beyond." It was in
part a way to resolve the most pressing epistemological dilemma
of the time—the disjunction between subject and object. In fact,
the sublime experience itself is an attempt at the farthest perceptual extreme to reconcile subject and object, self and nature. Ernest Lee Tuveson has argued in *The Imagination as a Means of
Grace: Locke and the Aesthetics of Romanticism* that such sublimation was an important process in resolving the isolation left
in the wake of the disestablishment of Christian world order. For

9. Horace Walpole, *Anecdotes of Painting in England . . . to which is added
The History of Modern Taste in Gardening*, 4:137–38.

the moment subject and object are interfused, the comparing faculties cease, and unity at last may result. And the objects most capable of initiating this conjunction are those most beyond the constraining power of the intellect: the vastness of the skies, the expanse of the sea, huge mountains. The *sub*lime thus came to imply the *sur*real, and what started as an aesthetic became a metaphysic.

Given this as the direction of eighteenth-century aesthetics, we may now see that what makes Wordsworth and Turner so important is that they proclaimed in poetry, prose (especially Wordsworth's newly found fragment, "The Sublime and the Beautiful"), and painting that sublimity can be achieved by perceiving objects once thought either picturesque or else beyond the pale of perception. Wordsworth and Turner were unique in teaching the century to "feel with the eye," and their influence was profound. They secularized the sublime. As Leslie Brisman has written in *Romantic Origins*:

> We speak of the domestication of the sublime among the Romantics, and imply by the process a movement away from an earlier, undomesticated, *unheimlich* art to a later cultivated simplicity whose significance may depend on our awareness that more majestic forms have been borrowed for incidents from common life. The paradox revolves around the ambiguity of natural origins and their first or revised temporality. On the one hand the eighteenth century idea of the sublime is the original one, and the attempt to generate emotion like it out of incidents less remote or incidents of a new, fancied remoteness is a derivative. On the other hand, Wordsworth and his heirs believed that both everyday incidents and the new forms of romance they explored could compete with the old high art for an original—an earlier—place in consciousness.[10]

To understand how important this romantic shift was, let me very briefly condense the history of the sublime prior to the nineteenth century.[11]

10. Leslie Brisman, *Romantic Origins*, pp. 18–19.
11. Although much has been written on the sublime, I consider these the most important general studies, at least for an interpretation such as mine: Samuel Holt Monk, *The Sublime: A Study of Critical Theories in Eighteenth-Century England*; Christopher Hussey, *The Picturesque: Studies in a Point of View*; Kenneth Clark, *Landscape into Art*; Walter John Hipple, Jr., *The Beautiful, the Sublime*,

Longinus was supposedly the first to discuss the sublime, but in fact he said precious little about what was to be considered sublimity. His concern was for rhetorical style, and as a matter of fact, it was only after Boileau's *Traité du Sublime* (1674) that the English translated περι Υψους as "sublime."[12] Prior to this, the title of Longinus's work was built around such words as *eloquence, loftiness in speech, elegancy*, terms certainly more descriptive of his concerns than the title "On the Sublime" ever indicates. However, it must be acknowledged that Longinus, in one almost throwaway passage, does discuss what later became central in romanticism:

> Wherefore not even the entire universe suffices for the thought and contemplation within the reach of the human mind, but our imaginations often pass beyond the bounds of space, and if we survey our life on every side and see how much more it everywhere abounds in what is striking, and great, and beautiful, we shall soon discover the purpose of our birth. (chap. 35)

Longinus was neglected as an aesthetician until the neoclassical theorists became interested in what determined "taste" in art. Here, as R. S. Crane first mentioned, theories of the sublime developed in two directions: on one hand, the rhetorical sublime was investigated by critics like Dennis, the Warton brothers, Lowth, Young, Reynolds, Duff (to name only a few), who used the concept to investigate "qualities of the soul in art" (taste, rules, traditions), while another group, composed of figures like Addison, Hume, Akenside, Baillie, Burke, Gerard, and Reid, attempted to explain sublimity as an affective response to natural phenomena (states of consciousness, pleasures of the imagina-

---

and the Picturesque in Eighteenth-Century British Aesthetic Theory; Elizabeth Wheeler Manwaring, *Italian Landscape in Eighteenth Century England: A Study Chiefly of the Influence of Claude Lorrain and Salvator Rosa on English Taste, 1700–1800*; Edward Malins, *English Landscaping and Literature, 1660–1840*; John Robert Watson, *Picturesque Landscape and English Romantic Poetry*; Appleton, *Experience of Landscape*; John Barrell, *The Idea of Landscape and the Sense of Place, 1730–1840*; and James A. W. Heffernan, "Reflections on Reflections in English Romantic Poetry and Painting."

12. The two English translations of *On the Sublime* prior to Boileau's *Traité du Sublime* were John Hall, *On the Height of Eloquence* (1622), and John Pulteney, *Of the Loftiness and Elegancy of Speech* (1680).

tion, and so on.[13] It is this second group we are interested in, and
it is, of course, Edmund Burke who is here the most important
for his transformation of the ideas developed by Addison (*Spectator*, nos. 411–21) into a coherent pattern.

Burke's thesis in his *Philosophical Enquiry into the Origin of
Our Ideas of the Sublime and Beautiful* is deceptively clear. After
discussing what constitutes "taste," he separates the sublime
from the beautiful: the beautiful is small, smooth, polished,
light, and delicate, while the sublime is huge, rugged, irregular,
dark, and chaotic. Pleasure emanates from perceptions of the
beautiful, but what can come from the sublime? For Burke,

> Whatever is fitted in any sort to excite the ideas of pain and danger,
> that is to say, whatever is in any sort terrible, or is conversant with
> terrible objects, or operates in a manner analogous to terror, is a
> source of the *sublime*; that is, it is productive of the strongest emo-
> tions which the mind is capable of feeling. I say the strongest emo-
> tion, because I am satisfied the ideas of pain are much more power-
> ful than those which enter on the part of pleasure. (pt. 1, sec. 7)

But why would anyone want to experience this sublime? The answer is that within terror there is an element of delight, provided
of course that there is no real threat of personal harm. Hence a
painting of a shipwreck, or a fire, or an avalanche, or an erupting
volcano is sublime to a viewer in the gallery, but not to "real-life"
sailors, citizens, and farmers who presumably are experiencing
the catastrophe. The viewer's delight is complex; it is partly the
thrill of "there but for the grace of God go I," partly the result
of overcoming anxiety, and partly the joy of moving out of self-
consciousness into something beyond. It is this last aspect that
fascinated the poets and painters in the early nineteenth century.

As one could have predicted, there was in aesthetic scholarship the typically spirited debate over where sublimity resides—
in the object itself (Addison) or in the perceiver (Alison)—but as
things developed this became almost beside the point. What is

13. On the distinction between the "rhetorical" and the "natural" sublime, see
Ronald S. Crane's review of Samuel Holt Monk, *The Sublime: A Study of Critical
Theories in Eighteenth-Century England*, p. 165.

clear, what is revolutionary, is that here, for the first time, an acknowledgment was being made that what had previously been a religious experience (transcendence) is actually a perceptual phenomenon. It is visual first, then visionary. It is literally spectacular. This "displaced Protestantism," as Bloom has called it, suggests that a higher consciousness is possible, that the spiritual unity denied to mankind in the Fall is at least partially recoverable—at least temporarily. The sublime is a redemptive experience, what Schiller saw at the center of romanticism—*die Kunst des Unendlichen*, an individual aesthetic experience, democratic, amoral, an especially reconciliatory event. All it takes is the willing man of feeling and the grandeur of objective nature. What Locke had separated would finally put us together.

III. The Sublime in Pre-Romantic Art

Each epoch has its peculiar handwriting or handwritings, which, if one could interpret them, would reveal a character, even a physical appearance, as from the fragment of a fossil palaeontologists can reconstruct the entire animal. . . . And what else is handwriting but the concentrated expression of the personality of an individual? Of all the sciences or pseudo-sciences which presume to interpret the character and destiny of man from signs, graphology is surely the one which has the soundest foundation. Handwriting is taught, and certain of its characteristics belong to the general style of the period, but the personality of the writer, if it is at all relevant, does not fail to pierce through. The same happens with art.—Mario Praz, *Mnemosyne: The Parallel Between Literature and the Visual Arts*

The usual method of approaching romantic sublimity is via the history of aesthetics or faculty psychology, but I think a more fruitful approach, at least for my purposes, is by interpreting the handwriting of art. What is singular about the sublime experience is that it represents movement across precincts of consciousness. Martin Price has rather grandly called the sublime "a surpassing of conventions of reasonable limits, an attempt to come to terms with the unimaginable."[14] I hope to show by looking at visual and verbal texts (romantic "handwriting") that this is not entirely true. The surpassing of limits does "throw the mind back on itself," but the experience does not become inexplicable, or how can it ever be described, let alone conceived? The moment of the sublime is that moment just before the visible dissolves and with it the poet's ability to "make sense" of impressions in words.[15] But it is *not* apocalyptic or mystical or millennial or unimaginable.

Milton, of course, was the master of the sublime image, and this is why so many romantic poets tried to imitate and so many romantic painters tried to illustrate his works. Here is the standard example proffered by eighteenth-century aestheticians:

> On heavenly ground that stood, and from the shore
> They view'd the vast immeasurable abyss,
> Outrageous as a sea, dark, wasteful, wild,
> Up from the bottom turn'd by furious winds,
> And surging waves, as mountains, to assault
> Heaven's height, and with the centre mix the pole
>   Silence, ye troubled waves, and thou deep, peace,
> Said then th'omnific Word, your discord end.
>   Nor staid; but on the wings of Cherubim
> Uplifted in paternal glory rode
> Far into Chaos, and the world unborn;
> For Chaos heard his voice: him all his train
> Follow'd in bright procession, to behold
> Creation, and the wonders of his might.

14. Martin Price, "The Sublime Poem: Pictures and Powers," p. 194.

15. Usually the sublime was thought to be visual (spectacular), and this caused aestheticians at the end of the century some concern. Could it be aural as well? Burke and others claim yes, but it is far more difficult to explain: the best they could say was that it was "dead sound," like the pause between thunderclaps, or else a shrill roar, like Wordsworth's "stationary blast of the waterfall." So Leigh Hunt, for instance, was clearly distressed by what he took to be the botching of sublimity at the end of Mozart's *Don Giovanni* and felt the need to reprimand the stage director. This may also be why Beethoven, who was clearly concerned about interpretations of sublimity, described the progression of the Sixth Symphony with program notes. He wanted the listener to be aware that these sounds should go to the very threshold of hearing. I make this point because sublime/ sublimation is a vision/visionary experience not from theory, but from practice.

> Then staid the fervid wheels, and in his hand
> He took the golden compasses, prepar'd
> In God's eternal store, to circumscribe
> The universe, and all created things:
> One foot he center'd, and the other turn'd
> Round through the vast profundity obscure,
> And said, Thus far extend, thus far thy bounds,
> This by thy just circumference, O world

Initially the painters, from Joseph Wright of Derby to John Martin, had an easier job of it—all they had to do was to "copy" Milton's text. The poets had problems. After all, most of them did not have the brazenness to stand beside God and look *down* on the horizon. What characteristically happened to the first poetic generation after Milton was that, desirous of achieving his heroic scale, they called up the personified muse (Solitude, Liberty, Fancy, Death) to release them from constrictions, but that was about as far as they could go. For example, here is William Collins with a prayer to music:

> Arise as in that elder time,
> Warm, energic, chaste, sublime . . .
> O bid our vain endeavors cease;
> Revive the just designs of Greece.
> Return in all thy simple state.

or Edward Young celebrating man's transcendent possibilities:

> Who looks on That, and sees not in himself
> An awful Stranger, a Terrestrial God? . . .
> I gaze, and, as I gaze, my mounting Soul
> Catches strange Fire, Eternity, at Thee;
> And drops the World—or rather, more enjoys:
> How chang'd the Face of Nature! how improv'd!
> What seem'd a Chaos, shines a glorious World,
> Oh, what a World, an Eden; heighten'd all!
> It is another Scene! another Self!

or James Thompson encountering his "other" self:

> He comes! he comes! in every breeze the power
> Of philosophic Melancholy comes!
> His near approach the sudden-starting tear,

The glowing cheek, the mild dejected air,
The softened feature, and the beating heart
Pierced deep with many a virtuous pang declare.
O'er all the soul his sacred influence breathes,—
Inflames imagination, through the breast
Infuses every tenderness, and far
Beyond dim earth exalts the swelling thought.
Ten thousand thousand fleet ideas, such
As never mingled with the vulgar dream,
Crowd fast into the mind's creative eye.
As fast the correspondent passions rise.

As Martin Price has shown in detail, in each case we can witness a nascent romantic interest in sublimation—a struggle to get free, to get loose, to get to the threshold, to frame the visionary encounter; but it never quite works. In part this is because the poet is constrained by the demands of personification, in part because he cannot go "up" into the realm still consigned to the Christian mythos, and he cannot go "in" because that is not "poetic." It was William Cowper who near the end of *The Task* came closest to capturing a sublimity freed of received myth and form. Here is the almost sublime, almost threshold, vision as it starts in the actual world:

Rivers of gladness water all the earth,
And clothe all climes with beauty; the reproach
Of barrenness is past. The fruitful field
Laughs with abundance.

The scene is set firmly in nature, in the world of forms, and soon the lifting occurs. First the poet loses the controls of "right reason,"

Content indeed to sojourn while he must
Below the skies, but having there his home.
The world o'erlooks him in her busy search
Of objects, more illustrious in her view;
And occupied as earnestly as she,
Though sublimely, he o'erlooks the world;

then the inner spirit is set free:

Its warfare is within. There unfatigu'd
His fervent spirit labors. There he fights,
And there obtains fresh triumphs o'er himself.

This has all the promise of natural Methodism, if you will, "en-thusiasmos" for the common man, yet it is so vague and image-less. What was needed was a sense of form and order, albeit an imaginary one, by which to establish a new temporal and spatial disposition. What was needed was the painter's eye, a sensitivity to image, not Milton's time-worn imagery and phraseology. What was needed was a new sense of the daemonic, what Geoffrey Hartman has called the ability to picture "the confrontation with a second self in the form of genius loci or persona."[16]

What also limits neoclassical descriptions of sublimity, what al-lows the sublime to degenerate into the gothic on the one hand or the picturesque on the other, is an unwillingness (inability?) to take risks, to see in a new way. What was needed was visionality, not visuality—a landscape not only of the external world but of how the perceiver saw that world. The artist must return himself to participate in his "text" not as a spectator but as an organizer. The artist needed to leave his Claude-glass at home, needed to stop climbing those hills in search of downward "prospect," needed to stop "sweeping the horizon from commanding height"; in short he needed to commit himself.[17] Essentially, as Ruskin later pointed out, the pathetic fallacy might well be the price of new vision. When the painter is overly concerned with propor-tion, order, taste, good sense, and keeping himself "at a dis-tance," no sublimity can result. This is true as well with the poet whose dedication to objectivity overrides his fidelity to feeling. Ironically, the separation of the artist from his work was the tri-umph of Augustan criticism, but as long as the artist believed himself to be primarily a technician, no landscape could contain sublimity and no poem could describe it. The one thing that Col-

16. Geoffrey H. Hartman, "Romantic Poetry and the *Genius Loci*," in *Beyond Formalism*, p. 333.
17. Of the many introductions to the importance of prospect in eighteenth-century poetry and painting, I have found the most succinct to be Barrell, *Landscape and the Sense of Place*, pp. 1–63.

lins, Dyer, Cowper, and Thomson needed, the one thing that
Richard Wilson, Thomas Rowlandson, Francis Wheatley, and
Francis Towne lacked, was a willingness to be incomplete, to al-
low inequilibrium, to be visionary and spectacular.

It is to emphasize the importance of vision in the romantic
sublime that I have sought to pair off painting and poetry, not as
illustrations of each other but as examples of a change in "handwriting." I believe one can find a vocabulary of vision, a correspondence of sight, a sense of pattern that is romantic, for
indeed, as Diderot said, "one does discover the poets in painters and the painters in poets." The poems I have chosen—
Wordsworth's *Yew Trees*, Coleridge's *The Rime of the Ancient
Mariner*, Byron's *Manfred*, book 1 of Keats's *Endymion*, act 4 of
Shelley's *Prometheus Unbound*—are "about" sublimity only in
the broadest sense, and I have attempted to link them with
paintings that all deal with the world "out there" just at the edge
of imagelessness—Joseph Wright's *A Cavern: Evening*, J. M. W.
Turner's *The Slave Ship—Slavers Throwing Overboard the
Dead and Dying*, John Martin's *Manfred and the Witch of the
Alps*, Alexander Cozens's *The Cloud*, and John Constable's *Study
of Clouds and Trees*. With the exception of Wordsworth and
Wright, these artists are all exploring the horizon, and in these
works the reader/viewer is lifted up to, and often almost over,
that threshold. True to the dual nature of the "sublime," as the
"eye" goes up and out, we are vouchsafed an inner vision, a psychological vision, as the "I" goes down and in.

IV. The Psychological Structure of Sublimity

> Wordsworth would never have had any great effect on me, if he had
> merely placed before me beautiful pictures of natural scenery. Scott
> does this still better than Wordsworth, and a very second-rate land-
> scape (i.e., landscape painting) does it more effectually than any
> poet.—J. S. Mill, *Autobiography*

Mill is correct. If sublime *effect* is what you are after, it will
always be initially produced more efficiently by the painter.

Even so, the painter's two-dimensional sublimity ultimately depends on a deeper structure. Although recent criticism has often become mired in the rhetoric of "altered states of consciousness," I should discuss this concept at least in passing, for it is the psychological corollary of the visual experience: it is the down and in part of the experience.

An "altered state of consciousness" is quite simply one in which the individual "clearly feels a *qualitative* shift in his pattern of mental functioning, that is, he feels not just a quantitative shift (more or less alert, more or less visual imagery, sharper or duller, *etc.*), but also that some quality or qualities of his mental process are different."[18] This shift is pronounced and often traumatic. In each of the poems I will discuss, there is a clear-cut change in the "hero of consciousness" or "aesthetic hero," as he is sometimes known, before the sublime experience can occur. This is because the "sense sublime" is something created by the perceiver. In Coleridge's words: "I meet, I *find* the Beautiful—but I give, contribute, or rather attribute the Sublime. No object of Sense is sublime in itself; but only as far as I make it a symbol of some Idea. The circle is a beautiful figure in itself; it becomes sublime, when I contemplate eternity under that figure."[19] Hence the Ancient Mariner falls into a "swoon"; Manfred becomes "senseless"; Endymion starts to "dream"; Prometheus "wakes up"; and even Wordsworth must forget his conscious self, for all are participating in acts in which normal, waking awareness is set aside so that the imagination can function and the altered level of awareness be achieved. But, as we shall see, "normal" consciousness is in no way obliterated; rather it is momentarily subverted.

In Western psychology we generally recognize only two major states of mental functioning, consciousness and subconsciousness. In fact, as Carlyle perceptively claimed in *Characteristics* (1830), making this basic distinction was one of the major achievements of the early nineteenth century. Today, although we are able to distinguish gradations of control within each major

18. Charles T. Tart, "Introduction" to *Altered States of Consciousness*, p. 2.
19. S. T. Coleridge, "Unpublished Fragments on Aesthetics," ed. Thomas M. Raysor.

division (for instance, we recognize the difference between dreaming and sleeping, stupor and coma, reverie and daydreaming), we still generally insist on just these two major levels, conscious and subconscious. When we separate and label gradations of consciousness, we are creating what is called by psychologists a metapsychology, that is, a system of awareness levels. For instance, a contemporary metapsychologist, Stanley Krippner, has constructed a system that includes some twenty mental states within the two major modes of consciousness. The highest or most "ego liberated" of these states is what he calls "expanded consciousness," and he remarks that today this state is "most frequently brought about experimentally by the use of psychedelic drugs and plants."[20] Keats described something rather similar in the "Pleasure Thermometer" passage in *Endymion*, except that nature was viewed, not digested.

In the early nineteenth century these experiences of expanded states of consciousness were also generated, but only occasionally, by drugs. The romantic artists were fascinated with attaining and holding what they considered to be a new level of consciousness. In fact, as Michael Pafford has shown in *Inglorious Wordsworths*, the nineteenth century was full of secular enthusiasts eager for what they took to be ecstasy for the common man. They did not know this, but the "new" state they achieved was not peculiar to the West. Eastern religions had been based on the same search for elevation to the threshold and then release. In Zen it was "satori" or "kensho"; in Yoga, "samadhi" or "moksha"; and in Taoism, "the absolute tao." So in a historical sense it was predictable that, in the generations of romantics that followed, artists like Allen Ginsberg and Alan Watts would go to the East to achieve what the first generation had often found just above nature. In fact, in the twentieth century there have usually been three routes to sublimity: for many it has been through the Eastern religions, but for D. H. Lawrence, Henry Miller, and others it was through the mythology of sex; while for William James, Aldous Huxley, and the collegiates of the early 1970s it was through drugs. In fact, the word *psychedelic* (*psyche*, "mind"; *delos*,

20. Stanley Krippner, "Altered States of Consciousness," in *The Highest State of Consciousness*, ed. John White, p. 5.

"manifesting") is an appropriate description of the psychological effect of the sublime experience whether found by Wordsworth on Mount Snowdon or experienced pharmacologically by the hippy in Haight-Ashbury. Only the retellings differ.[21] Of course, it is in the language and depth of those retellings that we find what is particular to romanticism and singular about the poets.

It is in this context that one can best understand the great revival of Plato and the Alexandrine Neoplatonists at the turn of the nineteenth century. Plato had analyzed something like the sublime in the *Symposium* and *Phaedrus*, and Plotinus had popularized this sublime; as we will see, Platonic mythography very often in the nineteenth century became the vehicle of description. But even when the romantics attempted to retell their experiences in Platonic myths they encountered the same negative attitudes toward heightened consciousness that are prevalent today. In fact a century later we are still reticent to admit even in our language that such states could exist. For example, although Sanskrit has about twenty different words to express elevated consciousness well below the transcendent, we have precious few. The Western, Christian world has had a long-standing fear of what ultimately has been considered an antisocial experience or a bizarrely religious one. One need only recall the treatment of the Quakers or the Methodists, whose "inner light" experiences made them outcasts for generations, to realize how deep our fear of somebody else's sublimity is. In part, this is because we have insisted on treating expanded consciousness as a religious phenomenon. It is not. It is a shift of consciousness that occurs, as Blake said, only "when the doors of perception are cleansed."[22]

To have some idea how hard the Western world has pushed

21. R. A. Durr, *Poetic Vision and the Psychedelic Experience*, compares the descriptions of drug-induced sublimity with those of the romantic poets and finds startling similarities.

22. Blake, as I intend to show in Chapter 1, was not interested in the sublime (at least as I'm defining it), but surely, as Kenneth Walker has said, "It is strange that Freud [the other great romantic allegorist], who discovered so much about subconscious states, should not have postulated the existence of levels of consciousness *above* as well as *below* the level on which we usually live." See "The Supra-Conscious State," in White, ed., *The Highest State of Consciousness*, p. 15. But Freud, for all of his revolutionary theories, did not tackle experiences that even for him might have proved too ethereal. He referred to the sublime in passing as the "oceanic feeling"; and that, as far as he was concerned, was that.

against recognizing this "released" state of consciousness, one need only review the history of Western "mysticism," for that is how we have often labeled sublimation. The "mystic" experience is of course *beyond* the threshold, but we continually confuse the "sub-" and "supra-" liminal. In romantic criticism this state of consciousness is usually described as "apocalyptic," and a generation or so ago we were continually being told of Wordsworth's apocalyptic vision, or Shelley's, or even Keats's, and it was assumed that really nothing more could be said. At the poetic extreme was John Clare; at the pictorial extreme was Richard Dadd—and both were considered "divinely mad." In fact, we almost have to categorize them as "mad" or sacred because no sane person should find such release without losing his mind or gaining religion. As R. D. Laing has said, we have tended to fear this kind of sub-liminal experience instead of realizing that it is a mode of perception, a level of consciousness: "The person going through ego-loss or transcendental experiences may or may not become in different ways confused. Then he might legitimately be regarded as mad. But to be mad is not necessarily to be ill, notwithstanding that in our culture the two categories have become confused. It is assumed that if a person is mad (whatever that means), then *ipso facto* he is ill (whatever that means)."[23] Alan Watts saw another problem in calling this kind of experience "mystical," or apocalyptic, for considering it so "confuses it with visions of another world, or of Gods and angels."[24] To say that a "released" state of consciousness is "mystical," then, is to say that it is either mad and can be forgotten or is religious and cannot be understood. In either case, we have refused to confront supraconscious experiences as really occurring in the here and now, as something not privileged but open to all.

I think it possible to consider the perception of ᵗʰᵉ sublime as simply one in a number of sub-threshold experiences, except that this particular one occurs rather late in the development of individual consciousness. In this sense it is a rite of passage in which the romantic "hero of consciousness" must move to some new level of awareness. As we shall see in the poetry, this protagonist

23. R. D. Laing, *The Politics of Experience*, p. 96.
24. Alan Watts, *This Is It and Other Essays on Zen*, p. 54.

is not usually the ephebe of puberty (here Endymion is the exception) but rather the mature man (the Ancient Mariner, Manfred, Prometheus); in fact he is the poet himself. Although his initial response to experiencing his new level of awareness is fraught with anxiety, the results are ultimately self-actualizing. Geoffrey Hartman has explained this paradox using the term *liminal* where I would have preferred "*sub*liminal":

> During this *liminal* or *marginal* phase the candidate is segregated and exposed to spirit-powers directly without forms or mediations available to men in society. He discovers in this way both his individuality and his isolation, both selfhood and the meaning of society.
>
> If we reflect that marginality is dangerous not because it is empty but because the absence of conventional social structuring allows room for an irruption of energies society has not integrated, then we see how similar this state is to the "chaos of forms" which art explores. The artist is surely the liminal or threshold person par excellence.[25]

Victor Turner, the anthropologist, has pointed out that this kind of experience is always an ordeal, especially for the budding artist, because the "liminar" (again, I would have preferred "*sub*liminar" because the artist is not yet on the threshold—he is still a "candidate") must realize his own lack of individuality and control. He must be merged, made part of some "process structure" beyond the self. In a sense, then, the experience of the sublime is an initiation, unique in that the welcoming structure is not communal but psychological and the expression of the initiation is not through social ritual but through individual art.[26]

What exactly *is* this experience? Is it common or uncommon, constricting or liberating, learned or known, physical or metaphysical? First let me give an example in nonpoetic form. Bernard Berenson, the art collector/critic, man of letters, latter-day romantic, described something rather like the romantic sublime: "It was a morning in early summer. A silver haze shimmered and trembled over the lime trees. The air was laden with their fragrance. The temperature was like a caress. I remember—I need not recall—that I climbed up a tree stump and felt suddenly immersed in Itness. I did not call it by that name. I had no need for words. It and I were one." [27] The experience has to do with a kind of ego loss, or a loss of self-consciousness, if you will, and a simultaneous connection to something outside the self. It is of short duration, hard to explain (but not inexplicable, as Wordsworth first showed in *Tintern Abbey*), and ultimately pleasant. Here is another example, this time from Richard Bucke, a Canadian physician who went on to write one of the more interesting books on the subject, entitled *Cosmic Consciousness*. Visiting England in the spring of 1872, he had this experience while walking down a country road:

> All at once, without warning of any kind, I found myself wrapped in a flame-colored cloud. For an instant I thought of fire, an immense conflagration somewhere close by in that great city; the next, I knew that the fire was within myself. Directly afterward there came upon me a sense of exultation, of immense joyousness accompanied or immediately followed by an intellectual illumination impossible to describe . . . I saw that the universe is not composed of dead matter, but is, on the contrary, a living Presence; I became conscious in myself of eternal life. It was not a conviction that I would have eternal life, but a consciousness that I possessed eternal life then; I saw that all men are immortal; that the cosmic order is such that without any peradventure all things work together for the good of each and all, that the foundation principle of the world, of all the worlds, is what we call love, and that the happiness of each and all is *in the long run* absolutely certain. The vision lasted a few seconds and was gone; but the memory of it and the sense of the reality of what it taught has remained during the quarter of a century which has since elapsed. [28]

This sounds very much like a very prosaic and even trite Shelley, or Wordsworth, or Whitman, or D. H. Lawrence, or Coleridge, or Thoreau, or Yeats, for it is—although I hesitate to use this exhausted phrase—a secular epiphany. What Bucke described is a

27. Bernard Berenson, *Sketch for a Self-Portrait*, p. 18.
28. Quoted from a privately printed account of the experience by William James in *Varieties of Religious Experience*, p. 399.

lifting out of self-consciousness into selflessness. Call it "mystic" as Dean Inge hyperbolically did, or "adamic," "numinous," or a "peak-experience" as Marghanita Laski, Rudolph Otto, and Abraham Maslow have; the descriptions tend to be trite because they are so encoded with religious abstractions.[29] But the experience itself surely is not. A final example is from Schiller, who attempts to analyze the complex flow of emotions:

> The feeling of the sublime is a mixed feeling. It is at once a painful state, which in its paroxysm is manifested in a kind of shudder, and a joyous state, that may rise to rapture, and which, without being properly a pleasure, is greatly preferred to every kind of pleasure by delicate souls. The union of two contrary sensations in one and the same feeling proves, in a peremptory manner, our moral independence. For as it is impossible that the same object should be with us in two opposite relations, so it follows that it is we *ourselves* who sustain two different relations with the object. It follows that these two opposed natures should be united in us, which, on the idea of this object, are brought into play in two perfectly opposed ways.[30]

I have in these examples attempted to stay away from what the poets themselves reported simply because quoting only the poets would have given the impression that this is an experience unique to romanticism. It is not, but many of the most interesting discussions of it are from the romantics. And the best critical explanations of the experience are only now being generated. Of these I think Albert O. Wlecke's distillation of Coleridge's view is most succinct: "The 'sense sublime' refers to an activity of the esemplastic power of the imagination during which consciousness becomes reflexively aware of itself as an interfusing energy

29. The best general works on the subject of elevated consciousness are by Marghanita Laski, *Everyday Ecstasy* and *Ecstasy: A Study of Some Secular and Religious Experiences*. Michael Paffard has, in *Inglorious Wordsworths*, detailed some similar experiences reported in the works of nineteenth- and twentieth-century literary figures such as Walter Pater, C. S. Lewis, Basil Willey, and A. L. Rowse.

30. Friedrich von Schiller, "The Sublime," in *Essays Aesthetical and Philosophical*, p. 133. For more on the Reason's inability to function in processing the sublime, see Neil Hertz "The Notion of Blockage in the Literature of the Sublime," in *Psychoanalysis and the Question of the Text: Selected Papers from the English Institute 1976–77*, ed. Geoffrey H. Hartman, pp. 62–85.

dwelling within the phenomena of nature." This definition is
even more revealing when coupled with Andrew Wilton's rather
too grand description of the effect of the sublime in Turner:
"There is no boundary beyond which things animate and inani-
mate no longer qualify as sublime: sublimity is the elevated
thought and inspired perception that resides in the mind of the
beholder, and suffuses everything it touches with grandeur."[31]
When the experience succeeds, the perceiver is released from
the anxieties of isolation and achieves momentary unity with
both his inner "self" and the world "beyond." But it does not last;
the threshold soon collapses and we are returned to the mundane.

The list of artists in the nineteenth century who had these experiences, and felt the need to record them, is not inconsider-
able. Little did Wordsworth realize, when he turned to that tree
to pull himself back from the "abyss" of altered consciousness,
that he would be fostering a generation of secular Herberts and
Crashaws. When one realizes that Tennyson also had a lifetime of
these experiences (as recorded from the early Burkean poem "On
Sublimity" to the more complex passages of *In Memoriam*) and
that he, along with Wordsworth, held the laureateship for most
of the century, one can only conclude that what had begun as an
abrupt turn in aesthetics in the eighteenth century had become
not only acceptable but a prerequisite of poetic vision.

When we attempt to fit the sublime experience into a romantic
metapsychology, the states of consciousness might be organized
like this:

liminal	mystic consciousness
sublime	elevated consciousness
natural	normal consciousness
subnatural	dream consciousness

31. Albert O. Wlecke, *Wordsworth and the Sublime*, p. 8, and Andrew
Wilton, *Turner and the Sublime*, p. 97.

While Western artists have always felt free to explore the sub-
natural world, the land of dreams, few ever dared go above.
Those who have (Dante, Milton) did so with requisite timidity
and caution, for the world above nature is the domain of God and
his angels. God is both immanent in nature and transcendent to
it, but God is singular and unique in the skies. Little wonder
then that Thomson, Collins, Cowper failed to visualize sublimity
in poetry. They were conditioned not to; the individual had
no claim to the world above. Like their landscape-painter colleagues, the most they could be was picturesque.

Northrop Frye contends that the shift in cosmic mythology
that finally allowed for the "secular sublime" to be in-visioned in
art was made by the end of the eighteenth century. Prior to that
time the poets, scientists, and theologians all worked within a supernatural structure that was based on such organizing concepts
as the Chain of Being and the Ptolemaic universe. The supernatural hierarchies that these concepts implied were maintained
even after they were proved faulty, partly because no one wanted
to tamper with a world picture that was so intertwined with morality. Frye describes the pre-romantic paradigm:

> On the top level is God, and the place of the presence of God is
> heaven. The only language that can describe this top level is analog-
> ical language, and . . . the imagery of heavenly bodies was central
> to the analogy. Next come the two worlds of nature, an upper world
> . . . where man was originally intended to live, and a lower world of
> physical nature, established as man's environment after the fall of
> Adam.

Below these, of course, on the bottom level, was Hell. This was a
very logical and conservative purview of the world, with a ready-
made morality incorporated within it: "up" is good; "down" is
bad; and "middle" becomes an ethical concept. There is simply
no room for any subliminal experiences. Man knew his place and
should stay in it. Frye continues:

> In the Romantic period this schema becomes profoundly modified.
> We can still trace the schema on four levels, but the structure be-
> comes much more ambiguous. In the first place, the tendency to

moral conventionalizing disappears: all four levels can be seen as
either ideal or demonic, or as anything between. Secondly, we have
traced the process by which the imagery of the sky ceased to have a
special kind of significance attached to it, and became simply assimilated to the rest of nature.[32]

No longer bound up in the valuative terms of the Christian hierarchy, the heavens opened up; as A. D. Nuttall has shown, they
became "a common sky."[33] And this sky developed into almost as
much a storehouse of nonreligious imagery and emblems as the
natural world had been a generation earlier. Within a matter of
years, poets became free to populate and animate the skies with
their own creations, as they had not been able to do since the
sixteenth century.

It is with considerable reason that the early nineteenth century abounds with cloud paintings and pictures of skies. The
poets, however, had a more difficult time of it, and Shelley's *The
Cloud* shows why. The poets needed something with defined
image, with specificity, something locatable: they needed a
new mythopoesis. They solved this problem by often populating
their skies with daemons. These "daemons" had nothing to do
with Christian "demons"; rather they became—in psychological
terms—projected registers of changes within the protagonist.
They are the images of sublime process. Anton Raphael Mengs,
ironically one of the most influential codifiers of neoclassicism,
first noticed how the ancients pictured spirits between the gods
and men, remarking that "at last they found the medium between deity and humanity [and] it was then that the art arrived at
the most sublime degree."[34] The romantics were, in this sense,
reviving the classical tradition, but for different reasons. What
Charles I. Patterson says about these spirits in Keats's poetry is
equally true in the poetry of Coleridge, Byron, and Shelley:

> The term "daemonic realm" is used herein simply as a metaphor for
> a particular area of activity of the human consciousness influenced
> by much that wells up from the unconscious; for, of course, Keats

32. Northrop Frye, *A Study of English Romanticism*, pp. 24–25.
33. A. D. Nuttall, *The Common Sky: Philosophy and the Literary Imagination*.
34. Anton Raphael Mengs, *Works*, trans. Joseph d'Azara, 1:34.

did not literally believe in daemons but used the idea of a daemonic world as an objective correlative to an inner proclivity within man. The term denotes trance-like states of mind like some of those which psychologists and psychiatrists now discuss. The daemonic state in Keats' poetry is a sharply focused trance in which a person still perceives specific objects and situations vividly and concretely.[35]

In fact the spirits of this "daemonic level" became almost a leit-motiv appearing above the poet-protagonist in response to changes in his perception. They became the "signification" of sublimity. So the poet of *Alastor* runs into them on his peregrinations through consciousness. They are the "wild images" he sees above the ruined temples of Ethiopia, "where marble daemons watch / The Zodiac's brazen mystery" (lines 118–19). Or they are the "fair fiends" floating through both the cosmic ether and the poet's own "deep mind." Sometimes the two worlds—the external spirit world and the internal psychic world—are so beautifully dovetailed that they seem to be one:

> . . . two eyes,
> And seemed with their serene and azure smiles
> To beckon him. (489–92)

These daemons are also akin to the ministers of cosmic thought that Coleridge describes both in *Limbo* and here in his *Religious Musings*:

> Contemplant Spirits! ye that hover o'er
> With untired gaze the immeasurable fount
> Ebullient with creative Deity!
> And ye of plastic power, that interfused
> Roll through the grosser and material mass
> In organizing surge! Holies of God!
> (And what if Monads of the infinite mind?) (402–8)

In fact, Coleridge even describes the subliming process in his *Apologia Pro Vita Sua*:

> The poet in his lone yet genial hour
> Gives to his eyes a magnifying power:

35. Charles I. Patterson, *The Daemonic in the Poetry of John Keats*, p. 11.

Or rather he emancipates his eyes
From the black shapeless accidents of size—
In unctuous cones of kindling coal,
Or smoke upwreathing from the pipe's trim bole,
 His gifted ken can see
 Phantoms of sublimity.

A long list could be made of the instances when these spirits appear as the poet-protagonist turns inward. Even Childe Harold, who confesses that he has "thought / Too long and darkly, till my brain became, / In its own eddy boiling and o'erwrought, / A whirling gulf of phantasy and flame" (3. 7), tries to cast this world outward "til he had peopled the stars." But in vain, for he learns—as does Manfred—that he has no control of the spirits "out there" because he has no control of them in his mind.

These spirits (daemons, genii, tutelary spirits) do not just appear in the major poetry of Byron, Coleridge, Keats, and Shelley, they appear in a distinct and repeatable hierarchy of places and powers. They usually inhabit five strata—subterranean, aquatic, terrestrial, aerial, and ethereal—that represent levels of consciousness, the height and depth of the sublime. What is important to remember is that they all are below the threshold of transcendence and that they form only a small structural part of the metapsychological paradigm. If we now go back to try to fit these spirits into the romantic metapsychology, the levels might look something like this:

liminal		mystic consciousness
sublime	{ ethereal aerial daemonic	elevated consciousness
natural	{ terrestrial aquatic	normal consciousness
subnatural	{ subterranean	dream consciousness

It was by experimenting with these spirits that the romantic poet was able to do what his late neoclassical counterpart could only attempt: he was able to give form to vision, structure to the sublime.

An interesting but peripheral question is, Where did the poets find these supernatural worlds and how were they constructed? Were they the ab ovo creation of the imagination or were they borrowed from older mythologies, from other attempts to construct analogies for consciousness? As I mentioned previously, the organization and characterization of the spirits were primarily drawn from the works of Plato and especially of the Neoplatonic mystics.[36] And these works were being translated and promulgated by one of the more eccentric English Platonists, Thomas Taylor. Most of the poets knew Taylor, and they certainly had read his esoteric speculations on the workings of the lower heavens.[37]

36. Around the turn of the nineteenth century a renewed interest in the operation of ancient cosmologies resulted in translations of the Neoplatonic mystics, many of whom had never before been translated into English. They appeared not solely because the poets were demanding new vehicles, but rather because of a general public fascination with the mythologies of other cultures. Many hoped that by studying different mythologies certain primordial truths might be unfolded. As Walter Evert has said in *Aesthetic and Myth in the Poetry of Keats*:

> Romantic adaptation of received myth verges on a chapter in the history of poetry and ideas that has only recently been receiving the attention that it deserves, the mythological syncretist movement of the eighteenth and early nineteenth centuries. Engaging the energies of serious theologians, lay scholars, and a fascinating assortment of the lunatic fringe, it had an intellectual vogue that has perhaps been underestimated simply because its primary assumption has been discredited (i.e., that all the world's religions and mythological systems derive from an Ur-myth which embodied a universal system of natural religion). (p. 20)

Although the theologians never found their Ur-myth, the poets were introduced to esoteric cosmologies that were well adapted to their needs for new metaphors. This was a remarkable example of serendipity, for the romantic poets, fascinated by states of consciousness, were provided translations of the Neoplatonic philosophers, who had been equally fascinated by how inner consciousness was linked to the outer workings of the universe. In addition, the romantics found they had a reading audience that was eager for poetic treatment of myths that were thought to embody eternal verities. This kind of romantic myth criticism was popular a decade or so ago, for instance, see Wallace Brown, "Byron and the English Interest in the Near East"; Edward B. Hungerford, *Shores of Darkness*, pp. 106–62; and Albert J. Kuhn, "English Deism and the Development of Romantic Mythological Syncretism."

37. A word or two must be said of Thomas Taylor. At the turn of the century Taylor was the major link between Plato, the Neoplatonists and the romantics. If

This cosmic system that Taylor was translating was well adapted for use as a psychological gestalt. When the Neoplatonists looked to the horizon, they saw a flowing pyramid of interanimating powers that all ultimately emanated from the supreme power called the "One"; when the poets looked within, they saw a remarkably similar process: what they called the Imagination is analogous to the One. A multiplicity of feelings and thoughts were linked to this liminal force, which was itself imageless and unfathomable. Just as the ancient philosophers saw layers of spirits moving helixlike from the One, so the poets perceived levels of consciousness moving out from the psychological locus of the Imagination. More important, the Neoplatonic hierarchy provided for the poets what the painters were discovering in the atmosphere at the horizon: an image to mirror states of consciousness.

I do not mean to imply here that the romantic painters did not have a conceptual problem of considerable magnitude as well. Theirs was a problem of substance as well as of point of view, or in terms of the eighteenth-century painter, a problem of "station" and "arrangement." To picture the sublime in landscape, one must look in and up, but painters of the eighteenth century had only recently learned to look out, to paint the picturesque complete with all its imperfections. A major shift was in the offing, for as Gerald Finley has contended:

---

it is true that each generation translates Platonic philosophy according to its own tastes, then what Taylor translated and how he translated it may be important. He had a fondness for the Alexandrian Mystics (Plotinus, Porphyry, Iamblicus, and so on), who were especially interested in describing the animating powers in the universe. It was via Taylor's translations that Coleridge constructed the world above the Ancient Mariner, Byron his world above Manfred, and Shelley his world above Prometheus. See my "The World above the Ancient Mariner," "The Supernatural Structure of Byron's *Manfred*," and "The Metaphysical Pattern of Act IV, *Prometheus Unbound*." In these articles I argue in far more detail than I will here that the romantics borrowed their "celestial furniture" from Taylor's translations, but I make no case, as I hope I do here, for the aesthetic and psychological reasons. The best works about Taylor are Frank B. Evans, "Thomas Taylor, Platonist of the Romantic Period," and Kathleen Raine, "Thomas Taylor in England" in *Thomas Taylor: Selected Writings*, ed. Raine and George Mills Harper, pp. 3–49.

By the later eighteenth century British landscape painting, with combined aims of greater truth and increased expressiveness, began to change. The rhetorical conventions of the Picturesque were challenged and discarded, as a widening and deepening of natural effect and emotional content became more immediate and compelling goals. One manifestation of this change occurs in paintings and watercolours of the "landscape sublime." With mounting confidence artists sought to convey through their painting the sensual impact and stunning immediacy of freshly observed nature.[38]

This is the movement that Ronald Paulson considers central in eighteenth-century art; it is the movement from "emblem to expression" that continued well past the turn of the century until by the 1830s it had reached the edge of expressibility, until it became Impressionism.[39] In American painting it developed into what is now generally called Luminism, the conclusive phase of nineteenth-century American landscape painting. Robert Rosenblum has carried this idea even further, arguing:

> The line from the Romantic Sublime to the Abstract Sublime [abstract expressionsim] is broken and devious, for its tradition is more one of erratic, private feeling than submission to objective disciplines. If certain vestiges of sublime landscape painting linger into the late nineteenth century in the popularized panoramic travelogues of Americans like Bierstadt and Church, the tradition was generally suppressed by the international domination of the French tradition, with its familiar values of reason, intellect and objectivity. At times, the countervalues of the Northern Romantic tradition have been partially reasserted (with a strong admixture of French pictorial discipline) by such masters as van Gogh, Ryder, Marc, Klee, Feininger, Mondrian; but its most spectacular manifestations—the sublimities of British and German Romantic landscape—have only been resurrected after 1945 in America, where the authority of Parisian painting has been challenged to an unprecedented degree. In its heroic search for a private myth to embody the sublime power of the supernatural, the art of Still, Rothko, Pollock and Newman

38. Gerald Finley, "The Genesis of Turner's 'Landscape Sublime,'" p. 156.
39. Ronald Paulson, *Emblem and Expression: Meaning in English Art of the Eighteenth Century*. Morse Peckham charts the development of romanticism into Impressionism in *Romanticism: The Culture of the Nineteenth Century*.

should remind us once more that the disturbing heritage of the Romantics has not yet been exhausted.[40]

Although this may be overstating the case, the shift in sensibilities that characterizes modernism began with the romantic painter's movement away from a middle ground prospect, complete with requisite coulisse, deflected vistas, sky dado, secondary vantage points, and silhouettes, to the "landscape sublime," with its intense concentration on the magnetic area of the horizon. In this movement away from the picturesque, the European (the Dutch and especially the Italian) landscape painters, given such low priority by Reynolds in his *Discourses*, were elevated and admired by the English artists. The major influence of Claude, the Poussins, and especially Salvator Rosa—although it seems so trite and clichéd in retrospect—was that they were willing to lift the eye at a time when so many other heads were tipped to the ground.[41] The fascination of both artists and ordinary observers for the Claude-glass, the slightly convex and blackened mirror used to make vistas out of common views, bespeaks this

40. Robert Rosenblum, "The Abstract Sublime." This thesis is developed in full in *Modern Painting and the Northern Romantic Tradition: Friedrich to Rothko.*
41. Barrell, *Idea of Landscape*, described the Claudean encounter with the horizon thus:

> There developed, then, the habit of seeing landscape as arranged into the sort of compositional patterns employed by Claude and his followers. . . . A landscape by Claude employs, in the first place, a fairly high viewpoint— high enough, that is, for a distant horizon to appear above any rising ground between it and the viewpoint: and the first impression which everyone must receive, I imagine, on seeing a Claude landscape, is one of tremendous depth. The eye, attracted by an area of light usually set just below the horizon, travels immediately towards it over a long and often steeply contoured stretch of intervening land. The initial movement in all Claude's landscapes is this one, from the foreground straight to the far distance; and it must I think be understood as a rapid movement, an immediate response to the way the picture is organized. . . . We look at the horizon before we become aware of the painting as "a world designed for the imagination to enter and wander about it"; and the discovery we make then, that the objects are deliberately arranged to lead the eye from foreground to horizon, is the discovery of *how* the eye was immediately attracted to the horizon, of how an effect already experienced was achieved. (pp. 7–8)

growing interest in generating "spectacular" effects.[42] Additionally, I think it was no accident that British watercolor landscapes were first produced near Norwich, where the dull East Anglian plains almost forced confrontation with the sky, for English painters had to look seriously at space, at the horizon, at the clouds, even beyond the clouds, if they wanted to express the sublime.

This new focus on the horizon, this lifting of the eye/I, was not without risk. During most of the eighteenth century, topographic poetry, picturesque painting, and landscape gardening were synchronic.[43] Prospect poetry, in which the poet climbs a hill, looks around until he finds an interesting, or commanding, vista, and then paints a word-picture of it, mimics the progress of the painter and, for that matter, the landscape architect. The "scenic vista," as a condensation of an experience in nature, is central in neoclassicism: Sir John Denham's *Cooper's Hill* is an example of this, as is Richard Wilson's *A Distant View of Rome from Monte Mario*, as is "Capability" Brown's Stowe garden. Picturing the sublime unsettled the stasis of scenic vistas. Compare these works to Wordsworth's description of the Gondo Gorge, Turner's painting of *The Fall of an Avalanche in the Grisons*, and the fact that the American wilderness was thought to be the archetypical garden, and it is clear that some revolution in taste did occur.[44]

42. The Claude-glass is discussed and illustrated in Deborah Jean Warner, "The Landscape Mirror and Glass." A Claude-glass could be a colored lens instead of a mirror, but the mirror seems to have been more commonly used.

43. This thesis has been most recently developed in John Dixon Hunt, *The Figure in the Landscape: Poetry, Painting and Gardening in the Eighteenth Century*, and continued in Ronald Paulson, *Literary Landscape: Turner and Constable*.

44. The impossibility of constructing a romantic (sublime) garden had interesting consequences; not only did it necessitate a trip to the Lake District with Gilpin's *Guide* in hand, it also gave new meaning to the Grand Tour. No longer could this be a Mediterranean experience climaxing in Greece, but now it had to include excursions into Northern Europe as well. In fact, the Tour itself instigated interest in sublimity, for reports of "grand vistas" on the Continent (as in *Childe Harold*, canto 3) only augmented the interest in new aesthetic categories. I am not going to discuss the American interest in the sublime (or the English fascination with American landscape) other than to point out that here in the New World, indeed, the sublime garden did exist. And it was the landscape of the

The horizon then was essentially one of the new focuses of romantic sight, one of the new contrasts to be studied, one of the new margins perhaps to be crossed. Existing as it does at the edge of our world, the horizon is by its very distinctness, magnitude, and finality an apt image of all that "in here" and "out there" imply. Let me conclude with two more quotations: the first general and philosophical, made by one of the most astute observers of the literal romantic "scene," and the second specific and painterly, made by one of the most important practitioners. Here is John Ruskin in *Modern Painters*:

> The fact is, that sublimity is not a specific term,—not a term descriptive of the effect of a particular class of ideas. Anything which elevates the mind is sublime, and elevation of mind is produced by the contemplation of greatness of any kind; but chiefly, of course, by the greatness of the noblest things. Sublimity is, therefore, only another word for the effect of greatness upon the feelings. Greatness of matter, space, power, virtue, or beauty, are thus all sublime; and there is perhaps no desirable quality of a work of art, which in its perfection is not, in some way or degree, sublime.[45]

And here is Thomas Cole in his *Essay on American Scenery*:

> There are two lakes . . . situated in a wild mountain gorge called the Franconia Notch, in New Hampshire. . . . Shut in by stupendous mountains which rest on crags that tower more than a thousand feet above the water, whose rugged brows and shadowy breaks

Northeast in particular that was assimilated into the visions of the painters of the Hudson Valley and Catskill Mountain schools as well as into the literary landscapes of Irving, Cooper, and Bryant. Of course, the English were more appreciative than the "natives"; in fact, they were downright enthusiastic. The romantic poet Thomas Moore, confronting Niagara, wrote (in a letter to his mother, 24 July 1804): "I felt as if approaching the very residence of the Deity; the tears started into my eyes; and I remained, for moments after we had lost sight of the scene, in that delicious absorption which pious enthusiasm alone can produce. We arrived at the New Ladder and descended to the bottom. Here all its awful sublimities rushed full upon me. My whole heart and soul ascended toward the Divinity in a swell of devout admiration, which I never before experienced. Oh! bring the atheist here, and he cannot return an atheist. I pity the man who can coldly sit down to write a description of these ineffable wonders; much more do I pity him who can submit them to the measurement of gallons and yards. . . . We must have new combinations of language to describe the Fall of Niagara."

45. Ruskin, *Modern Painters*, 1:41.

are clothed by dark and tangled woods, thay have such an aspect of deep seclusion, of utter and unbroken solitude, that, when standing on their brink a lonely traveller, I was overwhelmed with an emotion of the sublime, such as I have rarely felt. It was not that the jagged precipices were lofty, that the encircling woods were of the dimmest shade, or that the waters were profoundly deep; but that over all, rocks, wood, and water, brooded the spirit of repose, and the silent energy of nature stirred the soul to its inmost depths.[46]

Exactly how the romantic artist achieves the sense of elevation described by Ruskin in the locale elaborated by Cole—literally and figuratively "on the brink"—is the subject of this work. As is so often the case in attempting to define romantic trends, we need first to look at Blake, who shows by exaggeration what was later to be accepted in relative moderation.

46. Thomas Cole, "Essay on American Scenery," p.7.

1

Blake: The Anti-Sublime

Allegory addressed to the Intellectual powers, while it is altogether hidden from the Corporeal Understanding, is My Definition of the Most Sublime Poetry.—William Blake to Thomas Butts, 6 July 1803

For William Blake the romantic sublime was not one of the roads to the palace of wisdom. As a matter of fact, he had little use for the sublime either as a moral or as an aesthetic category; Blake's vision is finally apocalyptic or liminal, not sublime. How could Blake have cared about sublimity (at least the way I have restricted it) when he was such an epistemological monist that the natural world of forms had no independent existence? The whole logic of the sublime is based on an attempt to join what Locke had rent asunder—to join subject and object, if only for a moment. This distinction was lost on Blake, for he was more than happy to separate subject and object, imagination and matter; in fact he insisted on it. Additionally, Blake would have been skeptical of the "sublime" (in the eighteenth-century sense) because the experience, initially a high-energy confrontation of subject and object, finally results in a return to the senses. In other words, it returns us to ourselves, albeit with expanded awareness; it does not release us permanently. We go up to the horizon, but not beyond. This is the opposite of what should happen: the sublime (now Blake's term) must transcend "Corporeal Understanding" forever.

Several critics have claimed that, Blake's own words notwithstanding (and he issues a good many of them on this subject, especially in his running gloss to Reynolds's *Discourses*), he is often concerned with sublimity well within the romantic sense.[1] Here

1. I suppose the safest thing to say on this subject is what Hugh Haughton said in his review of Thomas Weiskel's *The Romantic Sublime*, namely that Blake be-

40

in his poetry, for instance, is a rather romantic description of a
bird just breaching the horizon:

> The Lark sitting upon his earthly bed, just as the morn
> Appears, listens silent; then springing from the waving Cornfield,
> loud
> He leads the Choir of Day: trill, trill, trill, trill
> Mounting upon the wings of light into the Great Expanse,
> Reechoing against the lovely blue & shining heavenly Shell,
> His little throat labours with inspiration; every feather
> On throat and breast and wings vibrates with the effluence
> Divine.
>
> (*Milton*, 2. 62–68)

But we must notice that the bird presumably flies out of the natural world into the Beyond: this is not the pathway of the sublime.

A better example might be *The Tyger*. Here, as Morton Paley
has argued, Blake is very much in the tradition of eighteenth-
century sublimity.[2] And Paley is correct, for the tiger is imag-
istically close to such "standard" pieces of sublimity as Stubbs's
lion, Copley's shark, or Ward's lioness. But if the imagery and
rhetoric are based on the aesthetic principles of Burke and especially Dennis, what about the theme? I think we need to be cau-

---

lieves in the "sublime *without sublimation*," but this almost begs the question.
Blake can be traditionally sublime when illustrating "sublime" artists like Gray,
Young, Blair, and Milton, but when left on his own, I think he is genuinely visionary, that is, not metaphoric at all. It is always clear in Blake's paintings and poetry
whether he is above or below the horizon (threshold); he is rarely in-between. He
wrote of this movement beyond the threshold in *Milton*:

> that everything has its
> own vortex; and when once a traveller thro' Eternity
> Has pass'd that Vortex, he perceives it roll backward
> behind
> His path, into a globe itself infolding like a sun,
> Or like a moon, or like a universe of starry majesty,
> While he keeps onwards in his wondrous journey on
> the earth.
>
> (1.549–54)

Thus I would contend that Blake is the only genuinely "apocalyptic" romantic
poet spurning all intermediary stages of perception. His "divine vision" can only
be expressed through allegory; see Preface, *Blake's Sublime Allegory: Essays on
"The Four Zoas," "Milton," and "Jerusalem,"* ed. Stuart Curran and Joseph A.
Wittreich, pp. xiii–xvii.

2. Morton Paley, "Tyger of Wrath."

tious here because the effects of what I'm calling romantic sublimity are not simply astonishment, but enlightenment. The
sublime experience takes us "up to the threshold," provides momentary release from tension, and then returns us to ourselves
with greater awareness. However, Blake is not concerned with
our return—witness the incessant questionings, almost as if he is
demanding no resolution. Rather, it seems to me, he finally
wants to "tease us out of thought," and the sublime language
("dread hand," "dread feet") and sublime imagery ("forests,"
"distant deeps," "furnace," "stars [throwing] down their spears,"
to say nothing of the "tyger" itself) are simply the means to another end. Or take another example: the speaker in *The Crystal
Cabinet* may well achieve sublimity, the third-fold vision, but he
misses ecstasy, and that for Blake is sufficient to return him to the
World of Generation, presumably to try again until he gets it
right. Blake's interest is clearly not in heightened consciousness
per se, but in experience beyond consciousness, a movement
into the world of pure Intellect. He will not tarry at the edge; he
wants the world beyond.

A comparison of Blake's painting *The Arlington Court Picture*
with his poem *The Mental Traveller* may illustrate/illuminate his
skepticism of both eighteenth-century and romantic concepts of
sublimity. But before we look at Blake's two views we need to realize that the sublime has two opposites: the finite or mundane,
and the infinite or mystical. Either extreme denies sublimity, for
the sublime experience (actually a "moment") depends on our
willingness to "let go" of the nominal world and then quickly
catch it again. If we become merged with the infinite, the process of sublimation ceases. The awareness of altered consciousness is replaced by an entirely new consciousness, and although
this new consciousness may be what Blake wants, it is not at all
what the moral aestheticians or romantic poets had in mind.

Now, with this in mind, let us consider the specific verbal and
visual texts. Three enigmas have bothered scholars for years:
what happens in *The Mental Traveller*? what does Blake mean by
"infinity"? what is his *Arlington Court Picture* about? I think
these three puzzles are part of Blake's continuing examination of
what he considers the futility of sublimation in the world of Natu-

ral Religion. *The Mental Traveller* has proved elliptical beyond belief; the most accepted key to its meaning, the Orc cycle as described by Northrop Frye, has always seemed too simple to explain the last half of the poem. *Infinity* and *eternity*, two of Blake's favorite words, have resisted all specific definitions. And *The Arlington Court Picture* loosed a flood of criticism a decade or so ago reminiscent of what preceded the cracking of Linear B. I hope to show that these three cruxes can be explained in part by Blake's adaptation of a symbol just then coming into public knowledge, the symbol of infinity (∞), and that he used this in part to satirize the growing interest in the secular sublime. The symbol, suggesting as it does the infinite continuation of time (the drawn line) and the expansion and contraction of space (the area between the lines), became one of Blake's more ironic images; it became his visual paradigm of the World of Generation. The "sublime experience" occurs at that moment when time and space are at their most expansive, at the threshold; but instead of stopping, the cycle only continues its endless motion. To understand this process it may help to examine these three cruxes separately.

I. *The Mental Traveller*

. . . these States Exist now. Man passes on, but States remain for Ever; he passes thro' them like a traveller who may as well suppose that the places he has passed thro' exist no more, as a Man may suppose that the States he has passed thro' Exist no more. Every thing is Eternal.—Blake, *A Vision of the Last Judgment*

It is paradoxical that although Blake hated diagrams, one often has to consult one's own schema to explain points in his poetry otherwise impenetrable to criticism. We can be thankful that Blake himself provided many such schema via his engravings, for Blake the engraver often best glosses and explicates Blake the poet. But it is unfortunate that often when we need Blake the engraver the most, we are left with only Blake the poet. So it is interesting and informative to try to construct our own schema or map to "see"what happens in *The Mental Traveller*. And a number of critics have attempted just that.

The first and most important of these critics is Northrop Frye, who proposed that the poem was a condensation of the Orc cycle.[3] There has been some uneasiness with this interpretation, for, as I indicated above, the circle schema has not been able to encompass the second half of the poem. John H. Sutherland sounded the quiet alarm in the midfifties: "The parallels [between *The Mental Traveller* and the Orc cycle] are genuine and instructive, particularly during the early part of the poem; however, the Male Babe's experiences are more complex than Orc's simple rise, stagnation and fall."[4] But those who, like Harold Bloom, favor the cyclical explanation continue to see the poem working in perfectly measured circles or, aptly enough, "revolutions": the Male baby (creative impulse, liberty . . .) growing, consolidating, falling; then the Female baby (materialism, oppression . . .) doing the same.[5] Substitute whatever you think Blake may be allegorizing in the male, place its opposite in the form of the female, and you have the single-cycle/two-stroke Blakean engine. Here it is as diagrammed by Hazard Adams:[6]

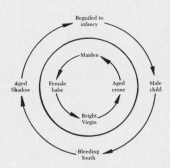

3. Northrop Frye, *Fearful Symmetry: A Study of William Blake*, pp. 207–35.
4. John H. Sutherland, "Blake's *Mental Traveller*," p. 139.
5. Harold Bloom, *Blake's Apocalypse: A Study in Poetic Argument*, pp. 289–96.
6. Hazard Adams, *William Blake: A Reading of the Shorter Poems*, p. 98.

I am not suggesting that the concept of circularity is not in the poem—it certainly is; witness the last stanza—but I am convinced that there is more going on in the poem and that a more accurate schema can be devised. The circle gives no indication of the expansion and contraction of space, which is obviously an important part of the process, for when the Old Man takes the Female Babe in his arms,

> The Senses roll themselves in fear,
> And the flat Earth becomes a Ball;
>
> The stars, sun, Moon, all shrink away,
> A desert vast without a bound,
> And nothing left to eat or drink
> And a dark desert all around. (st. 16–17)

Space wildly explodes and contracts as both Male baby and Female baby grow and die. As Adams himself admits:

> Stanzas 17 and 22 invite us to think of the world of the cycle or the great shell as a constantly expanding and then contracting balloon-like form. While time moves in a wheel, space expands or contracts, becomes coldly remote or imaginatively immediate. Approaching the moment of the male's birth back into the world of Beulah and a protective mother, space comes together toward a visionary point; and the voids between the planets, the "orbed Void of doubt," the "abstract Voids between the Stars," disappear into the innocent vision.[7]

But his diagram can explain only time. The best he can do is, in his own words, "suggest an imperfect spatial metaphor."

If ever there was a description of the sublime, this expansion almost to the point of cosmic burst is it. What could be more sub-

----

7. Ibid., pp. 96–97.

lime than the still moment before The End—in fact this was a common theme in nineteenth-century painting and poetry. But we must remember that the world the Mental Traveller is telling us about is the fallen world of the "cold earth wanderers." Infinity, Eternity, Sublimity here do not mean what they do in the cosmic schema of, say, *Jerusalem* or *Milton*. This is the world inside the "black globe," below the "retrific" roof, forever beneath (in my terms of the sublime) the horizon.

To explain change in this world Blake needed a new image, a metaphor to express endless expansion to the point of explosion, then rapid contraction. He needed something, as Adams has said, that was circular, or better yet oblate. Perhaps what he needed was a circle depressed at the poles, something like this:

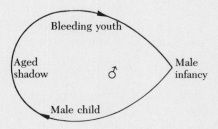

This bulb gives the sense of the circularity of time (the line) and also of the expansion and contraction of space (the space between line). Sublimity—but of course for Blake this is a false sublime—occurs as space balloons outward, just at the moment before contraction. Additionally, this schema fits Blake's continuation of the Space/Time paradigm, developed later in *The Four Zoas* and *Jerusalem*, where Orc expands to become Urizen, then Urizen contracts to explode again into Orc.

But what about the Female diagram? What about the Rahab-Vala process? It seems to work the same way, both in time and space, but is staggered with the Orc cycle so that the Male Youth is cared for by the Old Woman. In other words, the beginning of

the Male cycle is the end of the Female. The Female cycle looks
like this:

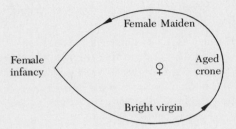

If we put these two oblate circles together we get something like
this:

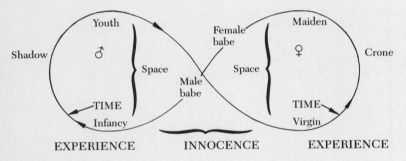

If this looks remarkably like a familiar symbol, it may not be entirely by accident. In 1655 John Wallis, an Englishman, introduced the symbol ∞ to signify infinite number, or infinity. At the
beginning of the eighteenth century Wallis's symbol had become
incorporated into calculus, and as Cheyne's *Philosophical Principles of Natural Religion* attests, as early as 1705 it had become
quite popular.[8]

Now I admit there is a good deal of critical conjuring in my
argument thus far, and so before I continue to argue that Blake
not only knew of this symbol but may even have attempted to use
it as the symbolic keystone in other works, it may be useful to

8. See Florian Cajori, *A History of Mathematical Notations* 2:44–48.

consult the only other critic who has dissented from the perfect circle/cycle explanation of *The Mental Traveller*. When W. B. Yeats wrote his commentary on the poem in 1893 with Edwin Ellis, he was confused by what was going on in the poem. However, by 1925, in the first edition of *A Vision*, things had changed:

> When Edwin J. Ellis and I had finished our big book on the philosophy of William Blake, I felt that we had no understanding of this poem [*The Mental Traveller*]: we had explained its details, for they occur elsewhere in his verse or his pictures, but not the poem as a whole, not the myth, the perpetual return to the same thing; not that which certainly moved Blake to write it; but when I had understood the double cones, I understood it also. The woman and the man are two competing gyres growing at one another's expense.[9]

As Kathleen Raine has stated, "This invocation of the gyres to explain the man and woman who move alternately from youth to age, from age to youth, may seem to explain the obscure by the more obscure. However (as Raine admits, although she ultimately holds to the full circle theory), this is not finally so.[10] Yeats's gyres do show a similarity to Blake's connnecting oblate circles, especially if they are turned ninety degrees and pulled apart:

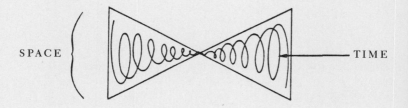

SPACE   TIME

The perning action *in* Yeats's gyre corresponds to the tracing action *around* Blake's oblate circle; in other words, time moves in a line, space moves in pulses.

9. William Butler Yeats, *A Vision*, p. 134. For more on Yeats's own views on the sublime, see chap. 5, "Yeats' Dialogues with the Voice of Enchantment," in Stuart Ende, *Keats and the Sublime*.

10. Kathleen Raine, *Blake and Tradition*, 1:307. For Raine's subscription to the full circle theory, see p. 323.

Yeats claimed that both he and Blake fashioned their diagrams from ancient myths, but he wisely never told what myths. Perhaps, as has been suggested, they were derived from Plato's *Politicus*, or from the esoteric designs filtered through the Neoplatonists and translated into English by Thomas Taylor at the turn of the nineteenth century.[11] But there is no definite proof that Blake did not "borrow" his own paradigm elsewhere. Admittedly, he may have gotten the cyclical theory from Swedenborg, but that theory explains only changes in time (birth-life-death-birth); it simply cannot explain changes in space.

Could it be that Blake refashioned the circular diagram, made it conform to the new symbol ∞ in calculus, and that Yeats, not really knowing the why and where of the symbol, recognized that it helped him explain his own theory of organic change? Is it conceivable that Blake did not depend wholly on Swedenborg or the ancient mythologists for his scheme, that he fashioned the complete Orc "cycle" from contemporary developments in calculus? I think so, for Blake was fascinated by developments in calculus and had at his disposal books that explained these new changes in mathematics, parts of which we know he read.

II. The Sign of Infinity

"Mathematic Form is Eternal in the Reasoning Memory"
—Blake, *On Virgil*

Keynes set the approximate date of *The Mental Traveller* as 1803 (from a fair copy in the Pickering manuscript), but those who hold that Blake had read Thomas Taylor's translation of Plato's *Politicus* say 1804.[12] We do know the poem was written after the turn of the century, probably before 1805. F. B. Curtis, working on a not entirely different matter, has shown that Blake

11. For instance, see Kathleen Raine and George M. Harper, "Introduction," to *Thomas Taylor the Platonist*, as well as Harper's *The Neoplatonism of William Blake*.
12. Raine, *Blake and Tradition*, p. 306.

knew about a recent development in calculus known as the "flux-ion" or "moment." A "fluxion," the smallest unit of change (the opposite of infinity), interested Blake because he "wished to es-tablish the existence of these 'moments' as instants of poetic crea-tion, and as the time-units of mercy and protection."[13] For Blake to learn as much as he did about these moments, Curtis contends (on both textual and historical grounds) that he probably read at least two sources: a series of reviews on La Croix's work *On the Differential and Integral Calculus* that were appearing in the *Monthly Review* for 1800 (vols. 28, 31, 32); and the squibs on cal-culus and assorted matters in the *Encyclopedia Britannica* (3d ed., 1797). The *Monthly Review* articles appeared during Blake's Felpham period and may have been in William Hayley's library; the *Encyclopedia* definitely was there.[14] It is also very possible that Blake had read parts of Hutton's *Mathematical and Philo-sophical Dictionary* (2 vols., 1795–1796), which had a lengthy section on the sign of infinity. Joseph Johnson, publisher of Hut-ton's *Dictionary*, was a personal friend of Blake's, especially dur-ing this period. It is, as Curtis states, "quite possible that Blake, avid reader as he was, browsed through a copy of this work whilst on one of his many visits to Johnson's shop at St. Paul's Church-yard, with newly engraved plates tucked under his arm."[15]

I go into this detail because if we accept—only as a premise—that Blake had the infinity sign in mind as he was constructing a design of *The Mental Traveller*, it may help us understand the poem as a critique of sublimity. In the first place, we are told that the world to be described is the fallen world, the world of eternal generation and decay. As Adams notes: "The speaker of the poem is reporting upon the fallen world from the point of view of eter-nity. The people he describes are human forms fallen into materi-alism. The traveler is speaking as if he has returned from a jour-ney into the fallen world, which is *also* a land of men, though

13. F. B. Curtis, "Blake and the 'Moment of Time': An Eighteenth Century Controversy in Mathematics," p. 463.

14. The contents of Hayley's library were sold by auction on 13 and 14 Febru-ary 1821 by the bookseller Evans of Pall Mall. The catalog of this sale is now in the British Museum, and it lists the seven volumes of Aiken's *Annual Review* un-der item 3; Curtis, "Blake and the 'Moment of Time,'" p. 465, n. 20.

15. Curtis, "Blake and the 'Moment of Time,'" pp. 465–66.

considerably different from the eternal land of men."[16] This is the world of Experience, a world of constant change, a world without contraries, without progress, just change—in fact, an infinity of change. It is a world in which sublimity may carry us up to the edge of new awareness but never beyond. We are always returned to where we started with no new knowledge. We remain trapped forever below the liminal. This is a truly *infinite* world, a world with beginning, perhaps, but a world certainly without end, without escape. If the Male baby is born in Innocence, he soon becomes the old tyrant in Experience, and if the Female baby is born in Innocence, she becomes the old hag of Experience. Where is the release, the escape? This is the mock sublime (at least for Blake), the almost at-the-threshold experience, and it is the most "cold earth wanderers" will ever have.

Blake's pattern is, of course, more sophisticated than I have made it seem, for as time changes, space constricts and expands in a kind of giant pulse. As time swings back to start a new cycle, a kind of systolic rhythm occurs: space breaks apart, then congeals, then explodes again. Still, what more appropriate symbol is there for this eternal flow than the sign-symbol of infinity?

III. The *Arlington Court Picture*

. . . the picture is a literal illustration of a book that is still to be identified. —Archibald G. B. Russell[17]

The *Arlington Court Picture* is becoming to the critics of Blake's paintings what *The Mental Traveller* has been to the critics of his poetry: a critical touchstone testing the ruggedness of a variety of interpretations. So far nothing has proved genuine; there are as many different explanations as there are explainers. The painting has been interpreted as a Neoplatonic allegory, as a

16. Adams, *William Blake*, p. 87.
17. As quoted by Geoffrey Keynes, "Blake's Vision of the Circle of the Life of Man," in *Studies in Art and Literature for Bella da Costa Greene*, ed. Dorothy Miner, p. 207.

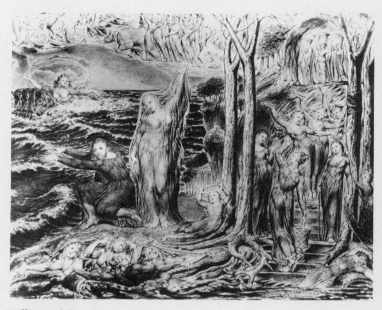

William Blake, *The Arlington Court Picture*, 1821. Arlington Court, a property of the National Trust, London.

picture of the soul's descent into the material world, as a retelling of the Book of Revelation, as a moment of truth in the fallen world, as a picture of the redemptive act, as a vision of the circularity of life, as an explanation of the unconscious, and as a rejection of the cycle of corrupt life.[18] For a painting uncovered only in 1947, this work has elicited a considerable number of critical interpretations, most of which have been unable to agree on major points, let alone the minor ones. More "meaning" has been wrung from the *Arlington Court Picture* in three and a half

18. See, respectively: Raine, *Blake and Tradition*, vol. 1, chap. 3; S. Foster Damon, *A Blake Dictionary*, pp. 86–87; John Beer, *Blake's Visionary Universe*, pp. 286–94; Robert Simmons and Janet Warner, "Blake's *Arlington Court Picture*: The Moment of Truth"; John E. Grant, "Redemption Action in Blake's *Arlington Court Picture*"; Keynes, "Blake's Vision", pp. 202–8; George Wingfield Digby, *Symbol and Image in William Blake*, chap. 2; and Anne K. Mellor, *Blake's Human Form Divine*, pp. 256–78.

decades than from most works of art in a century. The only point where all agree is that this is indeed a splendid painting, in fact, one of Blake's finest.

Perhaps it is best simply to look at the painting first, before any symbolic reading, for it is rare that any two Blake scholars will see the same things. In explaining Blake's paintings there is always the greatest controversy over the human forms because critics want so badly to fit them into their idea of Blake's mythic allegory. So, for instance, Professors Digby and Mellor say the man center-left is Albion or Jesus; Professors Simmons and Warner say it is Los; Professor Beer says Christ; Professor Damon says Luvah; and so on. So let us just *look* at the geometry of the picture and note only those designs we can all see, before mounting the hobbyhorses.

First of all, the picture is divided into three parts: the left side, right side, and bottom. The left side extends from the left margin to "axle-trees," which split the picture in half. These trees seem to be as firmly anchored in the firmament as they are in the earth, being supported both from above and from below. The right side extends from trees to right margin and is made up of three sets of women. At the bottom there is a river extending across the whole scene in which float three women who carry a rope over their heads. This rope is to be cut by a female on the far left. In front of these women is a horned man. Finally in the lower center of the painting is a brightly lit child holding up a halolike skein of thread.

Let me take each one of these parts and describe what is obvious, as opposed to symbolic, in each. On the left side there is a man crouched near the ocean dressed in a red robe (the only bright color in this otherwise almost monochromatic painting). He seems about to dive into the water (notice the position of the feet). All critics agree that the ocean represents the Sea of Time and Space: such consensus should make contrarians uneasy, but I think I agree. A trough of water leads out to a woman in a chariot tended by two men, one on either side. The chariot-woman's hands arc up, continuing a circle formed by the trough, toward a man asleep (dreaming? dead?) in another chariot. If my assumptions about the placement of the sublime vision are correct, then here above the horizon, above the threshold, should be something liminal, something extraordinary. But no, if this is sublime, it is a very sleepy sublime indeed. The older man seems distracted, and his scepter—sign of his power—has fallen to his side, while the horses who presumably have pulled this chariot are being unharnessed by four women. There are steps in front of these women that lead back down to earth. So the circle that started in the outreached hands of the kneeling man in red runs through the trough, up the arms of the chariot-woman, through the sleeping man, back down the stairs, and ends in the flow of the woman next to the kneeling man.

The right side is made up almost entirely of females. First, bottom right, a woman sleeps (dead?) in the river, exactly at the opposite point in the picture from the old man asleep (dead?) in the chariot. Above this woman is a woman carrying a bucket *up* the stairs who seems to be gesturing to two women, one on either side of her. This woman seems to be entering a circular route that is described first by the thread being drawn from the center child's skein and then by the arms of the women holding shuttles, that is, their uplifted arms are part of the circumference of this circle. Higher on the hill are angelic women (note the wings) carrying jugs on their heads. Here again we are at the horizon, the point of sublimity, but there is no release, for over the heads of the jug-carrying women is an arc of earth that flows down to the sea. We almost enter the liminal, but not quite.

Below this promontory lounge two women and perhaps a man with a beard. One of these maidens empties her vase, and the liquid flows down the hill. These women seem younger than the other women, and they are naked. Below them (above the child in the center) is a girl, younger still, resting on a promontory that continues the circular land flow that we saw above the heads of the angelic jug carriers. This is not obvious, but it is apparent on second look: a repeated motif of liquid seems to be forming a cycle—the water in the river is also the liquid in the bucket, which is also the liquid in the jugs on the heads of the angelic women, and which is finally returned to the sea by the female who is overturning the vase.

It is only when we look at the bottom third of the painting that the mythic symbolism seems obvious, and again we find all critics in agreement. The three women handling the rope are the Three Fates of classical mythology. Clotho, who presides over birth, draws the rope from the coil; Lachesis, who controls life, passes it over her head; and Antropos, who decides death, cuts the rope with her shears. Who the man is we cannot say (Tharmas, perhaps, judging from the symbolism), and the river seems to be the River of Generation. So perhaps here below we are seeing a theme that may be redoubled in the upper sides of the picture—namely the eternal cycle of life, male on one side, female on the other, meeting in the middle with the child.

The last component is the child in the lower center. This child has been overlooked by most critics, perhaps because they have made the erroneous assumption that the child is a female and hence part of the right side. A few important things first need to be considered: the child is sexless in appearance, neither male nor female, at least not yet; over the head is a halo of white, and the whole body is cast in light; the look on the face is beatific, note the uplifted eyes and tilted face; and finally the feet can be seen as part of the circle that is to continue through the body of the robed man. The thread from the "halo," however, leads to the circle that will be continued through the three female weavers. Both circles thus seem to meet in the child's form. This "halo" may prove ironic, suggesting, as Wordsworth might say, how the "Shades of the prison house begin to close / Upon the growing boy [girl?]." In this context it should be noticed that the child's leg recapitulates, indeed merges with, the root structure of the trees.

Could it be that we are seeing the infinity sign again, the male on the left, the female on the right, the androgynous child in the middle? Are we getting an illustration two decades later of the schema developed in *The Mental Traveller*? Perhaps a few more observations, this time more subjective, are in order here. Let us return to the left side of the painting. As Digby and Mellor have pointed out, the man in the robe bears a striking resemblance to Christ (compare portrayals of Jesus from Blake's *Para-*

dise Lost and *Paradise Regained* plates).[19] Christ, we recall, was the man crucified into the life cycle by the old woman in *The Mental Traveller*: "She binds iron thorns about his head / She pierces both his hands and feet." Also, the red robe, the only bright color in the painting, may suggest Orc and revolution. If the man in the robe is indeed Jesus/Albion/Orc, could it be that the old man in the chariot is Urizen? The Urizen figure of *The Mental Traveller* comes to great wealth and powers at the expense of the others, whom he has suppressed, but he also becomes an Aged Shadow slowly fading from life (stanzas 8, 9). What is interesting in the painting is that the nimbed man with the fallen scepter looks much like the robed man. In fact, Digby, I think without quite understanding why, says they are one and the same, "double aspects of the same man."[20]

Between these two figures is the character in the sea with the outswept arms. Who knows who he/she is? Again, each critic has his favorite explanation—the female moon goddess, Vala, the condensed circle of man's life—the list is as long as the number of critics. I think her sexual importance is obvious and cannot be neglected, but for obvious reasons I also like to believe John Grant:

> Probably the most decisive vindication of the Sea Goddess, in her being if not in all her consequences, is to be found in her close physical resemblance to the spiritual self-portrait of Blake himself which is drawn with the Upcott autograph. The Upcott figure is presumably of the opposite sex (though it could be an androgyne), but its posture is very similar and its face might even be that of the Conjurer in Red after he had had a rejuvenative shave.[21]

Indeed her face looks much like the face of the robed man, which as Digby and others have said, looks much like the face of the man in the upper chariot, which, I now add, looks much like the face of the infant and the face of the woman in the flowing dress. Blake could paint different faces just as he could paint trees with

    19. Digby, *Symbol and Image*, p. 65, and Mellor, *Blake's Human Form Divine*, p. 262.
    20. Digby, *Symbol and Image*, p. 65. See also p. 59.
    21. John E. Grant, "Studying Blake's Iconography for Guidance in Interpreting the *Arlington Court Picture*," p. 24.

firm roots in the ground. The question is, why did he paint those weird trees; and why did he give the people on the left side the same face? Could they be different aspects of the same person at different stages of life? emanations of the same character?

The robed woman in the center has divided the critics: she is Jerusalem to Digby and Beer, Vala to Keynes and Damon. To me she is simply the organ by which the infinite cycle continues. It is through her that both male and female must pass; hence she draws the man in the chariot down the stairs, through her body, to be reborn as the child who, then, depending on sex, goes left or right. Thus her marked resemblance to the Hellenistic Venus Genetrix, for she is indeed both the generative machine and the principle of continuous life.

On the right side I think the key is the route taken by the water, for there is no single female figure to follow as there is on the male side. It is almost as if Blake knew the female side would be initially more confusing and so provided a visual metaphor by which we can trace what is happening. The rising, carrying, and spilling of the water is analogous to the cycle of birth, life, and death. This explains the strange, atavistic water bucket, the ascending steps, and the organic arch over the water carrier's head, all of which reinforce the never-ending cycle of life. I admit that here the visual cycle seems obscure; but this is exactly as it was in *The Mental Traveller*. In fact, Mellor has also concluded as much: "This procession [of women water carriers] remains confined . . . endlessly repeating 'the cycle of generation' like the 'cold Earth wanderers' trapped in the fallen cycle of *The Mental Traveller*." [22] Let me stress that I am not asserting literal so much as thematic correspondence.

I also think it may be important that the women seem to get younger as they move counterclockwise along the circle (especially as the cycle descends to the child) and that the men get older as they move clockwise, which fits exactly into the infinity cycle that we saw in *The Mental Traveller*. The figure of the child in the center and the scene in the river at the bottom also reinforce this interpretation. The child does indeed, as Digby says

22. Mellor, *Blake's Human Form Divine*, pp. 267–68.

without explaining how, "link the two sides of the picture."[23]
Meantime the Fates at the bottom summarize both sides—the
infinite cycle of birth, life, death, and birth.

When we put all the general parts together, we have an interpretation of *The Arlington Court Picture* that has relatively little to do with Blake's esoteric mythologies but is rather self-
contained, based on what is in the painting. If we now try to fit all
the specific parts into the infinity paradigm we might see something like this:

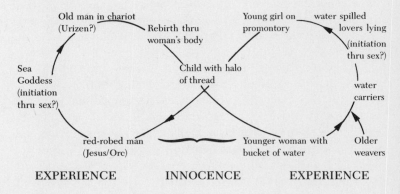

Old man in chariot   Young girl on   water spilled
(Urizen?)   promontory   lovers lying
         Rebirth thru   (initiation
         woman's body   thru sex?)

Sea   Child with halo
Goddess   of thread   water
(initiation   carriers
thru sex?)

red-robed man   Younger woman with   Older
(Jesus/Orc)   bucket of water   weavers

EXPERIENCE   INNOCENCE   EXPERIENCE

The possibility for escape, the possibility for achieving the sublime, occurs only in the upper corners, and there everything
is turned back down upon itself. There is a horizon, yes, but
nothing liminal beyond. As in Ecclesiastes, everything returns to
the beginning: the charioteer is to be drawn back down the
stairs, just as the angelic women are to pour their life-giving fluid
back down the hill to the ocean. The threshold may be sighted in
the world of "cold earth wanderers" but, alas, not experienced.
All is to continue as before. With this in mind I agree with those
critics who contend that Blake's intended title of the *The Arlington Court Picture* was "The Cycle of Life," not "A Vision of the
Cabbala," or "The Sea of Time and Space," or "The Spirit and the

23. Digby, *Symbol and Image*, p. 92. See also Keynes, "Blake's Vision,"
p. 206.

Bride Say Come."[24] For the painting shows, as does *The Mental Traveller*, the actual infinity of change that both male and female must undergo in the fallen world. And it shows this in a real tour de force by using the very sign it is trying to describe, the sign of ∞. It is by no means, as Professor Grant has suggested, the "Art of Clutter"; rather, I think it is one of Blake's best thought out and executed paintings on the incapacity of the fallen Imagination to break out of a world dominated by perverse concepts of space and time.

I take this conjunction of *The Mental Traveller* and *The Arlington Court Picture* as the mythic denial, the text to be overthrown, the challenge posed to romantic artists. Can they get out of the cycle of self-reflexive consciousness? Can they pass through the vortex? Can the poet move past the perceptions of "the cold earth wanderers"? Can the painter envision what is beyond the upper corners of *The Arlington Court Picture*? Can they escape the Blakean hourglass, let alone achieve what he clearly wants, namely a passage into the liminal? I should now like to turn to Wordsworth, who achieves the "sense sublime" well within this world and in so doing removes the romantic sublime from one horn, at least, of the dilemma.

24. See Beer, *Blake's Visionary Universe*, p. 288, n. 41; and Raine, *Blake and Tradition*, 1:75.

2

Wordsworth and Wright:
The Natural Sublime

And I have felt
A presence that disturbs me with the joy
Of elevated thoughts; a sense sublime
Of something far more deeply interfused,
Whose dwelling is the light of setting suns,
And the round ocean and the living air,
And the blue sky, and in the mind of man:
A motion and a spirit, that impels
All thinking things, all objects of all thought,
And rolls through all things.

(*Tintern Abbey*, 93–102)

What we read here is a copy text in the romantic literature of the sublime. As Carl Woodring has noted in "The New Sublimity in *Tintern Abbey*," what Wordsworth is describing, and the way he is describing it, signals a new ethos, a new way of separating this aesthetic category—the sublime—from the beautiful and the picturesque.[1] Wordsworth's approach does not at all conform to Burke's definition; there is nothing "rugged and negligent" here, nothing dark, angular, or severe. In fact we are not the least bit sure how much of the experience really depends on an external world at all, let alone one full of gloomy precipices and belching volcanoes. Wordsworth has made the sublime experience as dependent upon the observer as upon the observed, or to

1. Carl Woodring, "The New Sublimity in *Tintern Abbey*," in *The Evidence of the Imagination: Studies of Interactions between Life and Art in English Romantic Literature*, ed. Donald H. Reiman et al., pp. 86–100.

be more precise, on the interaction of the two, or, in the critical jargon of the 1970s, on the "interfusion/interface" of subject and object.

This epistemology based on "interpenetration" is already a critical cliché in Wordsworth studies: Geoffrey Hartman dealt with the general process of Wordsworth's aesthetic thought in *Wordsworth's Poetry, 1787–1814*; then James A. W. Heffernan narrowed the focus in "Wordsworth on the Sublime: The Quest for Interfusion"; and now Albert O. Wlecke in *Wordsworth and the Sublime* has explicated the specific text of *Tintern Abbey* to within an inch of its life.[2] It is a text now made ragged by overuse, but still very influential, as Thomas Weiskel has shown in his dense but thoughtful, quasi-Freudian interpretation.[3] Critics seem to have achieved not just exhaustion but also consensus on a number of points: that this quest for "interfusion" was one of Wordsworth's lifelong pursuits; that the real source of sublimity was not in Nature but within the perceiver; that the sublime mode of perception was a developing process growing progressively more sophisticated with repetition; and, most radical, that the sublime was becoming more than an aesthetic category. Thanks largely to Wordsworth, the sublime was becoming a psychological event capable of moral significance; it was being transformed back to the sacred.

Essentially, *sublimity* describes a level of consciousness Wordsworth achieved by momentarily understanding the unity of inner and outer. This perception took him up to the threshold of transcendence but did not provide release. The sublime consciousness is still tethered to language; the self is not lost, but momentarily merged. As James Scoggins has argued in *Imagination and Fancy*, the sublime is only "the grounds for visionary experience," not the experience itself.[4] Clearly, then, the development of the subliming self is a central theme in the growth of any ro-

2. Geoffrey H. Hartman, *Wordsworth's Poetry: 1787–1814*; James A. W. Heffernan, "Wordsworth on the Sublime: The Quest for Interfusion"; and Albert O. Wlecke, *Wordsworth and the Sublime*.

3. Thomas Weiskel, *The Romantic Sublime: Studies in the Structure and Psychology of Transcendence*.

4. James Scoggins, *Imagination and Fancy: Complementary Modes in the Poetry of Wordsworth*, p. 114.

mantic poet's consciousness, and, naturally enough, it is the central theme of *The Prelude*, from the boating incident at Hawkshead (Burkean sublime) through the Ravine of Gondo (romantic sublime) to the almost liminal experience on Mount Snowdon.

Someday critics will finally chart that movement up to, and then briefly at, the horizon which is the structure of *The Prelude*, but I would like to concentrate instead on one of Wordsworth's most important but critically neglected prose works, a fragment entitled "The Sublime and the Beautiful." This fragment has been unstudied for good reason: until it appeared in the Owen and Smyer *Prose Works of William Wordsworth*, it existed bound up in a pile of unpublished manuscripts in Dove Cottage Museum.[5] It is clearly a draft for an ancillary work to accompany Wordsworth's *A Guide Through the District of Lakes* (it is full of frequent and specific reference to locales in the Lake country and its environs); in fact, it was found bundled with the manuscript for *A Guide*, cataloged only as "Prose ms. #28."

Wordsworth's essay on the sublime has the chauvinistic purpose of elevating regional scenes in England to Alpine pretensions: in other words, one of Wordsworth's central arguments is that one needn't tour Switzerland when the Langdale Pikes are nearby. Since the "original sources of sublimity [are] in the soul of Man," not in the outside world, and since this experience depends on the imagination contemplating relative size, not "actual magnitude," it makes sense to stay at home and enjoy one's backyard. Had this fragment been published and promulgated, doubtless a generation of eager Alpinists could have unpacked their steamer trunks and headed up to the Lakes. As it was, the Reverend William Gilpin's tour guides published between 1783 and 1809 had already produced the first great influx of budding aestheticians into the Lake District, and Wordsworth was now simply raising the levels of expectation a notch higher; what Gilpin considered picturesque, Wordsworth could make sublime. This is not to say that the fragment was written in collusion with the Ambleside Chamber of Commerce, for it is clear that this tract,

5. Wordsworth's "The Sublime and the Beautiful" has been published as appendix 3 in *The Prose Works of William Wordsworth*, ed. W. J. B. Owen and Jane Worthington Smyser, 2:349–61.

like so much of Wordsworth's other prose, can be informatively read as both an exposition and a defense of his own poetry. Still, it provides not just a gloss to *A Guide* but, as critics are now discovering, a gloss to much in *The Prelude*. Additionally, it promises to become a most important work for critics because Wordsworth here details in specific terms his aesthetics of landscape.[6]

Wordsworth's exposition of the sublime shows more than a passing familiarity with, and assimilation of, earlier speculations; it shows remarkable originality. In this fragment he first states the requisites for the sublime:

> The body of this sensation [the sublime] would be found to resolve itself into three component parts: a sense of individual form or forms; a sense of duration; and a sense of power. The whole complex impression is made up of these elementary parts, & the effect depends upon their co-existence. For, if any one of them were abstracted, the others would be deprived of their power to affect.[7]

As Wordsworth then explains it, "individual form" refers most specifically to outline, and it is the one part of the sublime experience that clearly exists in the external world—at least initially. For instance, the horizon is intrinsically impressive, for its outline is obviously most distinct as it separates the huge forms of earth and sky. This effect is magnified if an otherwise flat horizon is occasionally broken by some vertical intrusions. As Wordsworth says in rather garbled prose:

> The influence of these lines is heightened if the mountain before us be not overtopped by or included in others but does itself form a boundary of the horizon for thus all these turbulent or awful sensations of power are excited in immediate contrast with the fathomless depth & the serenity of the sky or in contrast of another kind the permanent mountain's individual form is opposed to the fleeting or changeful clouds which pass over it or lastly the sense of grandeur which it excites is heightened by the powers of the atmosphere that are visibly allied with it. (note, 352–53)

6. See, for instance, W. J. B. Owen's "The Sublime and the Beautiful in *The Prelude*" and his "Wordsworth's Aesthetics of Landscape," as well as Stuart Peterfreund's "Wordsworth and the Sublime of Duration."

7. William Wordsworth, "The Sublime and the Beautiful," in *The Prose*

But Wordsworth has another criterion: duration. This is, I suppose, analogous to Burke's "succession and uniformity," which refers to the sense of redundancy in form that produces the effect of an endless continuation.[8] Hence a colonnade may encourage the eye to continue beyond the actual limits of the pillars, thereby confounding the Reason. Wordsworth's duration, however, has both internal and external components. In the world of forms it refers to a sense of "artificial infinity," existence through time and space, or rather beyond time and space. So one might experience duration by observing the stars or mountains or sea, providing, of course, the demands of individual form and power have been met. But duration is also internal and subjective: it refers to the lasting impression of a scene that is repeatedly viewed. Here Wordsworth clearly is subjectivizing the experience, asserting the particularity of the sublime based on the memory patterns of the perceiver.

Wordsworth here articulated in prose what he explains much better in poetry, most notably in *Tintern Abbey*, namely the importance of repeatability. This essentially is the aesthetic importance of the "spots of time," for they are the memory traces that reinform each new perceptive event. Tennyson may well have complained about the redundancy of the word *again* in *Tintern Abbey*, but we can now see how crucial it is.

> Five years have past; five summers, with the length
> Of five long winters! and again I hear
> These waters, rolling from their mountain-springs
> With a soft inland murmer.—Once again

Works, ed. Owen and Smyser, 2:351. Hereafter citations from this edition will appear parenthetically in the text.

8. Here is how Burke defines the phenomena of the "artificial infinite": "Succession and *uniformity* of parts, are what constitute the artificial infinite. 1. *Succession*; which is requisite that the parts may be continued so long, and in such a direction, as by their frequent impulses on the sense to impress the imagination with an idea of their progress beyond their actual limits. 2. *Uniformity*; because if the figures of the parts should be changed, the imagination at every change finds a check; you are presented at every alteration with the termination of one idea, and the beginning of another; by which means it becomes impossible to continue that uninterrupted progression, which alone can stamp on bounded objects the character of infinity" (pt. 1, sect. 9).

Do I behold these steep and lofty cliffs,
That on a wild secluded scene impress
Thoughts of more deep seclusion; and connect
The landscape with the quiet of the sky. (*Tintern Abbey*, 1–8)

Each new experience depends on its earlier referent; past antecedents determine present sensation. Again, in Wordsworth's prose:

> I cannot but, in connection with it [the sublime experience], observe that the main source of all the difficulties & errors which have attended these disquisitions is that the attention of those who have been engaged in them has been primarily & chiefly fixed upon external objects & their powers, qualities, & properties, & not upon the mind itself, and the laws by which it is acted upon. Hence the endless disputes about the characters of objects, and the absolute denial on the part of many that sublimity or beauty exists. To talk of an object as being sublime or beautiful in itself, without references to some subject by whom that sublimity or beauty is perceived, is absurd; nor is it of the slightest importance to mankind whether there be any object with which their minds are conversant that Men would universally agree (after having ascertained that the words were used in the same sense) to denominate sublime or beautiful. (375)

In a sense, then, everyone becomes his own sublimist. The experience shifts not as objects change, but as the perceiver does. While the lofty precipice may well startle the child into the sublime, the adult may respond equally to a softly contoured slope or even to "the meanest flower that blows." William Empson, in his comments on *Tintern Abbey*, has fun tweaking Wordsworth by asking exactly what was meant by the "sense sublime" or an "aspect more sublime." "More sublime than what?" Empson asks.[9] But the answer is clear: Wordsworth is referring to this sense of repetition, this internal reflexivity, this linguistic process by which the memories of the Wye Valley are "infused" with current perceptions. It is as if the sublime uncodes the memory, not to remind us of the past, but to expand the present.

9. William Empson, "Sense in *The Prelude*," in *The Structure of Complex Words*, p. 301.

To recapitulate: what makes these lines from *Tintern Abbey* a *locus sublimitatis*, if you will, is, first, that the poet is perceiving unique, specifically located forms—he even names them: "*This* dark sycamore," "*These* plots of cottage ground," "*These* orchard-tufts," "*These* hedge rows," "*These* pastoral farms." By virtue of their unique form and the poet's sensitivity, these objects have sufficient power to suspend the comparing and cataloging powers of the Reason. But there is nothing awesome or fearsome here, only a loss of self-consciousness and a growing sense of unity with these external forms. Second, the poet himself, now by virtue of his previous perceptions, informs the scene with a host of recollections, associations, and, ultimately, meanings. The resulting sense of elevation and transport may well *lead* to a "mystic experience," "ecstasy," "apocalypse," "transcendence," "*anima mundi*," "phenomenological intentional interpenetration," or whatever each new generation of critics may want to call it, but it is clear that this next event is beyond the pale of the sublime.

The sublime, we must remember, only goes to the edge of release, to the limit of language, to the horizon; it is still very much bound to the here and now, to the senses. It is a state of awareness, a state of elevated consciousness that is momentarily stopped at the threshold of something supraconscious.[10] Wordsworth explains this world at the edge in *Tintern Abbey*:

> —that serene and blessed mood,
> In which the affections gently lead us on,—
> Until, the breath of this corporeal frame
> And even the motion of our human blood
> Almost suspended, we are laid asleep
> In body, and become a living soul:
> While with an eye made quiet by the power
> Of harmony, and the deep power of joy,
> We see into the life of things. (41–49)

One can often be sympathetic with Ezra Pound's question, "Does Mr. Wordsworth sometimes use words that express nothing in

10. For a Kantian-Freudian interpretation of this kind of "blockage" in Wordsworth, see Neil Hertz, "The Notion of Blockage in the Literature of the Sublime," in *Psychoanalysis and the Question of the Text: Selected Papers from the English Institute, 1976–77*, ed. Geoffrey H. Hartman, pp. 62–85.

particular?," but this is not the case in *Tintern Abbey*. Here
there is a specific experience and, as Gene Ruoff contends, one
must stress

> the term *experience* because ideologically oriented analyses some-
> times obscure the point that what the romantics might call the sub-
> lime, the transcendent, or the divine was important precisely be-
> cause it was perceptually accessible, but only occasionally and
> fleetingly. But wherever there is access to the highest experience—
> in the bower, in the dream, or in childhood (to cite some persistent
> metaphors)—that experience cannot readily be brought back into
> the human community to become a vital part of man's social, histor-
> ical existence. The goal of the poet, after all, is not simply to ap-
> prehend the sacred, but to bring sacred experience into a meaning-
> ful relationship with the rest of human experience.[11]

If Wordsworth's contribution to psychology was to make every
man his own sublimist, his contribution to aesthetics was to make
every scene in nature a potential object of sublimity—even London can be seen as sublime, even something as common as a
break in an overcast sky.[12] However, I should now like to turn our
attention to a relatively unstudied poem, *Yew Trees*.[13] Published
about the same time Wordsworth was composing the essay on
the sublime, *Yew Trees* is an apt exemplum of his views on the
sublime. Here is the poem:

11. Gene W. Ruoff, "Wordsworth's *Yew Trees* and Romantic Perception," pp.
158–59.
12. Clearly London is a sublime scene in *Composed upon Westminster Bridge,
September 3, 1802*, primarily because human life is not stirring, but this is not the
case with London in book 8 of *The Prelude*; here sublimity exists within the process of human interactions. Wordsworth's sublime "moments" can be well below
what Hartman calls "apocalyptic pitch," as Kenneth R. Johnson elaborates in his
explanations of *A Night Piece* and *St. Paul's* in "The Idiom of Vision," in *New Perspectives on Coleridge and Wordsworth: Selected Papers from the English Institute*, ed. Geoffrey H. Hartman, pp. 1–39.
13. Although both Wordsworth and Coleridge singled out *Yew Trees* for its dis-
play of imaginative power, there has been a relative paucity of comments about it:
Raymond Dexter Havens, *The Mind of a Poet: A Study of Wordsworth's Thought*,
1:227, and Cleanth Brooks and Robert Penn Warren, *Understanding Poetry*, 3d
ed., pp. 273–79. Things, however, are changing as there recently have been two
fascinating articles on *Yew Trees*: first, Michael Riffaterre, "Interpretation and
Descriptive Poetry: A Reading of Wordsworth's *Yew Trees*," and an analysis by
Geoffrey Hartman, "The Use and Abuse of Structural Analysis: Riffaterre's Interpretation of Wordsworth's *Yew Trees*."

There is a Yew-tree, pride of Lorton Vale,
Which to this day stands single, in the midst
Of its own darkness, as it stood of yore:
Not loth to furnish weapons for the bands
Of Umfraville or Percy ere they marched
To Scotland's heaths; or those that crossed the sea
And drew their sounding bows at Azincour,
Perhaps at earlier Crecy, or Poictiers.
Of vast circumference and gloom profound
This solitary Tree! a living thing
Produced too slowly ever to decay;
Of form and aspect too magnificent
To be destroyed. But worthier still of note
Are those fraternal Four of Borrowdale,
Joined in one solemn and capacious grove;
Huge trunks! and each particular trunk a growth
Of intertwisted fibres serpentine
Up-coiling, and inveterately convolved;
Nor uniformed with Phantasy, and looks
That threaten the profane; a pillared shade,
Upon whose grassless floor of red-brown hue,
By sheddings from the pining umbrage tinged
Perennially—beneath whose sable roof
Of boughs, as if for festal purpose, decked
With unrejoicing berries—ghostly Shapes
May meet at noontide; Fear and trembling Hope,
Silence and Foresight; Death the Skeleton
And Time the Shadow;—there to celebrate,
As in a natural temple scattered o'er
With altars undisturbed of mossy stone,
United worship; or in mute repose
To lie, and listen to the mountain flood
Murmuring from Glaramara's inmost caves.

Although these yew trees are solidly in the mundane world of
the senses and in no way represent a break in horizontal forms (as
does, say, the precipice, volcano, waterfall), they become, thanks
to the poet, a fit object of the sublime. There is a paradox in all
this, for the powers of the imagination that perform the sublimation are the selfsame powers that are themselves transformed.
The trees at the end are not the same as they were at the begin-

ning, nor is the poet. And what about those spirits—how have they appeared? Sublimity, we recall, is not deduced, it is attributed; and the result of that attribution is the change within the perceiver that changes "reality" outside.[14] The interanimation of individual form, power, and duration coupled with the meaning-making desires of the poet have reordered the world in some new way. The question now is whether this reordering can be decoded by the reader, and Wordsworth implies, as I hope to show, that it cannot be decoded completely. Those "ghostly shapes" will always be there at the threshold, beckoning the poet into the world past language, into the liminal.

On the level of objects and things there is no doubt about the physical uniqueness of these yews: literary pilgrims have even assured us that they were indeed there for Wordsworth to see. Still one initially wonders what business such trees can have with any elevated state of consciousness. Yews, especially those in the Lake District, are not massive trees; I suppose the American counterpart would be the bristlecone pine. These are hardly the bull oaks or iron elms that a Burkean might demand. So it is clearly not their absolute size that impresses the poet but their relative position. One yew in Lorton Vale stands single, presumably shown off against lower shrubbery, while the four of Borrowdale are clustered together giving an impression of oneness. In addition, perhaps because they are evergreen, their coloration hides the fragile skeleton, giving the illusion of magnitude and massiveness. In any case, this much is clear; these yews are not sublime objects to the poet solely because of size or outline; their sublimity resides in the attributed qualities of power and duration.

Here Wordsworth clearly departed from received concepts of sublimity. These trees are not awesome and terrible; rather they can only be made so by the deconstructing powers of the imag-

14. One might keep in mind two comments on the sublime: one by Coleridge, "I meet, I *find* the Beautiful—but I give, contribute, or rather attribute the Sublime" ("Unpublished Fragments on Aesthetics by S. T. Coleridge," ed. Thomas M. Raysor, p. 532) and another by Wordsworth, "To talk of an object as being sublime or beautiful in itself, without references to some subject by whom that sublimity or beauty is perceived, is *absurd*" (*Prose*, 2:357).

ination. And they are made so most obviously by the poet's displacement of space into time.[15] Wordsworth seems to be playing
ironically with the yews' association with death, for it is their
ability to circumvent death, their resistance to decay and change,
that generates the power. Wood from such venerable trees as
these have furnished bows for the armies of Hotspur to battle
the Scots, as well as for those armies of Henry V to defeat the
French. Clearly this synecdochical association with past glories is
neither new nor startling; what is a shock is the poet's sense that
these trees of "vast circumference and gloom profound" have *actively* participated with mankind while remaining outside time.
Hence they are in a sense godlike, caring, and willful, yet exempt
from mortal constraints. They have never been loath to give up
their sturdy fiber for England; in fact, we get the sense they have
conspired with England against all foes.

It is clear that well before the poem is over these yews have
become iconic and deific. Michael Riffaterre has said of the results of their extraordinary duration:

> The repetitive sequence is like a hymn to the (hyperbolized) con-
> cept of Vegetable Life, as opposed to Mineral Life (fiberless,
> growthless), and as opposed to Animal Life. The yew is not de-
> scribed in relation to the tree of that name, but as an image of an
> existence closer to Eternity than ours—or, in Wordsworth's terms,
> more impervious to "decay" than ours. It simply carries on in a new
> language the first part of the poem, which stated this poetic vision
> in terms of human life transcended.[16]

15. This argument is put forward first in Brooks and Warren, *Understanding
Poetry*: "The size of the first yew tree, the aspect that makes it remarkable (the
"pride of Lorton Vale") is not measured for us in terms of feet and inches. The
dimension of space in converted into that of time: it is the mighty age of the tree
on which the speaker dilates" (pp. 274–75), and then in Riffaterre, "Interpretation": "Associations here do not work from outside history to text, but the other
way around. The text builds up a phantasm of history. Shift the sentence from
general to particular, from nouns to names, and in terms of time or space you
create an effect of reality. And if the reality be distant in time, then the effect of a
reality that deserves not to be forgotten. The whole "weapons" motif serves only
as a time marker, but a periphrastic one. In accordance with the principles of the
genre, it dates the tree by describing activities of yore, instead of just stating that
it is very old. The description of dated activities is the more effective if the text
adds a marker of fame, since in a time code *fame* is the equivalent of *durability*,
and is therefore a hyperbole of *ancient* if the time code is actualized in the past
tense" (pp. 232–75).
16. Riffaterre, "Interpretation," p. 237.

Hence what Wordsworth is attempting in the first twelve lines is to encode the image of the yew tree with attributes of divinity, instigating the process of sublimation, for it is the very essence of the sublime that the organizing powers of the Reason be blocked. The single yew, isolated out of time and change, mightily concentrated yet inexplicably linked to the fortunes of mankind, does become a "type and symbol of Eternity, / Of first, and last, and midst, and without end" (*Prelude*, 6. 639–40), simply because this is the only way the imagination can resolve the tension: these trees become daemonic.

This chain of association is now linked to the "fraternal Four of Borrowdale." Once again the emphasis is on power and duration:

> But worthier still of note
> Are those fraternal Four of Borrowdale,
> Joined in one solemn and capacious grove;
> Huge trunks! and each particular trunk a growth
> Of intertwisted fibres serpentine
> Up-coiling, and inveterately convolved;
> Nor uninformed with Phantasy, and looks
> That threaten the profane. (13–20)

The same strain of primordial god-stuff runs through these trees: not only are they in a "solemn" grove, but their mere existence "threaten[s] the profane." The wood is animate, serpentine, intertwisted, "inveterately convolved," unfolding its presence. Here before us is a sight that compresses divinity into nature.

The linguistic coding of the natural and supernatural prepares us for the jolt of the next and last image. Within these delphic trees is the secret grove, the temple, the shrine, the *omphalos*. This is not, however, the *locus amoenous* of a natural Eden, for there is an aspect of profound melancholy here; surely "pining umbrage" has the *penseroso* air reasserted by the decorations of "unrejoicing berries." There is a sense of the fallen world here in the "pillared shade . . . beneath [the] sable roof of boughs." This is the daemonic world at the threshold of new consciousness; this is the world of the "ghostly shapes" of Fear, trembling Hope, Silence, Foresight, Death the Skeleton, and Time the Shadow, the "phantoms of sublimity" that Coleridge claimed were the in/ sights of the poet with "gifted ken" (*Apologia Pro Sua Vita*).

The only analogy for this experience, at least in the West, is religious. These yew trees hold special knowledge for the poet; their "intertwisted fibres, serpentine / Up-coiling" betoken experience beyond the pale, beyond the senses. It is a world unseen save by those who come to worship and accept on faith what cannot be articulated. Here it may be instructive to look at Wordsworth's cancelled ending:

> Pass not the [? Place] unvisited—Ye will say
> That Mona's Druid Oaks composed a Fane
> Less awful than this grove: as Earth so long
> On its unwearied bosom has sustained
> The undecaying Pile; as Frost and Drought,
> The Fires of heaven have spared it, and the Storms,
> So for its hallowed uses may it stand
> For ever spared by Man!

Wordsworth clearly intended in this last stanza to reinforce the reverential as well as the venerable aspect of these trees, for the bower has become a fane. The profane has become sacred.

If the experience here is religious, then it comes from the poet's (critic's) attempt to make the sublime sensible. However much we may have been prepared, it is still a shock to be told what the poet may see inside: he may see ghosts at *noontime*. Possibly these ghosts are the poet's imaginative attempt to order experience at the threshold; in fact, the passage seems reminiscent of how Shelley tried to make sense of his confusion in a similar circumstance:

> No voice from some sublimer world hath ever
>   To sage or poet these responses given—
>   Therefore the names of Demon, Ghost, and Heaven,
> Remain the records of their vain endeavour,
> Frail spells—whose uttered charm might not avail to sever,
>   From all we hear and all we see,
>   Doubt, chance, and mutability.
>
>   *Hymn to Intellectual Beauty*, 25–31

Wordsworth shows in *Yew Trees* the same daemonmaking process that will reappear in the Ancient Mariner's vision, in Endymion's glimpse into the skies, and in the worlds above both Manfred and

Prometheus. It is the Imagination's attribution of mythopoetic order and proportion to confusion. Critics like Brooks and Warren who have had trouble piecing together the personified forms of Hope, Death, Time, and so on, into some intelligible pattern should first realize that these forms are the creations of the poet's symbolmaking powers.[17] They are what he creates, what he imagines, what he sublimes, not at all what would be there for anyone else. They are his individual attributions of order and structure, not necessarily allegorical or even coherent.

So *Yew Trees* is not really "about" yew trees at all but rather about the trip to the brink of the world beyond "sensible" perception. The poet remains at the edge still bound to language. As Geoffrey Hartman has written of this lack of closure:

> The in-between character of the Wordsworthian narrative voice can be interpreted in several, nonexclusive ways: as indicating a tension between mutism and oracular eloquence, or self-depletion (the self phantomized by a sublime experience) and self-redemption (through identification with the sublime), and so forth. Coming closer to Wordsworth's own terms, one could emphasize a split between humanizing and eternizing movements of thought: the poet, haunted by the "unimaginable touch of Time," puts himself or a surrogate beyond the "touch of earthly years."[18]

Clearly something will have to be sacrificed if the poet decides to cross into that liminal world; if he finds his way into the "natural temple" to the "altars undisturbed of mossy stone," he will have to give up the order and regularity of *this* world. He will have to give up language and thus give up art. So he keeps to the margin. Hartman continues:

> Consider the phenomenon of centroversion in Wordsworth: how his mind circles and haunts a particular place until released into an emancipatory idea of Nature. The yews, in this light, are *omphaloi*: boundary images, or signs of a liminal situation, a cultic and charged threshold. As we follow the poet's words we are kept moving along a border between natural and supernatural ideas; and

17. Brooks and Warren, *Understanding Poetry*, p. 278.
18. Hartman, "Use and Abuse," pp. 170–71.

there is no guarantee he might not go over the line into a dark and discontinuous fantasy.[19]

Here in essence is the paradox of the sublime: unity demands the loss of self, the abrogation of reason, yet it promises "mute repose," the merging of self and object, as well as the possibility of still higher consciousness. But what is the price for the possibility of a "peace that passeth understanding"? This is unresolved, but it clearly entails giving up the senses.

The embedded emblem that informs all the images in this poem is the cave. It is never mentioned as such, but it is there behind the image of the "natural temple," behind the image of the "capacious grove" and the "undecaying Pile." The journey here into the yew trees is the journey into the cave, across the threshold of light into darkness or, better yet, from profane darkness into spiritual light. In fact, the cave was clearly in Wordsworth's mind when he wrote the note to the poem:

> These yew-trees are still standing, but the spread of that at Lorton is much diminished by mutilation. I will here mention that a little way up the hill, on the road leading from Rosthwaite to Stonethwaite, lay the trunk of a yew-tree, which appeared as you approached, so vast was its diameter, like the entrance of a cave, and not a small one.[20]

One need only read Wordsworth elsewhere to find confirmation of this imagistic commonplace. Here, for instance, from the 1850 *The Prelude*:

> The curious traveller, who, from open day,
> Hath passed with torches into some huge cave,
> . . . looks around and sees the vault
> Widening on all sides; sees, or thinks he sees,
> Erelong, the massy roof above his head,
> That instantly unsettles and recedes,—
> Substance and shadow, light and darkness, all
> Commingled, making up a canopy
> Of shapes and forms and tendencies to shape

19. Ibid., p. 173.
20. *The Poetical Works of William Wordsworth*, ed. Ernest de Selincourt, 2:503.

That shift and vanish, change and interchange
Like spectres,—ferment silent and sublime!
That after a short space works less and less,
Till, every effort, every motion gone,
The scene before him stands in perfect view
Exposed, and lifeless as a written book!—
But let him pause awhile, and look again,
And a new quickening shall succeed, at first
Beginning timidly, then creeping fast,
Till the whole cave, so late a senseless mass,
Busies the eye with images and forms
Boldly assembled,—here is shadowed forth
From the projections, wrinkles, cavities,
A variegated landscape,—there the shape
Of some gigantic warrior clad in mail,
The ghostly semblance of a hooded monk,
Veiled nun, or pilgrim resting on his staff:
Strange congregation! yet not slow to meet
Eyes that perceive through minds that can inspire. (8. 560–89)

The vision into the cave is the vision into the buried self, into
the dark world of dreams, into consciousness itself. The model is,
of course, the Platonic cave, which was being transformed in the
eighteenth century into the Lockean image of the mind. From
the twilight inside we see both the dimly coruscating forms shadowed behind (subconscious) and the ever-streaming flow of light
outside (conscious). As M. H. Abrams asserts in *The Mirror
and the Lamp*, the cave was but one of the metaphors of the
mind revived by the romantics.[21] Movement between these two
worlds, inner and outer, dark and light, illusion and reality, subconscious and conscious, necessitates the crossing of the natural
threshold. As in Porphyry's Cave of the Nymphs, this passage
leads perilously from one state of consciousness to another, and it
is precisely this perilousness that engenders the sense of sublime.

Here it may be of more than passing importance that once
within the cave of the yew the poet listens in "mute repose" to
activity in caves still more remote: he listens "to the mountain

21. M. H. Abrams, *The Mirror and the Lamp: Romantic Theory and the Critical Tradition*, p. 58.

flood / Murmuring from Glaramara's inmost caves." Not only is
the cave motif redoubled, the cave within the cave, but now the
companion image of percolating water is introduced. Perhaps
this water is "a sufficiently apt symbol of the flowing of time, especially conceived of as issuing from a dim and inaccessible past,"
as Brooks and Warren suggest, but Wordsworth may have had a
more traditional coupling of images in mind.[22] These are the buried waters, hidden streams murmuring through Glaramara that
finally bubble up to the surface in springs. These two images, the
cave and the spring, are historically linked to the process of perception: the cave as the mind, the water as the stream of consciousness. In fact, the cave and the spring, symbolic of the nec-
essities of art, are said to exist on the holy mountain sacred to the
muses. Additionally, the spring is central to Platonism (especially
the Neoplatonists like Plotinus), in which, like the sun, it is lik-
ened to the processes of emanation. Clearly in all these myths
the image of the cave and the spring is synecdochical—an expression of consciousness itself.

Although these are ancient images, they were being revived in
late eighteenth-century art; in fact, they were becoming an important visual trope in both theoretical aesthetics and practical
application. The spring was always associated with the foun-
tainhead, but the cave was developing into the artificial grotto.
Although the cave might have served as a haven or hermitage
(Defoe's *Robinson Crusoe*) at the beginning of the eighteenth
century, it developed into something psychological (Pope's Cave
of Spleen as well as his Cave of Truth in *The Dunciad*, or the philosopher's cave in Johnson's *Rasselas*). By the turn of the century
"caverns measureless to man" were buried below the surface to
become the caves of Quietude and Solitude in *Endymion* and finally the Cave of Demogorgon in *Prometheus Unbound*. Equally
startling is what is simultaneously happening in the visual arts.
For the first time we start seeing *through* the cave in paintings as
in, say, Loutherbourg's *The Inside of the Cavern at Castleton*,
1778, as well as John Robert Cozens's *Alpine Ravine*, 1776, or
Robert Freebairn's *Neptune's Grotto*, 1807. This perspective of

22. Brooks and Warren, *Understanding Poetry*, p. 278.

seeing from inside out soon developed into the cavescapes of John Martin, Francis Danby, and J. M. W. Turner where it took on allegorical and symbolic meanings.

What happened is that the enclosed space of the cave, complete with the startling shift in light at the aperture, became an image of sublimity. That is why the cave so abruptly started appearing in all the arts; think of Fingal's Cave, Merlin's Cave, or Calypso's Grotto as they were either revived or conceived in romanticism. Here, for instance, is William Gilpin, the aesthetician, describing a cave in Castleton:

> A towering rock hangs over you; under which you enter an arched cavern twelve yards high, forty wide, and near a hundred long. So vast a canopy of *unpillared* rock stretching above your head, gives you an involuntary shudder. A strong light at the mouth of the cave, displays all the horrors of the *entrance* in full proportion. But this light decaying, as you proceed, the imagination is left to explore its deeper caverns by torchlight which gives them additional terror. . . . It is known by the names of the cathedral.[23]

Think as well of what occurred in the mid-1700s to the manufactured cave, the grotto, in landscape gardening. Pope built his grotto at Twickenham not as a folly but rather because it was one of the new forms in the art. The Hermitage at Chatsworth, St. Augustine's Cave at Stowe, and, most famous, the Grotto at Stourhead all show how rapidly this already iconic image was becoming assimilated into new aesthetic schemes.

I should now like to turn from the general to the more specific, to look at a cave that appears in a rather unlikely place: in the paintings of Joseph Wright of Derby. This painting, *A Cavern: Evening*, was completed in 1774, well in advance of the professionally sublime caves of Martin and Danby. It represents, I think, a development in romantic consciousness analogous to what we saw in Wordsworth's poetry. This painting and its companion piece, *A Cavern: Morning*, 1774, seem to me to signal a turning away of the sublime from dependence on external scenes to a more subjective and psychological definition of the sublime.

---

23. William Gilpin, *Observations, relative chiefly to picturesque beauty . . . in Cumberland and Westmoreland*, 2:215.

Joseph Wright of Derby, *A Cavern: Evening*, 1774. Smith College
Museum of Art, Northampton, Massachusetts.

Joseph Wright is certainly not known as a landscape painter; he
is justly famous for portraits and wonderfully lighted scenes of
men at the edge of empirical discovery (*The Alchemist, Academy
by Lamplight, Hermit Studying Anatomy, Philosopher Giving a
Lecture on the Orrery, Philosopher by Lamplight, An Experiment on a Bird in the Air Pump*), all representing threshold experiences in science. In the early 1770s, however, Wright traveled
to Italy and there, I think, became fascinated with the possibilities of picturing the sublime in landscape. Prior to his Italian
journey he had painted only one "pure" landscape (at least only

one that we know of), a picturesque scene that may have been intended as a background for some uncompleted study.[24] By the mid-1770s, however, he had painted several works—*The Earth-stopper*, *The Hermit*, and the *The Old Man and Death*—with expansive landscape backgrounds using similar forms. Doubtless there were other landscapes that have been lost, but this we do know: after Wright returned from Italy he became very much the budding romanticist, even making the requisite pilgrimages to the Lake District to paint not the picturesque, but the sublime.

So what he painted in Italy may have shown him possibilities he knew could be brought back home. The two natural subjects he painted in Italy were volcanoes and caves, two subjects most expressive of high Augustan and romantic sublimity. The former is Burkean and explosive, the latter Wordsworthian and implosive. On the subject of Wright's volcano pictures Benedict Nicolson, who assembled the monumental collection of Wright's oeuvre, has written that they "occasionally surpass sublimity by hinting at powers beyond the violent explosion, powers of malevolence in nature," and this is certainly true.[25] In addition, these vulcan eruptions are more clearly informed by Wright's unique knowledge of the blast furnace (as we still see in all those marvelous *Iron Forge* paintings) than by any contrived aesthetic design. Although in Wright's vision no one hangs over the lip of the volcano and no molten lava comes avalanching down over peasant hovels, it is clear that he is concerned with the dynamics of force and less interested in consequences.[26] These volcanoes are essentially tilted caves on fire.

Although Wright was initially intrigued with views of an erupting Mount Vesuvius (he painted it first from the edge looking

24. Benedict Nicolson, *Joseph Wright of Derby: Painter of Light*, 1: 75.

25. Although the primary influence on English gothic/sublime landscapists was Salvator Rosa, it is noteworthy that on Wright's Italian journey he carried Alexander Cozens's *A New Method of Assisting the Invention in Drawing Original Landscapes*. As I will explain later in the chapter on Keats, Alexander Cozens was the foremost prescriber of sublimity in landscape, even developing a system whereby patterns of light and shadow could be composed ("blotted" as he called it) to produce utmost effect. However, Wright's assimilation of Cozens is best seen in his late English landscapes, in which he is clearly making copies of Cozens's own views. See Nicolson, *Joseph Wright*, pp. 78–79.

26. Nicolson, *Joseph Wright*, p. 75.

down, then from the edge looking out, then from the middle distance, then from across the water with the requisite schooner in silhouette), after some ten different views he moved on to Naples. En route, he made what, in retrospect, was a most serendipitous side trip to the Gulf of Salerno, for there he came across the famous sea grottoes. These grottoes no longer exist because the neighboring rock has eroded away and the soft overhangs have fallen, but what a propitious sight they must have been for a young Englishman eager for exciting vistas. They were already something of a tourist attraction, gathering the same clientele who marveled at Vesuvius.

The experience was not lost. In the early 1770s Wright sketched two views in black chalk, then painted them—one at sunrise and the other at sunset. He later painted many other grotto scenes involving these visual prototypes, varying the subject matter somewhat to include some dubious foreground characters (bandits, melancholy damsels), but never changing the two central aspects. He always painted the cave from the inside looking out, and he always made the light outside too bright to see through. This creates an aura effect, making us blink as if we, accustomed to the cave darkness, now have to pause, momentarily stunned by the iridescence and whiteness, before we can proceed. The effect is rather like looking into the mouth of the volcano, except that here we are looking horizontally outward into blinding light as if into one of his flaring blast furnaces. It is what Wordsworth sensed, not ghosts at midnight but at noontide, a spectacular sight that cannot be cataloged by the Reason.

As Wright continued to experiment with this image of enclosed space opening into brightness, the grotto became transformed into the tomb. In *Virgil's Tomb* (1779), the ancient scholar is encaved with his studies lighted by a mysterious moon, while another *Virgil's Tomb* (1782) has only the empty grotto. There is no doubt which is more successful in achieving the sublime: the cave image depends on our ability to perceive ourselves within that tight space. Caught in that enclosure we must feel compressed, trapped between light and dark. It is surely of more than passing coincidence that while Wright was painting these cave scenes, he was also continuing a series of prison scenes begun in 1775 with *The Captive, From Sterne*.[27] The fascination with enclosed space and the sense of looking out through a hole into blinding light contain the same lighting as the blast furnace pictures now combined with the high gothic theme of a picture like *The Old Man and Death*: we are stopped, stymied, and strangely frightened.

I should like now to look again at *A Cavern: Evening*, which, along with its counterpart *A Cavern: Morning*, is one of the most impressive cave scenes in romanticism. I say this because it shows something quite extraordinary, something as exciting as what Wordsworth had shown at the end of *Yew Trees*. It shows that light is every bit as impressive as form, that one need not see a precipice, blasting waterfall, volcano, or typhoon; what one needs is the sense of threshold, a sense of boundary, a sense of liminality beyond. Our reaction to blasting light, whether it be through the grate of a prison cell, from the ironmonger's forge, from the mouth of a volcano, or flooding into a cavern, depends on a most fundamental reflex: the contraction of our pupils, and our concomitant panic at not being able to make out recognizable forms. We are stopped short by light, made momentarily powerless, at a loss for words.

Admittedly, any abrupt shift in light will cause us this momentary blockage, but the effect will be heightened when perceived through a dimly recognized form such as the opening to the cave. Ronald Paulson thinks the form itself is conducive to the sublimation:

> The cave is an open space embedded within a large impenetrable area of nature . . . it can be either looked into . . . or out of, as in the sea-grotto pictures. The arch is carved out of darkness as space, or the arch itself is man-made with natural space visible through it.
> The model for these works . . . would seem to be the Platonic cave with figures lighted by a fire inside and the cave mouth open toward the light. The Platonic metaphor—or its eighteenth-century version, the Lockean metaphor of mind itself, [is] a cell cut off from the out side world of sense impressions. . . . For Wright, with his interest in effects of sun and moonlight, the Platonic and

27. I am thinking especially of works like the two *Small Prison Scenes* (1787 and 1890) as well as *Interior of a Prison* (1788).

Lockean metaphors are related to the Plotinian one of poetic creation as a radiating sun—a power which 'gives a radiance out of its
own store' to the inert world it sees; and to the Cambridge Platonists' image of the 'the Spirit of man' as 'the Candle of the Lord'.
The Creator Himself is 'the fountain of light', who has furnished us
in this 'lower part of the World with Intellectual Lamps, that should
shine forth to the praise and honour of his Name. . . .' This is the
anti-empirical, anti-Lockean position in which man, as 'the Candle
of the Lord', sheds 'more light upon' the objects of the external
world than he 'receives from them'. And this will become Wordsworth's 'An auxiliar light / Came from my mind which on the setting
sun / Bestow'd new splendor.'[28]

Seeing these cave pictures as the image of the self-reflexive mind
contemplating itself may still be a bit farther than we are willing
to go, yet in the sense that Michael Riffaterre considers *Yew
Trees* the "mimesis of a visionary act," I think the same may be
said about these caverns of Joseph Wright.[29] We are seeing with
the eye through the eye, imagining the mind with the mind. We
do not know what lies beyond the aperture; we know only what
we can imagine. Language can take us only to the edge. It is
in this pre-liminal, sub-liminal area that Wordsworth sees his
"Ghostly shapes," and it is also here that we catch the full blast of
Wright's vision of luminescence.

One wonders if Wright was aware of the religious iconography
suggested by those up-reaching arches and the light pouring
through. Surely Wordsworth knew that the cave form was a religious topos; he even referred to the yew-enclosure as a fane or
a temple and interpreted activity there as worship. Certainly
the English and American painters were aware of the awesome
power of rising and setting sunlight flooding across religious borders. In all but one of Wright's cave scenes there is a distinct cathedral arch overhead, an arch that most probably was not actually there in "real life," for this sea grotto was formed by the flow
of water and so would have had a rounded top. In fact, in his one
purely imaginative cave painting (*Grotto with Waterfall*, circa

28. Ronald Paulson, *Emblem and Expression: Meaning in English Art of the
Eighteenth Century*, p. 196.
29. Riffaterre, "Interpretation and Descriptive Poetry," p. 253.

1776) Wright does round out the arch and thereby sacrifice the effect. What we should see when looking through the cavern is analogous to what we see in the gothic cathedral: we stand in the portal looking down the central nave to a wall of light above the altar in stained glass. All around us is the skeletal web that holds up vaulting space. All form conspires to give us both a surge of energy and a contrary feeling of weakness. One need only look at Turner's 1796 *Westminster Abbey* to see the cave consciously so transformed.

It is surely reductionistic to couple Wright's vision with Wordsworth's critical prose, but such a coupling does provide a commentary on the romantic fascination with articulating the sublime. All Wordsworth's criteria are met in this painting: the importance of individual form (the gothic peculiarities of this cave), the importance of power (the blasting of light through the opening)—these are indeed attributes Wordsworth had extracted from empirical studies. But Wordsworth listed a third criterion, duration, by which he meant a sense of stability in space and repeatability through time. His example is of the neverending ocean waves or a vista of sway-backed mountaintops that may produce a sense of "infinite self-propagation." This image of wavelike repetition, of change without end, is also involved, I think, in Wright's painting. For not only do we have the sense of seeing from a chamber out into space, but this sense is repeated in the reflective surface of the water. We are caught, so to speak, in a hall of mirrors. Arch and aperture exist in foreground, middleground, and background and are then seen once again reflected in the water. Like viewing the waves of the ocean or the undulating line of mountain crests, we have here the momentary sense of a redundancy without resolution.

In Wright's vision we stand at the threshold, as much on the edge of altered consciousness as Wordsworth halfway inside the yew-bower. We are momentarily perplexed by the awareness of something uncontrolled by Reason: we are caught at the brink. It is the same experience recorded by Wordsworth halfway up into Snowdon:

> . . . at my feet
> A hundred hills their dusky backs upheaved

All over this still ocean and beyond,
Far, far beyond, the vapours shot themselves
In headlands, tongues, and promontory shapes,
Into the sea, the real sea, that seemed
To dwindle and give up its majesty,
Usurped upon as far as sight could reach.

(Prelude, 1805, 13. 45–51)

But Wordsworth finally attempts to go still farther; he meditates until the event is transformed into an image of cosmic Mind, until the images become momentarily liminal or even apocalyptic and all descriptions fail. In making this transformation, however, he moves past the sublime; he moves up and over the edge into a qualitatively different form of consciousness. Although he later renounced this as "the tyranny of the eye," it is precisely this progress, the pushing past the aperture, moving over the horizon, that characterizes the direction of the romantic vision from Wordsworth onward. And we will now see this, developing by fits and starts, in the works of other poets and painters.

3

Coleridge and Turner:
The Sublime at the Vortex

I readily believe that there are more invisible than visible things in the universe. But who shall describe for us their families, their ranks, relationships, distinguishing features and functions? What do they do? Where do they live? The human mind has always circled about knowledge of these things, but never attained it. I do not doubt, however, that it is sometimes good to contemplate in the mind, as in a picture, the image of a greater and better world; otherwise the intellect, habituated to the petty things of daily life, may too much contract itself, and wholly sink down to trivial thoughts. But meanwhile we must be vigilant for truth and keep proportion, that we may distinguish the certain from the uncertain, day from night.—Thomas Burnet, *Archaeologiae Philosophicae*

Coleridge's choice of the above epigraph for *The Rime of the Ancient Mariner* was particularly appropriate, for it sets the cosmic stage for the activity that follows. We may read it as a very precise prose description of *The Rime*, the first part declaring that there is an unseen world above us, and the second hinting that a vision of such a world might expand the mind and enlarge the consciousness. But this headnote is important for another reason: Burnet here articulates the essential claim of the sublime—it allows us passage past "trivial thought"; it takes us to a new order of experience and then returns us to our enlightened selves.

The problem for the romantic artist wishing to explore sublimity was that the verbal and visual forms he had inherited from the Augustans were able to describe little more than "daily life." "Man" was the proper literary study of "mankind," and in the visual arts Sir Joshua Reynolds had made it clear that linear sim-

plicity was all—"a firm and determined outline" meant more
than how to paint; it meant what to paint.[1] But for the sublime to
be pictured, demarcations between objects, between colors, between what Burnet calls "visible and invisible things," must be
removed. The sublime experience takes us up to the threshold of
the "greater world" and logically cannot be described in the
terms of the ordinary.

The great achievement of Coleridge and Turner was their insistence on the rightness of their vision, their insistence that the
sublime could be separated from other experiences and made
an independent category. This insistence was by no means the
norm; in fact, asetheticians like Uvedale Price, in works like *Essays on the Picturesque, as Compared with the Sublime and the
Beautiful*, asserted that the sublime was always a synthesis of
other aesthetic states.[2] The elements could be changed, but the
formula remained the same: the sublime was inevitably "made
up" of something else. Even Kant and Hegel considered the sublime relative, as had Kant's mentor, Burke. Not so, however, for
Coleridge; for him this principle of comparison or synthesis had
no place:

1. Joshua Reynolds, *Discourses on Art*, ed. Robert Wark, p. 52. Color is also
"controlled" by line:

> To give a general air of grandeur at first view all trifling or artful play of little
> lights, or an attention to a variety of tints is to be avoided; a quietness and
> simplicity must reign over the whole work; to which a breadth of uniform,
> and simple colour, will very much contribute. Grandeur of effect is pro-
> duced by two different ways, which seem entirely opposed to each other.
> One is, by reducing the colours to little more than chiaro oscuro, which was
> often the practice of the Bolognian schools; and the other, by making the
> colours very distinct and forcible, such as we see in those of Rome and Flor-
> ence; but still, the presiding principle of both those manners is simplicity.
> Certainly, nothing can be more simple than monotony; and the distinct
> blue, red, and yellow colours which are seen in the draperies of the Roman
> and Florentine schools, though they have not that kind of harmony which is
> produced by a variety of broken and transparent colours, have that effect of
> grandeur which was intended. (p. 61)

2. Uvedale Price, *Essays on the Picturesque, as Compared with the Sublime
and the Beautiful* . . . , pp. 86–87, even defines the picturesque as the synthesis
of the beautiful and the sublime, mixing "the complacent languor" of the former
with "the oppressive terror" of the latter.

We call an object sublime in relation to which the exercise of comparison is suspended: while on the contrary that object is most
beautiful, which in its highest perfection sustains while it satisfies
the comparing Power. . . . It is impossible that the same object
should be sublime and beautiful at the same moment to the same
mind, though a beautiful object may excite and be made the symbol
of an Idea that is truly [sublime.][3]

In this important respect Coleridge was as revolutionary as
Turner. In fact, I think Elinor Shaffer correctly contends that
Coleridge here signaled a major shift in the standards of taste.[4]
Older critics like Clarence Thorpe, who gave a straightforward
Kantian synopsis of Coleridge's views of the sublime (as he
gleaned them from Coleridge's annotations of Herder's *Kalli-
gone*), overlooked Coleridge's really important contribution.[5] In
essence, where Kant sees the desultory "incapacitation of Reason," Coleridge finds the birth of Wonder. There is no "collapse"
for Coleridge when the sublime is perceived, but rather elevation and possible purification. In a sense what happened after the
turn of the century was a reconciliation of neoclassic and romantic tensions, for what the eighteenth century saw as the outer
limit of order, the nineteenth took as the beginning of new
experience.

I mention this because I think the displacement of the beautiful by the sublime is one of the major movements in Coleridge's
poetry. It is the central thrust in *Kubla Khan*, in *Dejection: An
Ode*, even in *Christabel*; it entails an experience beyond the
senses that does not generate terror and fear, as Burke has suggested, but instead produces insight and knowledge. This is not
to say that the experience is free of anxiety (for Coleridge it most

3. S. T. Coleridge, *Marginalia*, ed. John T. Shawcross (who suggested the
words in brackets), as quoted in Raimonda Modiano, "Coleridge and the Sublime," p. 115.
4. Elinor S. Shaffer, "Coleridge's Revolution in the Standard of Taste." For
more on Coleridge's contribution to the criticism of the sublime, see Modiano,
"Coleridge and the Sublime."
5. Clarence DeWitt Thorpe, "Coleridge on the Sublime," in *Wordsworth and
Coleridge: Studies in the Honor of George McLean Harper*, ed. Earl Leslie
Griggs, pp. 192–220.

certainly is not), but only that there is a final recession of discomfort and a nascent sense of composure. Angus Fletcher has explained the paradox:

> He [Coleridge] is caught in a psychosomatic paradox: though the threshold is temporally nonexistent, a phantom-place, the passage across this no-man's land seems to be more intense, experientially, than life either inside or outside the temple, inside or outside the labyrinth. The threshold unmakes the dialectic of inside and outside, replacing it by an unmediating passage between. Its motto: Readiness is all.
>
> The intensity of the rite of passage, or simply, of Montaigne's "passing," seems with Coleridge to raise an accompanying liminal anxiety—the existential vertigo that led Herbert Read to associate Coleridge and Kierkegaard. This anxiety characteristically feels like a border-crossing emotion. It manifests itself as uncertainty, as fear approaching paranoia, the fear that life processes will be blocked, that one will be arrested, pressed down, or suffocated in the manner of Poe's heroes (with whom Coleridge shares the terror of suffocation). As one approaches the border, this anxiety rises; as one crosses it successfully, the anxiety recedes.[6]

Fletcher cites sources for Coleridge's ideas among the German and French philosophers, but other critics have maintained that the eighteenth-century English aestheticians were the major influence. I think Coleridge's views, especially his systematic structure of sublimity, resulted as much from his reading of Plotinus, Iamblichus, and Proclus as from Gilpin, Price, or Knight. In addition, his views seem also to have been influenced by his conversations with Wordsworth.[7] Curiously, on the subject of the sublime, Coleridge had little regard for Edmund Burke, let alone for the Germans Schelling and Herder.[8] In short, I

---

6. Angus Fletcher, "Positive Negation: Threshold, Sequence, and Personification in Coleridge," in *New Perspectives on Coleridge and Wordsworth: Selected Papers from the English Institute*, ed. Geoffrey H. Hartman, p. 140.

7. According to Dorothy Wordsworth, her brother and Coleridge were discussing what constituted sublimity at least by 1803 when they made the tour of Scotland; see Dorothy Wordsworth's *Recollections of a Tour Made in Scotland*.

8. Coleridge had a poor opinion of Burke's essay *On the Sublime and the Beautiful* and was also unimpressed by Burke's introductory section on taste, which he regarded as "neither profound nor accurate"; *Table Talk*, quoted in Thorpe, "Coleridge on the Sublime," p. 214.

think a source study of his views would prove a feckless task, especially because his own categories are so clearly derivative. Typically, he starts with a list of aesthetic sets:

Where the perfection of form is combined with pleasurableness in the sensations excited by the matters or substances so formed, there results the beautiful. . . . When there is a deficiency of unity in the line forming the whole (as angularity, for instance), and of number in the plurality of the parts, there arises the formal.

When the parts are numerous and impressive, and are predominate, so as to prevent or greatly lessen the attention to whole, there results the grand.

Where the impression of the whole, i.e. the sense of unity, predominates so as to abstract the mind from the parts—the majestic.

Where the parts by their harmony produce an effect of a whole, but where there is no seen form of a whole producing or explaining the parts of it, where the parts only are seen and distinguished, but the whole is felt—the picturesque.

Those are all traditional categories, and they are clearly gradations of each other. But beyond them is one separated from the rest: "Where neither whole nor parts, but unity as boundless or endless allness—the sublime."[9]

Nature therefore can be commanding, grand, majestic, beautiful, and picturesque, but only rarely sublime. That is simply because boundlessness is not common in nature; in fact, it is an attribute only of what Coleridge calls the "deep sky, the open sea and the wide desert." Sublimity exists therefore essentially on the lines between earth and sky or sea and sky, namely at the horizon. Coleridge demands no terror, no comparison, no collapse of Reason, no "blockage," no gradations of the picturesque. For Coleridge this "metaphysical sublime" (as he elsewhere calls it) depends, initially at least, on the unobstructed vision of space. He goes on to give an example: "I should say that the Saviour praying on the mountain, the desert on one hand, the sea on the other, the city at an immense distance below, was sublime. But I should say of the Saviour looking towards the city, his counte-

9. Coleridge's list of aesthetic categories is recorded in *Letters, Conversations, and Recollections of Samuel Taylor Coleridge*, ed. Thomas Allsop and reprinted in the notes to *Biographia Literaria*, ed. John Shawcross, p. 309.

nance full of pity, that he was majestic, and of the situation, that it was grand."[10] Presumably had the Saviour looked away from the city he would have experienced sublimity. For a more personal example, we might look at a passage in Coleridge's own *Notebook* in which he describes the sea near Malta:

> The Sky, or rather say the Aether, at Malta, with the Sun apparently suspended in it, the Eye seeming to pierce beyond, & as it were, behind it—and below the aetherial Sea, so blue, so a *zerflossenes Eins*, the substantial image, and fixed real Reflection of the Sky—O I could annihilate in a deep moment all possibility of the needlepoint pinshead System of the Atomists by one submissive Gaze. . . . Thought formed not fixed—the molten Being never cooled into a Thing, tho' begotten into the vast adequate Thought.[11]

This coruscating sea is the visual icon of romantic liminality: it extends beyond the limits of the senses, it is ineffable, space seems boundless, distinctions between color and form are blurred. Its only spatial demarcation is the horizon, the threshold that separates it from the world above, from the Beyond. We are taken to this dissolving vortex in two central works of the sublime: Coleridge's *The Rime of the Ancient Mariner* and J. M. W. Turner's *The Slave Ship—Slavers Throwing Overboard the Dead and Dying—Typhon* [*sic*] *Coming On*, and so it is to these works that I should like to turn.

Most critics in our century have neglected the unseen world above the Ancient Mariner, feeling instead the need to understand, sometimes even to justify, the central events of the poem in terms of what actually occurs. Critics have been particularly concerned with the nature of the Mariner's crime, since little in the "visible" world would suggest such far-reaching consequences for such a seemingly minor crime. Like biblical Jobs, they have sought to justify the ways of Coleridge to man. An uneasy consensus has been reached in this century with most critics

10. Allsop, *Letters, Conversations, and Recollections of Samuel Taylor Coleridge*, p. 309. For more on Coleridge's views of the affective nature of the sublime, see his comments beginning "I meet, I *find* the Beautiful—but I give, contribute, or rather attribute the Sublime" in "Unpublished Fragments on Aesthetics," ed. Thomas M. Raysor.

11. *The Notebooks of Samuel Taylor Coleridge*, ed. Kathleen Coburn, 2:9.58.

agreeing with Robert Penn Warren that the nature of the crime must rest in the bird's symbolic meaning, not in the literal act itself: "The mariner did not kill a man but a bird, and the literal-minded readers have echoed Mrs. Barbauld and Leslie Stephen: what a lot of pother about a bird! But they forget that this bird is more than a bird. . . . The crime is, symbolically, a murder."[12] But Warren and others have never told us exactly how this bird fits into any greater symbolic pattern.

It is my contention that Coleridge deliberately chose a "trivial" act as the central crime in his poem and a punishment that he knew would be absurd in order to introduce us to the mysteries of the sublime. He chose an absolutely irrational act to force us, again in Burnet's words, "to contemplate in the mind . . . the image of a greater and better world." If this is true, the killing of the albatross would not be just a "symbolic" murder; to the initiates of that world within and beyond, the sin in killing the albatross would be perfectly clear. The killing disrupts the harmony at the vortex between levels of consciousness.

Coleridge's initial problem was how to create the world above the horizon; how to give form to what Geoffrey Hartman has called "the spectral confrontation."[13] When Coleridge tried to find a vocabulary of images to describe that world Beyond he turned to earlier systems of cosmic organization, particularly those of the Neoplatonists. What is essential to understand, however, is not that Coleridge borrowed from the spirit hierarchies of earlier philosophers but that he restructured them to cast light on the nature of the sublime experience. Far more than natural symbols might, these hierarchies enabled Coleridge to project the psychodrama going on within the Ancient Mariner's mind, just as Shelley would later attempt in *Prometheus Unbound*. Creating this second universe (the "new allegory" as Hartman calls it) above the Ancient Mariner permitted Coleridge to probe more deeply into questions concerning the nature of elevated

12. Robert Penn Warren, "A Poem of Pure Imagination: An Experiment in Reading," p. 26.
13. Geoffrey H. Hartman, "Romantic Poetry and the *Genius Loci*," in *Beyond Formalism*, p. 334. The passage I quoted in Chapter 1 from Coleridge's *Apologia Pro Vita Sua* (1–8) is a good description of this "outering" process.

consciousness. What he did was to create a daemonic world above and around the Mariner that mirrors the world within. Thus, structural changes in this outer world, which act as a kind of psychic register, reflect changes within the Mariner's psyche.[14] Coleridge was interested in these wispy daemons for a number of reasons. Throughout his life he sought a metaphor that could express his belief that the universe was both organic and hierarchal; that is to say, one in which all life was held together by filaments but organized in gradations. Or to use the commonest analogy from Neoplatonism, he was looking for a way to express a universe that was arranged like the rays of the sun—each ray sharing the same heat, but those closer to the source burning more intensely. Coleridge believed that although all life, visible and invisible, is interanimating, the quality of life differs. In his *Hints towards the Formation of a More Comprehensive Theory of Life*, Coleridge expresses this arrangement of life in a strangely cumbersome metaphor: "It has been before noticed that the progress of Nature is more truly represented by a ladder, than by the suspended chain, and that she expands as by concentric circles. This is, indeed, involved in the very conception of individuation, whether it be applied to the different species or to the individual."[15]

Occasionally, there are rungs in this ladder that are separated from the preceding ones by more than the usual interspace. In actual life this corresponds to the difference between the lower

14. The question Coleridge must have faced was how to construct this second universe, how to find the logically organized yet organic stuff that could act as a convex mirror reflecting psychological changes in the Ancient Mariner. Usually critics have admitted that Coleridge "creatively arranged" his spirit life—the daemonic realm—from the Neoplatonists. But a careful look at these airy spirits shows that, although the result may be creative, the arrangement of the daemons is not. In fact, Coleridge lifted these spirits almost in toto from their places in the ancients' cosmic plan. Because critics have passed this by so quickly, I think they frequently miss much of the significance of these daemons. The spirits are usually treated only as figments of the artistic imagination, not in their original context as the organic matrix between psyche and cosmos, the animated vortex. For an explanation of Coleridge's knowledge of this aspect of Neoplatonism as well as his sources, see John Livingston Lowes, *The Road to Xanadu: A Study in the Ways of the Imagination*, chap. 13.

15. S. T. Coleridge, *Hints towards the Formation of a More Comprehensive Theory of Life*, p. 70.

animal life and the highest mineral life. ("Rocks," says Coleridge, "share with man the gift of life.") Another such gap occurs between the most "individuated" animal and man:

> Man possesses the most perfect osseous structure, the least and most insignificant covering. The whole force of organic power has attained an inward and centripetal direction. He has the whole world in counterpoint to him, but he contains an entire world within himself. Now, for the first time, at the apex of the living pyramid, it is Man and Nature—the Microcosm! Naked and helpless cometh man into the world. Such has been the complaint from eldest time; but we complain of our chief privilege, our ornament, and the connate mark of our sovereignty. *Porphyrigeniti sumus!* In man the centripetal and individualizing tendency of all Nature is itself concentered and individualized—he is a revelation of nature.[16]

There is another such gap above man in this ladder of life, and this is the most interesting one in relation to *The Rime of the Ancient Mariner.* Just as Coleridge has measured his way through a throbbing hierarchy of subhuman life until he reaches man, he continues, now working by inference, to suspect that there is also a "new series" of powers that are superhuman. At the vortex or threshold of this "new series," differentiated from the rest by degree and kind, is the sublime. It is here, in the interspace above man and below the gods, on the horizon between this world and the next, that Coleridge created his peculiar amalgam of Neoplatonic and Christian spirits. One thing that should be remembered throughout the following explanation of the various invisible beings above the Ancient Mariner is that they are counterpointed within the Mariner as well. For as John Beer has said, they are symbolic of "the more mysterious energies of the mind and spirit," and so the ordering of the cosmos is analogous to the ordering of the psyche.[17]

It is apparent from his revisions of *The Rime* that Coleridge was struggling to clarify the psychological significance of the Mariner's experience. The most obvious of these efforts is the gloss, but still more revealing are his alterations of the epigraphic argument. The original argument of 1798 reads:

16. Ibid., pp. 85–86.
17. J. B. Beer, *Coleridge, the Visionary*, p. 111.

> How a Ship having passed the Line was driven by storms to the cold
> Country towards the South Pole; and how from thence she made
> her course to the tropical Latitude of the Great Pacific Ocean; and
> of the strange things that befell; and in what manner the Ancyent
> Marinere came back to his own Country.

The import is purely geographical: the passage traces the arc of
the voyage. In 1800 Coleridge delved deeper, now more concerned with describing the psychological voyage:

> How a Ship, having first sailed to the Equator, was driven by
> Storms to the cold Country towards the South Pole; how the An-
> cient Mariner cruelly and in contempt of the laws of hospitality
> killed a Sea-bird and how he was followed by many and strange
> Judgments: and in what manner he came back to his own Country.

Here we have the psychological circuit—sin, guilt, and partial
redemption presumably effected, in part at least, by the awareness of some "strange Judgment."

In 1817, the gloss and headnote were added in another attempt
to move the Mariner's tale from external to internal, from story to
psychodrama. Since the epigraph that Coleridge excerpted from
Burnet's *Archaeologiae Philosophicae* sets the cosmic and psychic stage beneath and through which the Ancient Mariner must
pass, we might look at it in detail. The following is the excerpt in
its entirety, including the many lines in the middle that Coleridge left out. As we shall see, some of the omitted lines have
been incorporated into both the poem and the ballad's gloss:

> I can easily believe, that there are more Invisible than Visible Be-
> ings in the Universe: and that there are more *Orders of Angels* in
> the Heavens, than *variety of Fishes* in the sea; but who will declare
> to us the Family of all these, and acquaint us with the Agreements,
> Differences, and peculiar Talents which are to be found among
> them? It is true, human Wit has always desired a Knowledge of
> these Things, though it has never yet attained it. The Heathen Di-
> vines have very much philosophised about the invisible World of
> Souls, Genii, Manes, Daemons, Heroes, Minds, Deities, and
> Gods, as we may see in Jamblichus's Treatise on the *Mysteries of the
> Aegyptians*, and in *Psellus* and *Pletho* on the *Chaldean Rites*, and
> everywhere in the *Platonic* authors. Some Christian Divines have

imitated these also, with Reference to the Orders of Angels; and the *Gnostics* have feigned many things in this Matter, under the Names of *Eons* and Gods. Moreover, the Cabalists in their *Jetzirah* (or World of Angels) range Myriads of Angels under their Leaders *Sandalphon* and *Metatron*, as they who are conversant in those Studies very well know. But of what value are all these Things? Has this Seraphic Philosophy any Thing sincere or solid about it? I know that *St. Paul* speaks of the Angelic World, and has taken notice of many Orders and Distinctions among them; but this in general only; he does not philosophize about them; he disputes not, nor teaches anything in particular concerning them; nay, on the contrary, he reproves those as puft up with vain Science, who rashly thrust themselves forward to seek into these unknown and unsearchable Things. I will own that it is very profitable, sometimes to contemplate in the Mind, as in a Draught, the Image of the greater and better World; lest the Soul, being accustomed to the Trifles of this present Life, should contract itself too much, and altogether rest in mean Cogitations; but, in the mean Time, we must take Care to keep to the Truth, and observe Moderation that we may distinguish certain Things, and Day from Night.[18]

Although we do not know what causes the Ancient Mariner wantonly to shoot the albatross, once we realize that the bird is in some way connected to the invisible world within and above, we know why the shooting was sinful: It disrupted the vortex that holds the worlds together; it broke—to use Coleridge's metaphor—the rungs. It breached the horizon.

Coleridge's selection of his motto clearly implies that the "sin" of the Ancient Mariner, in Burnet's terms, is a refusal to "contemplate in the Mind, as in a Draught, the Image of the greater and better World; lest the Soul, being accustomed to the Trifles of this present Life, should contract iself too much." For in an organic universe, all parts, including the psyche of man, are held together by the magnetic forces of sympathy. All must come beneath what Coleridge elsewhere calls the "suspending Magnet, the Golden Chain from the Staple Ring, Fastened to the

18. As quoted in *Coleridge Notebooks*, ed. Kathleen Coburn, "Notes," 1:ii, 100 H 22.9.

Footstool of the Throne."[19] To snap one link, even though this be
the result of a refusal to think and feel, is to disrupt the whole
system. The Ancient Mariner's sin is simply ignorance, "not
knowing" enough about consciousness, a refusal—in a sense—to
sublimate. He never considers that the animate universe might
be held together by nothing stronger than what the Neoplatonists called the "laws of hospitality" and that these laws could be
intuitively understood.

But Coleridge had considered it, and so had Thomas Taylor.[20]
It was via Taylor's translations of the Neoplatonists—Iamblichus,
Plotinus, Porphyry—that Coleridge learned about natal daemons and their cosmic cohorts above the threshold. For the time
being, what we need to remember about the daemons is, first,
that they are strictly ordered in a vertical hierarchy; second, that
they are capable of speaking the language of whatever country
they inhabit; and, third, that the daemons of the water sometimes take the form of birds.[21]

What happens in the lowest level in the world around the Ancient Mariner is that the Mariner unknowingly kills an animal
whose natal daemon or protective spirit is the Polar Spirit. The
gloss tells us that the Polar Spirit is not daemonic in the Christian
or Jewish sense of a fallen angel but is on loan from the Neoplatonic hierarchies.[22] In this system there are five orders of natural daemons, named for the levels they control: Ethereal, Aerial,
Terrestrial, Subterranean, and Aquatic. The Polar Spirit is quite
obviously in the last category. However, he seems to be a special

19. Beer, *Coleridge, the Visionary*, p. 167. He footnotes this: "Coleridge Notebooks in British Museum," 37.36.

20. For more on Thomas Taylor, see above, note 37 to my Introduction.

21. That the different genera of daemons are arranged in hierarchies can be
glossed in the works of any of these mystics, for example, Plotinus, *Enneads*, III 5
[50] 6, or Iamblichus, *De Mysteriis* . . . ; that they were able to speak the language of the country, see Lowes, *Road to Xanadu*, p. 214, n. 41; and that the
daemon can assume various forms, see Lowes, *Road to Xanadu*, chap. 3, n.
42–43.

22. The gloss claims (part 2) that the Polar Spirit "is one of the invisible inhabitants of this planet, neither departed souls nor angels; concerning whom the
learned Jew, Jesephus, and the Platonic Constantinopolitan, Michael Psellus,
may be consulted."

kind of Aquatic daemon, as his "territorial imperative" extends only as far as the Equator.

After the Ancient Mariner has partially expiated his sin, he starts to gain sight with his "inward eye," and the movement toward the sublime begins. In the first of his visions (for surely he cannot really "see" nine fathoms deep) he sees the submerged Polar Spirit starting to move the ship:

> Under the keel nine fathoms deep,
> From the land of mist and snow,
> The spirit slid: and it was he
> That made the ship to go.
> The sails at noon left off their tune,
> And the ship stood still also.
>
> The Sun, right up above the mast,
> Had fixed her to the ocean:
> But in a minute she 'gan stir,
> With a short uneasy motion—
> Backwards and forwards half her length
> With a short uneasy motion. (377–88)

This passage is problematic, for although the 1817 gloss informs us, "The lonesome Spirit from the south-pole carries on the ship as far as the Line, in obedience to the angelic troop," in the 1798 version it is by no means clear who is propelling the ship. The "troops of Spirits blest" who enter the bodies of the dead in 1817 are not mentioned in the earlier version, nor is it clear that the Polar Spirit is subordinate to them. It is not surprising that Coleridge redesigned his hierarchy to make the angelic powers superior to the tutelary Spirit of the Pole, for by 1817 a more orthodox Coleridge had begun to press the Christian hierarchies over his pagan systems.

The ship is convulsed when the Polar Spirit releases his hold. One imagines the daemon angrily moving the ship back and forth in "a short uneasy motion" as he realizes he has reached the equatorial line. Then the Polar Spirit, denied the vengeance he feels is rightfully his, angrily gives the ship one last violent shove before returning south. But as we are to learn from the next marginal notes, the spirit has obtained from the higher powers—the Christian hierarchy of saints and angels—a promise that the Mariner "hath penance more to do."

The Polar Spirit has a host of companions who all seem to be in his hierarchal interspace or "series," as Coleridge labeled it in the *Theory of Life*. Just after the Polar Spirit has been sent home, some of his cohorts are heard discussing the Mariner's fate:

> I heard and *in my soul* discerned
> Two voices in the air.
>
> "Is it he?" quoth one, "Is this the man?
> By him who died on cross,
> With his cruel bow he laid full low
> The harmless Albatross.
>
> The spirit who bideth by himself
> In the land of mist and snow,
> He loved the bird that loved the man
> Who shot him with his bow."
>
> The other was a softer voice,
> As soft as honey dew:
> Quoth he, "The man hath penance done,
> And penance more will do." (396–409; italics mine)

These are obviously not Aquatic daemons but ones living in the air above the horizon. According to the gloss, they are "the Polar Spirit's fellow-daemons, the invisible inhabitants of the elements." So presumably these are the Aerial or Ethereal daemons of the Neoplatonic system, lingering in the air just above earth and sea, just at the threshold.

The two voices who next speak as part 6 opens are quite clearly those of the "Polar Spirit's fellow-daemons." The Aether (which we will see again in Keats's *Endymion*) was much discussed among seventeenth-century scientists, including Burnet, who felt that this mysterious substance was the stratum of divine spirit that separated the upper regions of space from the Empyrean. In fact, it was only after the celebrated experiments of Michelson and Morley in 1887 that "ether" was reduced to mean-

ing only anesthetic gas. Yeats, for instance, was convinced that
Coleridge had lifted the concept of an ethereal layer of divine intelligences from Berkeley's *Siris*, and Beer, continuing this line
of reasoning, suggests that the flashing lights, fires, and darting
watersnakes all represent an incursion of the etheral into the natural world.[23] They may well be right, although the creatures who
live in this stratum also fit neatly into the Neoplatonic paradigm,
while representing an "outering" of inner experience. What is
important, of course, for my argument is that they are all in the
subliminal zone, all just at the horizon of new consciousness.

So in this "series" of the supernatural hierarchy are the Aquatic
and Aerial or Ethereal daemons, but it is soon discovered that
these are below another "series," just as the animals are below
man. This more powerful "series" is composed of the angels and
saints of the Christian mythology. As the Mariner is initiated
from innocence to experience, he becomes convinced that "his
kind saint" is the agent of his forgiveness, and we are led to believe that it is this same saint who sent the angelic troops to command the natural daemons.[24] After these angelic spirits have re-
animated the bodies of the dead sailors and have sailed the ship
through the night, they

> . . . clustered round the mast;
> Sweet sounds rose slowly through their mouths,
> And from their bodies passed.
>
> Around, around, flew each sweet sound,
> Then darted to the Sun;
> Slowly the sounds came back again,
> Now mixed, now one by one. (351–57)

23. William Butler Yeats, *Pages from a Diary Written in Nineteen Hundred
and Thirty*, p. 18, and Beer, *Coleridge, the Visionary*, pp. 114, 152.
    24. Incidentally, it is these angelic spirits who sail the ship, just prior to the
reentry of the Polar Spirit. In fact, the gloss tells us that the ship was propelled
"not by the souls of the men, nor by the daemons of earth or middle air, but by a
blessed troop of angelic spirits." Bruce R. McElderry, Jr., points out in "Coleridge's Revision of *The Ancient Mariner*," p. 89, that the 1817 gloss contains
mostly afterthoughts that were not in Coleridge's mind when he wrote the poem
and it is clear *only* from the gloss that the angelic band was "sent down by the
invocation of the guardian saint."

Since they return to the sun, they probably live higher in the cosmos than the daemons, closer in a heliocentric universe to the godhead, and they are, therefore, more holy and powerful. The next day they slowly come down to the corpses, again in the form of sounds, filling "the sea and air with their sweet jargoning." At first the Ancient Mariner sees them only as "crimson shadows" (line 485) playing across the water a short distance from the prow, but when he turns around and sees them "in their own forms of light," hovering over each corpse, he describes them as a "seraph band." How he knows exactly who they are, we are never told, but inasmuch as they are seraphim, the highest order of angels, presiding over the cherubim and a host of others, clearly there is another complete life "series" in the cosmos. They perhaps would represent the liminal experience, above the daemonic sublime, and hence are mystical in the Christian sense.

When the supernatural (or psychological) machinery finally is set up, we see a logically and rigorously organized system in which all is interanimated and interdependent, a system of personified states that stretches both up into the heavens and down into the psyche of the protagonist. The highest point is absolute Oneness, but it is linked to all below it. Schematically, the structure above the Ancient Mariner looks something like this:

Liminal Consciousness {	(God) "My kind saint" Seraphim Undifferentiated angels
Subliminal Consciousness {	Ethereal daemons Horizon/albatross/Polar Spirit
Normal Consciousness {	Ancient Mariner

The perception of the world at the horizon, this world at the vortex, is the experience of the sublime, and understanding this is the "rite of passage," the "voyage" of both Ancient Mariner and reader.

So the poem is indeed, as Robert Penn Warren has said, "a sacramental vision." It is a vision of the threshold, a vision we can understand only after we have first understood how the world

J. M. W. Turner, *The Slave Ship—Slavers Throwing Overboard the Dead and Dying—Typhoon Coming On*, 1839. Museum of Fine Arts, Boston, Massachusetts.

above the horizon is put together and how it is connected to the world within. We can see analogous imagery in the seascapes of J. M. W. Turner, who takes us visually to that same point where the redeeming action of *The Rime* occurs; he takes us to the line where sea and sky cleave.[25]

Of all the nineteenth-century landscape painters, Turner first comes to mind in any discussion of sublimity. It is not happenstance that one of the most interesting recent Turner exhibitions, assembled in 1981 by the Art Gallery of Ontario, the Yale Center

25. I am thinking especially of such seascapes as *Wreck of a Transport Ship* (ca. 1810), *Fire at Sea* (ca. 1835), and the series of *Sunrises* . . . (1835–1845) in which the horizon is shattered with light or fire or both. It is perhaps noteworthy that *Slavers* has a literary text lurking in the background for it now seems that Turner had a long passage from Thompson's *Seasons* (lines 980-1025) in mind. See T. S. R. Boase, "Shipwrecks in English Romantic Painting."

for British Art, and the British Museum, had as its organizing theme Turner's contribution to the sublime. In fact, Andrew Wilton's descriptive catalog, *Turner and the Sublime*, has successive chapters on "The Classic Sublime," "The Landscape Sublime," and, finally, as if to signal the unique contribution of Turner, "The Turnerian Sublime." Wilton justly singles out *Slavers* as one of Turner's most unambiguous attempts at sublimity, as it forces us to enter the explosive atmosphere between sea and sky.[26] This is, of course, exactly the same place Coleridge forces us to enter in order to follow the voyage of his mariner.

Unfortunately, the most notable similarity between *Slavers* and *The Rime*—the colors—cannot be seen in this black-and-white reproduction. Certainly one of the most important achievements in romantic painting (and poetry as well) was the breakdown of Augustan distinctions between colors. (In *The Prelude*, for instance, Wordsworth correctly calls these distinctions "puny boundaries" [2. 223], for what the outline, especially between colors, does is reduce visual sensation to the regular spectrum.) Angus Fletcher has explained the importance of this blurring at the margin:

> While epic tradition supplies conventional models of the threshold, these conventions are always subject to deliberate poetic blurring, and this shift from the distinct limen to the indistinct serves a double purpose. On the one hand, poets, like painters, may delight in the softening of outline because it permits an intensification of medium: thus Turner's mastery of the indistinct expresses a technical interest in medium which is remarkably parallel to that of his near-contemporary, Coleridge. On the other hand, and this is perhaps the fundamental and more substantial point, poets have wished to subtilize, to dissolve, to fragment, to blur the hard material edge, because poetry hunts down the soul, with its obscure passions, feelings, other-than-cognitive symbolic forms.[27]

Turner was, of course, misunderstood for this blurring, as was Coleridge. Robert Southey called *The Rime* "a Dutch attempt at German Sublimity," by which he meant it was too vague and in-

---

26. Andrew Wilton, *Turner and the Sublime*, p. 98.
27. Fletcher, "Positive Negation," p. 136.

distinct. Witness as well what William Hazlitt is really saying underneath this laudatory snippet about Turner:

> We here allude particularly to Turner, the ablest landscape-painter
> now living, whose pictures are, however, too much abstractions of
> aerial perspective, and representations not properly of the objects
> of nature as of the medium through which they were seen. They are
> the triumph of the knowledge of the artist and of the power of the
> pencil over the barrenness of the subject. They are pictures of the
> elements of air, earth and water. The artist delights to go back to
> the first chaos of the world, or to that state of things, when the wa-
> ters were separated from the dry land, and light from darkness, but
> as yet no living thing nor tree bearing fruit was seen on the face of
> the earth. All is without form and void. Someone said of his land-
> scapes that they were *pictures of nothing and very like.* (Hazlitt's
> italics) [28]

But this is just as much a misinterpretation of Turner's design as
Southey's statement was of Coleridge's. One might recall the an-
ecdote in which Turner asked how a certain patron had liked one
of his paintings and when told that the patron found it "indis-
tinct," Turner responded, "Then you should tell him that indistinctness is my forte." Turner's indistinctness is not casual; it is
the result of taking apart, deconstructing, decreating; it is the
very stuff of vision and is, I think, precisely what finally "makes
up" the sublime.

One can see this taking apart in Turner's use of color as well as
of form. The predictability of color—especially in the coloring of
sunlight—had become so codified in the eighteenth century that
the painted sky was a visual cliché. Reynolds was both reflecting
and prescribing the norm when he repeatedly insisted that "the
masses of light in a picture be always of a warm yellow color,
yellow, red, or yellowish white." [29] Decisiveness of outline as well
as distinction between color had militated against any sense of
sublimity in the lower atmosphere. Turner's genius, as John Gage
has made clear, was to demonstrate how chromatics influence

28. Robert Southey's comments appear in his "Review of Lyrical Ballads," p.
197; William Hazlitt is quoted by Lawrence Growing, in *Turner: Imagination and
Reality*, p. 13.
29. See above, note 1, for Reynolds's comments on light and color.

light as well as space. Now for the first time in English art, color became inseparable from light, and the skies—especially those painted by the end of the century—reflect this.[30] They become literally spectacular. Turner's supposed last words that "the sun is God" are not inappropriate, although perhaps apocryphal. Sunlight and color are more than painterly effects, they are the matrix that holds his abstracted vision together.

Slavers is full of explosive color; as James A. W. Heffernan has noted, Turner here "uses every color in the spectrum—plus black and white."[31] There is white foam and gray ocean to the left; yellow sun, orange clouds and black water in the center; then green and indigo waves to the right. Up above in the corner is the hint of blue sky. If one forgets the shapes and forms of the objects, looking at *Slavers* is like looking at the continuous spectrum with the distinguishing lines between the colors omitted.

One does not ordinarily think of *The Rime* as a poem of many colors, but it is; as a matter of fact, its coloring is remarkably like that of *Slavers*. There is the white of the albatross, the moon, ice, and mist; the green, blue, and white of the ocean; the yellow and red of the copper sun, as well as in the hair and on the lips of Life-in-Death; and the blue, green, black of the water snakes. The one dominant hue in the colorful richness of both *Slavers* and *The Rime* is, of course, red; but it is a very special red—it is the red of blood and the red of the sun illuminating the horizon. It may be noteworthy in this context that Turner actually wrote the words *Fire and Blood* above an early sketch of what was to become his oft-repeated sun, for it is precisely this iridescent red that floods the vortex of these two romantic works.

The appearance and disappearance of this color signal all the major events of *The Rime*, just as they signal the coming of a typhoon in *Slavers*. After the Mariner has shot the albatross, the sun turns "bloody," and from there on red is the prevailing color, almost as if the consequences of the Mariner's act have tinted re-

30. John Gage, *Color in Turner: Poetry and Truth*, p. 111.

31. James A. W. Heffernan, "The English Romantic Perception of Color," in *Images of Romanticism: Verbal and Visual Affinities*, ed. Karl Kroeber and William Walling, p. 146.

ality. This red is in the sea, it is in the air, it is in the shadows of the ship; everything finally turns a "still and awful red" (271). The same is true in Turner's painting; all the other colors are dominated by this red, every object is infused with its presence. As Heffernan says: "Like Turner's *Slavers*, then the seascape of *The Rime* is dominated by the color of fire and blood. Mirroring at once the guilt of the mariner and his purgatorial suffering, the pervasive redness in this poem also unifies the many-colored elements of his world."[32] But why should this color be conducive to the sublime? I don't think it is the color red that necessarily produces the effect; rather it is the way that red crosses boundaries and permeates other colors. In both painting and poem there is an aggressive violation of distinctiveness, of boundary and margin, a conscious perversion of the idea that outline must divide the "seven specific individual colors of the spectrum." Red is more than the chromatic matrix of these works, however; it is also thematically important, for it keeps our minds both consciously and unconsciously fixed at the horizon. It forces us to the vortex.

In both painting and poem, it is the blood-red sun that shatters the horizon and breaks the separation between natural and supernatural, real and daemonic. In both painting and poem, we look directly into the sun, not to the side, not into diffractions or reflections. This is something we do not normally do, for we know the sun will momentarily blind us, cause us discomfort, so we shade our eyes or look obliquely. But in these works we are not given that opportunity: we are stunned. Edmund Burke, who considered darkness so conducive to sublimity, makes only one exception, and that is for precisely this kind of visual phenomenon:

> Mere light is too common a thing to make a strong impression on the mind, and without a strong impression nothing can be sublime. But such a light as that of the sun, immediately exerted on the eye, as it overpowers the sense, is a very great idea. Light of an inferior strength to this, if it moves with great celerity, has the same power; for lightning is certainly productive of grandeur, which it owes

32. Heffernan, "Romantic Perception of Color," p. 147.

chiefly to the extreme velocity of its motion. A quick transition from light to darkness, or from darkness to light, has yet a greater effect.[33]

It is this oscillation between light and dark, sun and shadow, that the Ancient Mariner (and we as well) must experience. In this context Ronald Paulson, with Robert Penn Warren's comments clearly in mind, has made the following tantalizing comment:

> Turner makes use of similar lighting effects (which include gleaming serpents) but his sun is all-sufficient and requires no moon as complement. If he thought about Coleridge's sun I am sure it meant to him God's wrath and the Mariner's conscience, bloodying the sky in *Slavers* or exploding it in *Regulus*, aimed at the Mariner as the "glittering eye" of the "bright-eyed Mariner" himself is leveled at the wedding guest. The sun's significance depends on whether the viewer is sinner or penitent, and consequently on whether the sun itself is external or internal.[34]

Indeed, like the sublime, the impact of the sun does depend on who is seeing it and on which sun (inner or outer) is being seen.

Yet another quality makes Turner's *Slavers* and Coleridge's *Rime* analogous, and that has to do with what the colors of the sun produce—the disruption of the horizon. Coleridge had no qualms about sending the spirits of the crew floating up to and around the sun; he was clearly willing to have the sun burn away distinctions between line and color; he was even willing to have the sun ironically blind the Mariner, so that he finally is able to "see." But look at what Turner does: his sun makes a vortex so powerful that all the whirling energy of the storm is there becalmed. We are in the eye of the storm, in the eye of vision. Yet even this is deceptive, for the conical funnels of the sunlight metaphorically prefigure the avenging typhoon of the title. Caught on the edge of the funnel are the dismembered bodies of the slaves thrown overboard (as apt a metonymy as the Mariner's wa-

33. Edmund Burke, *A Philosophical Enquiry into the Origin of Our Ideas of the Sublime and Beautiful*, ed. J. T. Boulton, p. 80.
34. Ronald Paulson, "Turner's Graffiti: The Sun and Its Glosses," in *Images of Romanticism*, ed. Kroeber and Walling, p. 178.

tersnakes), while off to the left the offending ship is about to be consumed in the whorl.

The calm inside this hourglass of light is as disturbing as the chaos outside. It is the emptiness, the void, the almost obsessive quietude that makes the activity beyond the edges seem all the more hebephrenic. The black body just before us on the right, about to land in our laps, is reminiscent of the castoffs in Géricault's *Raft of the Medusa*, where the bodies of the wretched seem to extend beyond the margin (this time the canvas itself) to become part of our personal space. Turner supposedly added this still-manacled body as an afterthought, yet it is as striking an image as the tiny rabbit racing down the tracks ahead of the locomotive in *Rain, Steam and Speed*: it jolts us from our assumptions of distance and space; it makes us part of that vortex. It is, as Gerald Finley has asserted, a deliberate violation of categories, of demarcations, and so

> one must consider such views of the Immediate Sublime as attempts by artists to free themselves from an abstract, conceptualized view of nature such as was inherent in the structure of the classic landscape, and illustrated contemporaneously in picturesque views. To break from the confinement of classical rules was to locate a mode of representation that was not only more natural, but one in which the expressive potential was enlarged, by seeming to involve the spectator himself.[35]

In these late paintings Turner characteristically left the center placid, as becalmed as the Mariner's ship. We are stranded, like the Mariner himself, within the eye. John Dixon Hunt has called this the "sublime center" and contends that this "pool of emptiness" is Turner's final achievement, for at last "the sublime is released from the necessity of having a local habitation and a name."[36] I think this is true, for Turner's sublime takes on a visual independence of its own, topographically free of identification,

---

35. Gerald Finley, "The Genesis of Turner's 'Landscape Sublime,'" p. 163.
36. John Dixon Hunt, "Wondrous Deep and Dark: Turner and the Sublime," p. 152.

almost free of image, just as the Mariner's experience is almost
free of metaphor.

When we look back at *The Rime* and *Slavers* we can see it was
no accident that the romantic quest to picture the sublime should
have led to the sea. It is the sea, as Auden pointed out, with its
emblematic vagueness and seeming endlessness, that so stymies
the reason and so excites the imagination.[37] In a sense, the sea is
the inverted sky: a unique sight (in Coleridge's words) "where
neither whole nor parts, but unity as boundless or endless allness, [a sight of]—the sublime." So it is no accident that the
horizon, the boundary between deep sky and flat ocean, should
have such iconic and psychological significance. That this line
should be broken in these two central works prefigures a radical
development of romantic vision: the lifting of sight over the
edge. We will see this vision re-forming again in Byron's *Manfred* and Keats's *Endymion* until, finally, in Shelley's *Prometheus
Unbound*, the horizon is completely breached and we are taken
to the very edge of language, almost to the "deep truth" that is
"imageless."

37. W. H. Auden, *The Enchafed Flood: Three Essays on the Romantic Spirit*,
chap. 1.

4

Byron and Martin:
The Daemonic Sublime

John Martin is the greatest, the most lofty, the most permanent, the most original genius of his age. I see in him, as I have before said, the presence of a Spirit which is not of the world, the divine intoxication of a great soul lapped in majesty and unearthly dreams. Vastness is his sphere, yet he has not lost nor circumfused his genius in its space; he has chained and wielded and measured it at his will; he has transfused its character into narrow limits; he has compassed the Infinite itself with mathematical precision. Martin has borrowed from none. Alone and guideless he has penetrated the remotest caverns of the past and gazed on the primeval shapes of the gone world.—Edward Bulwer-Lytton, *England and the English*

Perhaps what Bulwer-Lytton says about John Martin is true, but one cannot compass "the Infinite" for long: even vastness has limits. Subjects of art, as well as works of art, have their own constraints in time and taste. The assumption that great art "endureth forever" and is "inexhaustible to criticism" is not just silly, it is dangerous, for it implies that art can exist in vacuo outside time. Subjects of art as well as works of art remain interesting only if certain conditions are met, and one of the most important conditions is that the audience remain fresh. Bulwer-Lytton was wonderfully fresh for the experience of John Martin's vision, but Thackeray, more jaded, mocked the "grave, old people [who] look dumbfounded into those vast perspectives and think that the apex of the sublime is reached there."[1]

1. William Makepeace Thackeray, "Picture Gossip," *Frazer's Magazine* (June 1845) as quoted in William Feaver, *The Art of John Martin*, p. 206.

Nothing so quickly trivializes great subjects as fashion, and it was one of Martin's (and Byron's) achievements that he made vastness too popular. This process is not extraordinary: think of the number of Liszt or Chopin preludes made into tunes by overplaying, or think of Michelangelo's *Moses* or Cellini's *Perseus* made vulgar by too much exposure. Can any of us ever look at the *Mona Lisa* and see her as Pater did? No, and not because we cannot be as perceptive, but because we cannot erase the mimeographed image of that face we have seen on dishtowels, record jackets, purses, ashtrays, waterbottles, or lunchboxes. Works of art are often more quickly trivialized by wanton overappreciation than by the cruelest criticism.

The transformation from art to decoration, from style to stereotype, was certainly operative with the Burkean sublime by 1815. The "popular" audience was making its desires felt in the marketplace and, thanks to new developments in technology, the market could satisfy these demands. The steam-driven press and cheap pulp made inexpensive editions available, and printmaking had become so inexpensive that every farmer's son could have his own *Sistine Madonna* or, better yet, one of John Martin's mezzotints in the parlor next to the most recent verse by Byron. This popularity almost destroyed Martin's critical reputation for the next two generations, as it almost did Byron's; in fact, some of Byron's best poetry, his short lyrics, have still not recovered. Martin's pictures are still being diluted by illustrators of what is now called the Fantastic or, more pompously, the Vienna School, who have made vastness into visual cant. But the change in audience is coming: when Martin was first put up to the Royal Academy he received not a single vote; in 1957 he was elected. I suspect that the cinema is having much to do with Martin's current resurgence, for the movies *Star Wars, 2001: A Space Odyssey, Close Encounters of the Third Kind,* and *Tron* have reaffirmed the joy of perceiving vastness, even though vastness must now be framed way above the horizon in "outer" space.

It is surely ironic that the sublime, which was central to both Martin and Byron, was partially what caused their all too rapid rising, shining, evaporation, and fall. They were so soon imitated into parody: Martin by the likes of Samuel Coleman and George

Miller and Byron by such poetasters as Thomas Campbell and Edwin Atherstone. Yet in their own ways they were knowledgeable about "picturing" the sublime, as I should like to show by comparing the structure of thresholds in Byron's *Manfred* and Martin's watercolor illustration *Manfred and the Witch of the Alps* (1837).

In his *Essays on the Barrenness of the Imaginative Faculties in the Production of Modern Art* (1833), Charles Lamb wrote of Martin's *Belshazzar*:

> His towered structures are of the highest order of the material sublime. Whether they were dreams, or transcripts of some elder workmanship, Assyrian ruins old, restored by this mighty artist, they satisfy our most stretched and craving conceptions of the glories of the antique world. It is a pity that they were ever peopled. On that side the imagination of the artist halts, and appears defective.[2]

For Lamb, "material sublime" was almost pejorative—he was referring to Coleridge's comment on Schiller to the effect that "Schiller has the material Sublime; to produce an effect, he sets you a whole town on fire, and throws infants with their mothers into the flames, or locks up a father in an old tower. But Shakespeare drops a handkerchief, and the same or greater effects follow."[3] In other words, what Lamb did not like about *Belshazzar* was that Martin had made the sublime too spectacular. I do not wish to excuse Martin from Lamb's backhanded compliment, but Martin himself supposedly had said of this painting that it was designed to "make more noise than any picture ever did before," and his offense, if any, is that he succeeded only too well.[4]

It is the *scale* of Martin's materiality that is usually so upsetting: his space, his hugeness, his febrile pitch, his subject matter so full of floods, lava-emptying volcanoes, whorls of sky-force be-

2. Lamb's essay appeared originally in the *Athenaeum*, 12 January–2 February 1833, *Works of Charles and Mary Lamb*, ed. E. V. Lucas, 2:226–34. Keats also used the phrase *material sublime* in his verse epistle "To J. H. Reynolds, Esq.," 25 March 1818 (printed 1848), *The Letters of John Keats*, ed. Hyder Rollins, 1:261.

3. S. T. Coleridge, *Table Talk*, 29 December 1822, as quoted in C. D. Thorpe, "Coleridge on the Sublime," in *Wordsworth and Coleridge: Studies in Honor of George McLean Harper*, ed. Earl Leslie Griggs, p. 218.

4. C. R. Leslie as quoted in Mary Q. Pendred, *John Martin, Painter*, p. 103.

yond compare—all this can so soon become kitsch, a kind of visual hoax of the imagination. The frisson is achieved by our being forced to contemplate not density but excess. Of course, the same was said of Byron, but Martin's reputation suffered more because his incessant run of mezzotints gave his diaphanous vision a certain repetitive dullness. The School of Catastrophe, with Martin as headmaster, initiated the images of Christian melodrama still extant today in so many Sunday School reward-books. One need only glimpse his biblical panoramas to see how much his vision of the "material sublime" has contributed to our own hackneyed sight.

Martin's nonbiblical works are ever so much more interesting. This is true even when he is being Vast. Think, for instance, of *The Bard* (1817) or *Sadak in Search of the Waters of Oblivion* (1812), where he is being "literary" (illustrating the works of Thomas Gray and James Ridley) but not sentimental—at least not oppressively so. Martin had the wonderful ability to translate word to picture, text to topography—even Wordsworth, who had little use for Martin's work, recognized his genius as an "analogous artist."[5] Martin's best illustrations are, I think, of *Paradise Lost*, because here he could be large without being huge; he could be grand without being grandiose; here he had a text that as Addison himself said properly demanded sublime illustration. Even though Milton had been habitually illustrated through the eighteenth century (by Medina, Cheron, Thornhill, Hayman, Westall, Fuseli, Burney, Barry, Hogarth, Blake), Martin's illustrations are almost without equal. He captured the shivering ecstasy and the horror, the architectonic magnitude of Satan's bureaucratic underworld as well as the pastoral wonder of Eden. The only problem is that when Martin moved above the horizon into the realm of Christian hierarchy his vision quickly degenerated into almost a parody of his biblical panoramas, almost self-imitation. *Satan Viewing the Ascent to Heaven* or *The Creation of Light* show how hesitant he was to "cross the threshold," to trust his own imagination to fill in the blanks. In fact, he was so

5. William Wordsworth as quoted by Henry Crabbe Robinson, 14 March 1835, *Diary*, ed. Derek Hudson, p. 140.

cautious in attempting to be religiously "correct" that the results are often ludicrous.[6]

It is a shame that Martin is best known for his excesses, for when he was not being biblical or professionally religious he could freeze the frenzy of wonder as well as Danby or Loutherbourg or even Turner. This, in essence, is why his vision was so compatible with Byron's. Byron saw the sublime for himself; Martin saw it through others, but it was visual and spectacular for them both. Martin Meisel explains this compatibility:

> The dematerialization of the sublime, its translation into subjective terms, doubtless found its most congenial medium in the poetry of the first third of the century . . . [and] it was Byron, externalizing that within which passeth show, who swept Europe as the poet of the subjective sublime, of an inner drama set among scenes of glaring material sublimity and intermingled sordidness. The relation between these flawed and shadowed sublimities is often heavily ironic in Byron. But interestingly this poet of unaccommodating inner states and outer substances was found to be better partnered by John Martin than by anyone else when the time came to attempt to realize his conceptions in the theatre.[7]

This partnership, albeit almost totally one-sided, was almost a decade old by the time Martin did his illustrations for *Manfred*. Martin's *Fall of Nineveh* depended on Byron for the image of Sar-

6. In his *Diary*, ed. W. B. Pope, Benjamin Robert Haydon justly mocked Martin's attempts to paint beyond sight: "No effort of the mind can entertain such a notion [painting God as the creator]; besides, it is the grossest of all gross ideas to make the power and essence of the Creator to depend on size. His nature might be comprehended in an ordinary-sized brain, and it is vulgar to make Him striding across the horizon and say the horizon is 50 miles long." But then Haydon himself continues into the hyperbolic: "There is nothing grand in a man stepping from York to Lancaster; but when he [Martin] makes a great Creator fifteen inches, paints a sun the size of a bank token, draws a line for the sea and makes one leg of God in it and the other above, and says: 'There! That horizon is twenty miles long, and therefore God's leg must be sixteen relatively to the horizon,' the artist really deserves as much pity as the poorest maniac in Bedlam" (pp. 10–11). This subject matter is clearly too grand even for Martin (although not for a Raphael or a Michelangelo), and here is one of the few instances where he does fail, I think, by being too safe, too iconographic, too "Christian."

7. Martin Meisel, "The Material Sublime: John Martin, Byron, Turner and the Theater," in *Images of Romanticism: Verbal and Visual Affinities*, ed. Karl Kroeber and William Walling, p. 215.

danapalus's self-destruction (as did Delacroix's image); surely the motif of *The Last Man* owes something to Byron's *Darkness* (as well as to others like Mary Shelley); *Belshazzar's Feast* has affinities with Byron's vision of *Belshazzar*; and in Martin's own 1826 note to *Deluge* he glossed his vision by reference to "that sublime poem," Byron's *Heaven and Earth*. Hence by the time Martin had decided to illustrate *Manfred* he was already a visionary companion of Byron.

I think Martin understood *Manfred* better than he understood *Paradise Lost*, certainly better than he did the Bible. His two illustrations, the famous *Manfred on the Jungfrau* and the not-so-famous *Manfred and the Witch of the Alps*, capture the essence of Byronic sublimity. In both, the necromantic hero is poised on the brink, at the threshold of new consciousness. There is a Vastness here at the edge that is not the frenzied space of Martin's earlier biblical scenes but the balanced vision of a man who has carefully understood the text and is attempting a visual analogue. There is a sincerity here in Martin's illustration that is often missing in his other works. The great scenes in *Manfred* are not active but contemplative, and Martin seemed to sense this by choosing two of the quietest scenes to paint. To appreciate how perceptive he was, however, we need first to look at Byron's drama.

Although in recent years there has been a resurgence of scholarly interest in Byron's verse dramas, little new knowledge has resulted. This is especially true of *Manfred*; although there is a new level of appreciation (witness the number of times it has been anthologized in the last decade), critical commentary has lagged. Perhaps this new interest in *Manfred* has arisen because scholars who have been uneasy about Byron's place in the nineteenth century have at last found a way to make him into a romantic. For *Manfred* is Byron's most "romantic" work, both in character and in theme. Here is an almost Faustian hero, who has spent his life pushing toward a union of himself and invisible forces beyond, a "Streben nach dem Unendlichen," a sublimater nonpareil.

Despite the romantic character of its hero, other attributes of *Manfred* make it comparable with *The Rime of the Ancient*

Mariner, Prometheus Unbound, or *Endymion.* Certainly most startling is that the world above the threshold shares obvious structural similarities with the subliminal worlds of Coleridge, Shelley, and Keats. The supernaturalism Byron created above Manfred, however, is more rigorously and logically organized than the universes of the other poets. While in the other poems the cosmologies often provide clues to possible interpretations, in *Manfred* the supernatural machinery is central. There is nothing extraneous in *Manfred's* heavens, no supernumeraries in the skies; things fit into one piece.

Like a neoclassicist, Byron built in *Manfred* a very sturdy chain of being; but like a romantic, he used this chain not to keep man in his place, but to show that there are certain links man can snap and certain ones he cannot. The spirit world above Manfred appears to be a projection of linked states of consciousness, and one can interpret the drama by understanding both how these spirits are organized and how they reflect psychological changes in the protagonist. Moreover, we can "see" a central part of this process pictured in John Martin's illustrations.

Only recently have critics suggested that the spirits that populate the outer world of Manfred are personified reflections of the protagonist's internal world. Usually these spirits have been discussed, if discussed at all, only in terms of an external mythology. This is understandable, and interpretations that treat the spirits as "external realities" in the poem make considerable sense. However, I think *Manfred* can also can be interpreted as a drama of the sublime; that is, these spirits, like the spirits of *Prometheus Unbound,* are to be taken as if "drawn from the operations of the human mind," as if representing an altered state of awareness. William H. Marshall has summed up the implications of either approach:

> If the Spirits are projections of Manfred's own mind rather than supernatural beings invoked as some have believed (offering an explanation in terms of psychology rather than of magic), then they cannot do for him what he is unable to do for himself, since their nature is limited by whatever may be the dimensions of his mind. If, on the other hand, the Spirits are drawn from a realm of being outside earthly existence, their inability to aid Manfred merely emphasizes

how he is representative of the human dilemma: through reason
and imagination man can aspire, but the limitations imposed upon
him prevent him from attaining the object of his aspiration.[8]

There is, I think, a third possibility, namely that both interpretations can be considered together, as a kind of tertium quid.
As with the ambiguous nature of "reality" in *The Rime of the Ancient Mariner, Endymion,* and *Prometheus Unbound,* this need
not be an either/or situation, for the psychological and mythological interpretations can complement one another. In *Manfred*
this correlation grows increasingly more complex as the play
progresses: in the beginning the spirit life seems to be totally outside the protagonist; at the end, it seems almost totally internal.
In other words, the play is "about" the subliming process, the
rising to a threshold of new awareness, and we witness the effects
of this "rite of passage" by observing changes in Manfred's interaction with the spirit world.

When the action of the play begins, all the spirits appear to be
operating independently of Manfred's mind. If we are to believe
both the explicit and the implicit stage directions, Manfred is
clearly drawing down spirits from specific locations in Nature.
The first set of spirits even tells us where they have come from:
the clouds, mountains, waters, earthquakes, and beneath the
earth's crust. Certainly there is no need to draw attention to such
specific locations if these spirits are only projections of Manfred's
psyche. Furthermore, Manfred conjures them with an obscure
magic, and much is made of his knowing the signs, charms, and
language necessary to invoke and/or control life in worlds beyond. Again this kind of emphasis would be unnecessary, even
detrimental, if we were to view the spirits solely as aberrations of
Manfred's mind. If this were an allegory of the subconscious
mind, these spirits should come floating before Manfred at their
command, not at his, as they do, say, in *Alastor.*

On the other hand, Manfred himself tells us at the beginning
that "There is a vigil, and these eyes but close / To look within"
(1.1. 6–7), which suggests that what follows will be an enactment

8. William H. Marshall, *Notes to Lord Byron: Selected Poems and Letters,*
p. 521.

of what he "sees." Still later, at the end of the same scene, Manfred "falls senseless." This physical change seems to trigger sublimation, for no sooner does the Ancient Mariner "swoon," Endymion "dream," or Prometheus "wake up" than they undergo a
change of consciousness and the psychodrama begins. The outer
eye closes; the inner one opens. As do his counterparts in this
subgenre, Manfred then wakes to startling new sounds. A voice
(presumably that of the seventh spirit) is heard incanting:

> Though thou seest me not pass by,
> Thou shall feel me with thine eye
> As a thing that, though unseen,
> Must be near thee, and hath been;
> And when in that secret dread
> Thou hast turned around thy head,
> Thou shalt marvel I am not
> As thy shadow on the spot,
> And the power which thou dost feel
> Shall be what thou must conceal. (1. 1. 213–22)

A "possessed" and understandably confused Manfred wakes half
into a world of mixed consciousness:

> my brain reels—and yet my foot is firm:
> There is a power upon me which withholds,
> And makes it my fatality to live;
> If it be life to wear within myself
> This barrenness of spirit, and to be
> My own soul's sepulchre. (1. 2. 22–27)

Still later Manfred relates to the Witch of the Alps a vision of
awful sublimity prefiguring that of *Prometheus Unbound*, a vision
that shows his vain attempts to draw back from the threshold of
this new world:

> My solitude is solitude no more,
> But peopled with the furies;—I have gnashed
> My teeth in darkness till returning morn,
> Then cursed myself till sunset;—I have prayed
> For madness as a blessing—'tis denied me.
> I have affronted death—but in the war
> Of elements the waters shrunk from me,

> And fatal things passed harmless; the cold hand
> Of an all-pitiless demon held me back,
> Back by a single hair, which would not break. (2. 2. 131–40)

By the end of the second scene the confusion of internal and external is complete: the furies and the demon are both within and without, and no amount of inventiveness on the critic's part is going to separate them and give them specific location.

The same confusion is true of the destinies, for like the witches in *Macbeth* they have power over the natural world—they have, so they say, deposed kings, sunk ships, and plagued cities—and now they want control of Manfred. They are joined by Nemesis, a Byronic caricature of a fury, who has been out snatching defeat from the jaws of victory and bringing chaos out of order. Again, at first glance these spirits seem to exist totally outside Manfred, but just after the hectic scene with Arimanes, Manfred hints that they might also be projections of his tortured mind. He speaks of the new level of psychic peace (Kalon) he has found "seated in my soul" (3. 1. 6–18). Presumably to get to this nonverbal peace he has to cross the bounds of consciousness: he has to sublimate.

This same confusion between inner and outer is true at the play's end when the daemons come to collect Manfred. The Abbot, who presumably suffers no aberrations of the mind, recognizes the spirits as being "out there" and evil. He tells them to go, but they refuse. However, Manfred gets rid of them by using a slightly different tack:

> —Back to thy hell!
> Thou hast no power upon me, *that* I feel;
> Thou never shalt possess me, *that* I know:
> What I have done is done; I bear within
> A torture which could nothing gain from thine:
> The Mind which is immortal makes itself
> Requital for its good or evil thoughts,—
> Is its own origin of ill and end—
> And its own place and time; its innate sense,
> When stripped of this mortality, derives
> No color from the fleeting things without,
> But is absorbed in sufferance or in joy,
> Born from the knowledge of its own desert. (3. 4. 124–36)

I think Stuart Sperry is correct when he considers Manfred's daemons as "a confrontation with his own persona, his latent realization of the danger of personal domination by the character of his own creating."[9] Hence the climax of the play is indeed this ultimate confrontation of the subliming self with the dross of consciousness.

Clearly, whatever "meaning" the play is going to have for us depends on how *we* wish to interpret all the supernatural elements, for their role in the drama is ambiguous: "reality" is in flux. Are we seeing into, and outside, Manfred at the same time? If we are only seeing one "reality," which one is it? We are, like Manfred, left hovering at the edge. Byron surely realized this problem, for he seems to have taken uncommon care in arranging the "phantastic" elements. Like the subliminal spirits in *The Rime of the Ancient Mariner*, these spirits in *Manfred* do not appear at random but are carefully arranged in hierarchies, building not only up to Arimanes and beyond but also into the psyche of Manfred. The metapsychological pattern that they form has been drawn with such un-Byronic caution that we might well look still more carefully at them.

Because these spirits may be central to our understanding of changes in Manfred's consciousness, because they may well represent what Geoffrey Hartman considers a central event in romanticism, namely the "confrontation with a second self in the form of genius loci," it may be helpful to see how Byron first conceived of his hero, and then to see how he fitted the spirit world above him.[10] Byron himself wrote of *Manfred* that it was "a very wild, metaphysical, and inexplicable" kind of drama in which "almost all the persons—but two or three—are spirits of the earth and air, or the water [and] the hero is a kind of magician [who] wanders about invoking spirits who appear to him and are of no use."[11] In the nineteenth century it was accepted that Byron had plagiarized the beginning of Goethe's *Faust*, and although he re-

9. Stuart M. Sperry, "Byron and the Meaning of *Manfred*," p. 198.
10. Geoffrey H. Hartman, "Romantic Poetry and the *Genius Loci*," in *Beyond Formalism*, p. 333.
11. "Letter to John Murray," 15 February 1817, Byron, *Works*, ed. Rowland E. Prothero, 4:52–53.

peatedly claimed that "his Faust I never read, for I don't know German; but Matthew 'Monk' Lewis translated of it to me *viva voce*," his claims went unheeded.[12] The influence of Shelley, Walpole, Coleridge, Maturin, Lewis, and Beckford was so blatantly obvious in his other works that it seemed only natural to accuse Byron of writing *Manfred* with *Faust* open before him. E. M. Butler in *Byron and Goethe* absolves Byron of what were thought to be his sins of commission by stressing that Goethe drew his Faust from the medieval Christian tradition, whereas Byron's Manfred is "a direct descendent of the mighty magicians of old, who had power over the spirits."[13] Professor Butler does not, however, attempt to explain whom she considers to be the "magicians of old."

To understand what kind of magician Byron intended Manfred to be, it is helpful to remember that at the turn of the century there was a revival of interest in Near Eastern mythologies and that in 1816 Byron, mainly as the result of his association with Shelley, became fascinated with the works of the ancient Neoplatonic mystics of Alexandria: Iamblichus, Plotinus, Porphyry, and a number of others.[14] Although Coleridge and Byron drew their "genii loci" from the same source, Byron stayed much closer to Neoplatonic cosmology, and so I should like to set his cosmic pattern up in some detail.

The Alexandrian Neoplatonists believed in a graduated cosmos emanating in steps from the One downward to the phenomenal world. The most obvious attraction of such a cosmic staircase is the potential for psychological correspondences. The basic principle behind all myth is that the outer world will mirror inner space, and the Neoplatonic mythologies are no exception. They simply are more organized and logical than most, providing a se-

12. "Letter to John Murray, June 7, 1820," *Letters and Journals*, 5:37.
13. Eliza M. Butler, *Byron and Goethe*, p. 33.
14. See Wallace Brown, "Byron and the English Interest in the Near East." There is also the possible influence of Shelley, for Mary Shelley wrote in the notes to her edition: "During this summer his [Shelley's] genius was checked by associations with another poet [Byron] whose nature was dissimilar to his own, yet who in the poems that he wrote at this time [*Manfred* and Canto III of *Childe Harold*] gave tokens that he shared for a period the more abstract and etherealized inspirations of Shelley."

ries of steps or thresholds that lead both up and out as well as down and into the self.

In retrospect it seems inevitable that these plateaus were eventually peopled by, as Byron said, "forms that can outlast all flesh." In *Manfred,* Iamblichus seems to be the most important recorder and creator of these forms. In the second century, Iamblichus wrote an elaborate description and defense of Chaldean theology, known as *On the Mysteries of the Egyptians, Chaldeans, and Assyrians,* which Byron had certainly heard of and probably had read.[15] Like his fellow philosophers, Iamblichus believed that at the very top of this cosmic pyramid is the One—the force of unity for all life. But far below this peak, Iamblichus claimed, there was a deity who is "first god and king," and from this deity—the point of divine sublimation—emanate the Rational and Universal Souls downward throughout the angelic, archonic, heroic, and daemonic orders to man.

The chief concern of Iamblichus's *On the Mysteries* is not, however, the topography of the cosmos or the psyche but rather how the magician can communicate with the daemons that exist in the lower material spheres or plateaus. This is of considerable importance, for the theurgist (a "white magician," as opposed to the goetist, or "black magician") is responsible for preserving material harmony on the earth: he is responsible for making things go. To do this he "energizes" the six different types of daemons: celestial, ethereal, aerial, aquatic, terrestrial, and subterranean, who in turn can control the four elements: earth, fire, air, and water. These spirits exist on their own thresholds within the Universal Spirit, until conjured up and out by the theurgist. Since the magician knows the sympathetic nature of things microcosmic to things macrocosmic, he can, by controlling the earthly "signatures" or emblems, control their supernatural counterparts as well. Man is capable of discovering these signatures because, as Iamblichus says, "we preserve in the soul collectively the mystic and arcane image of the gods, and through this we elevate the soul to the gods, and when elevated conjoin it as much as possi-

15. The translation he may have read was written by Thomas Taylor. Taylor's translations of the Neoplatonists were being widely read among the nineteenth-century literati. For more information on Taylor, see my Introduction, note 37.

ble with them."[16] Thus in the process of discovering the external
divinity we may be brought into contact with the gods (2. 11).
Again, it is easy to see how such a schema almost begs for a psychological interpretation; if things work this way on the outside,
might they work the same way inside?[17]

For our purposes the most important facets of Iamblichus's argument are, first, the hierarchy of daemonic powers and their
singular characteristics; second, the insistence on the inherent
dualism of man, the insistence that he is endowed with two souls,
one sensual, of the body and fated, the other transcendent, im-
mutable, and of the gods (8. 6. 7. 8); and third, the idea that the
magician can "sublime" himself out of the material world by
conjuring.

The most direct reference in *Manfred* to Iamblichus and his
turbid vision of the universe is one that has been understandably
overlooked by scholars who were more concerned with other aspects of the play. Manfred, having conjured up "The Witch of the
Alps," says,

> I made
> Mine eyes familiar with Eternity
> Such as, before me, did the Magi, and
> He who from out their fountain dwellings raised
> Eros and Anteros, at Gadara,
> As I do thee. (2. 2. 89–94)

Byron himself glossed this as referring to Iamblichus, and Hartley
Coleridge further elaborated in his 1829 edition of Byron's po-

16. As quoted in Taylor's Notes to Iamblichus, *On the Mysteries*, 2d ed., 7. 4.
Notations will appear hereafter in the text in parentheses (section numbers first,
then chapter numbers).

17. Every Neoplatonist places these daemons differently in the cosmic structure. For Iamblichus, these daemons existed between the two extremes of divine
genera, namely the gods and human souls, and thus are the median link in the
chain of command over nature. They have both productive and operative powers
(1. 5); both are ministers of fate (1. 20; 2. 1) and the means of nature (3. 15). They
can be still further divided by habitat and intelligence: the aquatic, terrestrial,
and subterranean daemons are rational, willful, and conscious. The other three,
celestial, ethereal, and aerial daemons, can be invoked and are willful enough to
perform tasks that are evil, but they are not willful enough to exert a force of their
own. Iamblichus denied them fixed form, saying that they assume whatever
shape they are invoked into or whatever form pleases their imagination (1. 8, 16).

etry.[18] Although this tells nothing of the magic practiced by Manfred, it does establish a link between Byron and Iamblichus or his explicators. One of the most famous of these explicators was Michael Psellus, who, as we have already seen in the gloss to *The Ancient Mariner*, was one of Coleridge's important sources. Psellus classified the daemons as the "igneum," or fiery spirit of the upper air; the "aereum," or the aerial spirit of the air surrounding man; the "terreneaum," or earthly spirit; and onward through the orders of "aquarium et merinum," "subterraneaum," and the "lucifugum," or light-fleeing spirit.[19]

Looking at the spirits Manfred invokes in act 1, one finds that this supernatural pattern is undisturbed. The first spirit is celestial: "From my mansion in the cloud, / Which the breath of twilight builds" (1. 1. 51–52). The second spirit is ethereal, drawn from a lower sphere from which it controls mountaintops with avalanches and glaciers; the third is aquatic, from "the blue depth of the waters, / Where the wave hath no strife" (1. 1. 76–77), and the sixth is the "lucifugum," saying only, "My dwelling is the

18. Byron, *The Poetic and Dramatic Works of Lord Byron*, ed. John Nicholas and J. C. Jeaffreson, with notes by Lord Byron, p. 147. In his edition of Byron's poetry Hartley Coleridge relates this story told by Eunapius about Iamblichus:

It is reported of him that while he and his scholars were bathing in the hot baths of Gadara, in Syria, a dispute arising concerning the baths, he, smiling, ordered his disciples to ask the inhabitants by what names the two lesser springs, that were fairer than the rest were called. To which the inhabitants replied, 'that the one was called Love, and the other Love's Contrary, but for what reason they knew not.' Upon which Iamblichus who chanced to be sitting on the fountain's edge where the stream flowed out, put his hand on the water, and, having uttered a few words, called up from the depths of the fountain a fair-skinned lad, not over-tall, whose golden locks fell in sunny curls over his breast and back; so that he looked like one fresh from the bath; and then, going to the other spring, and doing as he had done before, called up another Amoretto like the first, save that his long-flowing locks now seemed black, not shot with sunny gleams. Whereupon both the Amoretti nestled and clung round Iamblichus as if they had been his own children . . . .'. After this his disciples asked him no more questions.

In Byron, *Works: Poetry*, ed. E. H. Coleridge, 1:105, quoting Eunapius Sardiani, *Vitae Philosophorum et Sophistarum*.
19. "De Daemonibus" in Marcilio Ficino, *Opera Omnia*, 2:1939–45. If Byron did not read Taylor's translation, I think it likely that he did read Ficino's translation of Iamblichus, *On the Mysteries*. Ficino's translation also includes dissertations on daemonology by Proclus, Plotinus, Porphyry, and Psellus.

shadow of the night, / Why doth thy magic torture me with light?" (1. 1. 108–9).

According to Iamblichus, these spirits have no bodies of their own but can assume bodies on command (1. 16), and they are also without passions (1. 10, 11). As in *The Rime of the Ancient Mariner*, the daemons in *Manfred* never appear physically and are distinguished only by their voices. In unison the seventh spirit and the six daemons claim, "We have no forms, beyond the elements / Of which we are the mind and principle: / But choose a form—in that we will appear" (1. 1. 182–84). When Manfred is unable to choose a form, it is the seventh spirit, not the six daemons, who has the power or will to assume physical shape.

Since the daemons are the productive and operative executors of nature (1. 5), they have power only over the four elements, not over the mind or psyche of man. It must be remembered that these are the lowest sublunar genera; they exist just at the edge of expanded consciousness. Above them are the corporeal, intellectual, and divine gods, all of whom do have power over man. Therefore it is perfectly consistent that these daemons refuse Manfred's plea for "oblivion, self-oblivion," saying,

> We can but give thee that which we possess:
> Ask of us subjects, sovereignty, the power
> O'er earth—the whole, or portion—or a sign
> Which shall control the elements, whereof
> We are the dominators,—each and all,
> These shall be thine. (1. 1. 140–45)

Next higher in Byron's chain of being is the enigmatic seventh spirit of the "star which rules thy destiny" (1. 1. 110). Typical of the bewildered interpretations of this spirit is Andrew Rutherford's comment: "If this spirit rules the star under which Manfred was born, has he controlled or influenced the hero's life? Was it he or some external fate, who was responsible for that dire change?" Rutherford continues, saying that this type of ambiguity is characteristic of the play's supernatural element, "so that in the play there is serious confusion or obscurity in the metaphysics."[20] He later concludes that this spirit suggests "a devil trying

20. Andrew Rutherford, *Byron: A Critical Study*, pp. 80, 81.

to win the hero's soul," but it is obvious from the play that the star does not control Manfred, nor does Manfred control the star (1. 1. 125–28). Once the cosmic pattern has been understood, the role of the seventh spirit is understandable. The Neoplatonists believed that everyone received a personal daemon at the hour of birth, and this daemon then controlled both body and environment.[21] These "celestial animals of the gods" exist in higher heavenly spheres and therefore are more powerful than the other daemons since they are closer to the "One," but they are managers, not dictators, of fate.

Manfred's star, however, has become "A wandering mass of shapeless flame, / A pathless comet, and a curse, / The menace of the universe" (1. 1. 117–19), which serves to heighten the awfulness of Manfred's predicament in much the same way that Childe Harold's birth "beneath some remote inglorious star" substantiates his claim to melancholy. Byron's use of star lore is probably not drawn directly from the Neoplatonists; more likely it is a syncretism of ancient and then-current astrological beliefs. What is interesting, however, is that the seventh spirit's place in the threshold structure of *Manfred* is consistent with his place in the hierarchies of the Alexandrian mystics.

Thus far—through act 1, scene 1—the spirits have existed outside Manfred and been powerless to aid him. They have been executors of nature only, the "genii loci," in no sense helpmates. Perhaps Byron objected to the unquestioning faith of his contemporaries in the palliative powers of nature; in any case, these spirits of nature are at best only temporary slaves. At the end of the first scene, however, with the eerie "Incantation," the action takes the first turn from external to internal nature as the self is sublimed toward new consciousness. The seventh spirit has just appeared in the form of Astarte, and Manfred is so shocked that he "falls senseless." The incantation follows, and although we never learn whose voice chants the magical song, the import of

21. See, for instance, Apuleuis, *De Deo Socratis*, which goes through the usual doctrine of the intermediary spirits, ending with the highest, most august class of daemons, the guardian spirits that watch over every man. Appropriately, Byron placed this spirit in Manfred's star, so as to make it physically higher than the other daemons. In fact, the seventh spirit even admits that it ruled the star that ruled Manfred's destiny (1.1.110).

the words is clear. We are, from now on, going to be dealing with
psychological as well as supernatural phenomena. The eye that
once looked outward "now closes to look within."

Manfred awakens from this transformation realizing that

> The spirits I have raised abandon me,
> The spells which I have studied baffle me,
> The remedy I recked of tortured me;
> I lean no more on superhuman aid. (1. 2. 1–4)

Again, as in scene 1, he implores Nature to provide release but
finally realizes that it is he, not she, who must compromise and
accept. Finally, a desperate Manfred prepares his own release by
planning to leap from the cliff. This is the initial climax of the
drama—the first scene John Martin chose to illustrate—and it
is resolved just as the nameless spirit has promised: Manfred
cannot finally escape consciousness; he is trapped below the
threshold.

> I feel the impulse—yet I do not plunge;
> I see the peril—yet do not recede;
> And my brain reels—and yet my foot is firm:
> There is a power upon me which withholds,
> And makes it my fatality to live,—
> If it be life to wear within myself
> This barrenness of spirit, and to be
> My own soul's sepulchre. (1. 2. 20–27)

Although this reading is by no means conclusive, it does suggest
that the spirits we are now to encounter fit into not only a cosmic
pattern but also a psychological one. Indeed we find that as we
move higher up through the "daemonic realm" we start to move
deeper into Manfred: the characters become more personalized,
more the projected persona, and less the wispy, amorphous
voices. Above the daemons and Manfred's star, both chronologi-
cally and spatially, is the Witch of the Alps. Once again Manfred
conjures her presence by use of a theurgic sign, but unlike the
invisible daemons previously conjured, she has a form that "The
charms of earth's least mortal daughters grow / To an unearthly
stature, in an essence / Of purer elements" (2. 2. 15–17). As the

ruling principle of material beauty, or as the "venus genetrix," it
is implied (2. 2. 153–58), she controls the purpose of the six
daemons. In other words, she would probably be at the level of
"god" in the Neoplatonic hierarchy, but her role is more important structurally: she binds the Neoplatonic and the Zoroastrian,
allowing Manfred opportunity to explain "my sciences, / My long
pursued and superhuman art," and to refer obliquely to Astarte,
his "heartcrushed love."

As we shall see, Martin also chose this scene to illustrate, and
with good reason, for in terms of the psychodrama, it is here that
Manfred consolidates the turn inward, refusing the anodyne of a
life lived in eternal nature. Again Byron seems to be almost play-
fully toying with the romantic view of nature as release by having
Manfred contemplate a life completely outside himself, with this
"Beautiful Spirit! in [whose] calm clear brow, / . . . is glassed se-
renity of soul" (2. 2. 25–26). When the Witch asks why she has
been called, Manfred answers,

> To look upon thy beauty—nothing further.
> The face of the earth hath maddened me, and I
> Take refuge in her mysteries, and pierce
> To the abodes of those who govern her—
> But they can nothing aid me. I have sought
> From them what they could not bestow, and now
> I search no further. (2. 2. 38–44)

When he realizes that such a life of the senses demands that he
"swear obedience to [her] will, and do / [Her] bidding" (2. 2.
156–57), he discharges her. Manfred is now more alone than
ever. On the supernatural level he has transcended the world
of the Intermediary Spirits, and on the psychological level he
has refused a lotus-eater's life in Nature. He is now prepared to
confront both the buried parts of his self and the "unnatural"
universe.

This unnatural universe takes on a singularly malicious quality
when Byron draws from the mythologies of Zoroastrianism to
complete the cosmic pattern. The cosmos of the Zoroastrian religion that Byron knew was one split and united by the constant

tensions between good and evil. Ormazd, the lord of goodness
and light, wages constant war against Ahriman, the lord of evil
and darkness. Beneath these great patriarchs extend vast sublunar worlds of spirits, who are good or evil depending on whose
hierarchy they are in, Ormazd's or Ahriman's. This dualism is
marked and distinct, and man is given the choice of worshiping
either the good or the evil. The six major spirits presided over by
Ahriman are collectively called the "daivas" (from which the
Christian "devil" is derived, just as "demon" is derived from the
Neoplatonic "daemon"), and it is they who implement the pol-
icies of evil through the offices of still lesser spirits.[22] Not only is
the system of thresholds maintained as it is in Neoplatonism, but
even the same numerology is employed, except that now the six
spirits are actively and consciously malefic, whereas in Neoplatonism they are noisy but innocuous.

After Manfred has refused the solace of submission to the
Witch of the Alps (2. 2. 165) he appears in the court of Arimanes
(2. 4), presumably of his own volition, for there is no mention of
his being conjured "up" or of his conjuring Armanes "down." Byron himself glossed "Arimanes" as being Ahriman, the evil principle of Zoroastrianism, and he wrote elsewhere that Manfred "at
last goes to the abode of the Evil Principles *in propria persona* to
evocate a ghost, which appears, and gives him ambiguous and
disagreeable answers."[23] It is obvious from the text that Arimanes
controls the three destinies, the six spirits (not to be confused
with the six daemons of act 1), and Nemesis.

There is also no doubt that evil extends throughout Arimanes's
hierarchy. On the lowest level the three destinies pride themselves on freeing a captive usurper so that he can return to the
destruction of his nation and on causing a tempest to wreck a ship
so as to kill all but one traitor, who is to be saved. Next higher is
Nemesis, a malicious Puck, who has just returned from

> repairing shatter'd thrones
> Marrying fools, restoring dynasties,

22. For instance, see George Foot Moore, *History of Religions*, 1:357–405;
John Walters Waterhouse, *Zoroastrianism*, and Robert Ernest Hume, *The
World's Living Religions*, pp. 205–10.
23. Byron, *Works*, ed. Rowland E. Prothero, 4:54–55.

Avenging men upon their enemies,
And making them repent their own revenge;
Goading the wise to madness. (2. 3. 62–67)

Later, when Manfred wishes to speak with "the Phantom of Astarte," it is Nemesis who, with the approval of Arimanes, "uncharnels" her spirit. From this evidence Maurice Quinlan believes that Nemesis bears

> a resemblance to Druj Nasu, the corpse-fiend of Zoroastrian belief who is described as a personification of the spirit of corruption, decomposition, contagion, and impurity, which in the shape of an abominable fly, takes possession of the dead body and spreads contagion everywhere.[24]

But it seems doubtful, judging from his other demonic characterizations, that Byron intended to be so specific. Otherwise, why did he choose a name like *Nemesis* that is freighted with such mythological, and even Platonic, implications? It is more likely that Byron here fashioned another artistic syncretism of pagan and Zoroastrian beliefs. It may be inconsistent, and even illogical, to use the name of a minister of justice in a completely demonic context, but it is unmistakably effective.

Surrounding Arimanes are six spirits whose proximity to the godhead indicates that they are the six spirits who minister the will of the evil principle to the lower spirits, in this case to the three destinies. In Zoroastrian mythology each of these six spirits is charged with the working of a specific evil, but in *Manfred* they seem to have no function other than to pester Manfred with commands to kneel and praise Arimanes.[25] One thing they do,

24. Maurice Quinlan, "Byron's *Manfred* and Zoroastrianism," p. 730, quoting A. V. Williams Jackson, *Zoroastrian Studies.*
25. Quinlan, ibid., considers these six spirits to be the six "daemons" conjured down by Manfred in the first act, but I think he is mistaken. The "daemons" are not evil but rather the executors of nature. Quinlan erroneously claims (p. 731) that the spirits can perform only at night, citing the sixth daemon's statement that "my dwelling is the shadow of the night, /Why doth thy magic torture me with Light?" (1.1.108–9). But as we have seen, this is Byron's representation of the light-fleeing or "lucifugum" daemon. Likewise, Quinlan believes the seventh daemon to be Aeshma, a Zoroastrian spirit, but again it is clear that the seventh daemon is the spirit of Manfred's star. This makes a considerable difference in interpretation, for if Quinlan is correct, Manfred has been determined from birth

however, is to provide Manfred with an opportunity to allude to a still higher (in fact, the highest) power in the hierarchy. Manfred demands that Arimanes

> bow down to that which is above him,
> That overruling Infinite—the Maker
> Who made him not for worship—let him kneel,
> And we will kneel together. (2. 4. 46–49)

Whether or not this "overruling Infinite" is Ormazd, as Quinlan supposes, or the Neoplatonic One, or what Iamblichus calls "First God and King" makes little difference. What is important is that this power establishes the topmost or innermost limit which, even in this imperfect universe, holds redemption/salvation/divine sublimation for those who resist the compromise with chaos.

It has become something of a critical commonplace to regard Byron's 1816 and 1817 works as emotionally cathartic and therefore not as carefully structured as his later poetry. It is true that *Manfred* was written during a period of intense domestic turmoil (the references to his relations with Augusta Leigh are too obvious to miss), yet, in spite of all the biographical material, Byron constructed a cosmic, psychological, and mythological system of some complexity. Although he was not the "profound philosopher" that Coleridge might ask a poet to be, Byron did work within the metapsychology he constructed. Expressed schematically, the pattern of thresholds would look something like this:

> Ormazd—the One—Sun ⎫
>   Ahriman   ⎪
>   "Daivas" or six spirits ⎬   Zoroastrian
> Nemesis   ⎪
> Three destinies   ⎭   act 2
>
> Witch of the Alps—"Venus Genetrix"
> seventh spirit—Manfred's star

---

and therefore is not responsible for his actions. But if the spirit only represents Manfred's star, then its control has extended only to Manfred's time and place of birth, not to his will.

celestial
ethereal
aquatic   six daemons   Neoplatonic
subterranean
aerial   act 1
light-fleeing

What is intrinsic to both Neoplatonism and Zoroastrianism is dualism: in Zoroastrianism, it is a dualism of good and evil in the cosmos; in Neoplatonism, it is a dualism of the higher and lower souls of men. As we have seen, in the first act Manfred's magic, made possible by the control of his "higher soul," allows him some power over the material daemons. But this power is useless, for the six daemons can direct only the forces of nature, not the will of man. In the second act we learn that it is the selfsame detested will that prevents Manfred from succumbing to the evil forces of Arimanes. So, ironically, what saves Manfred from capitulation to evil is the same thing that he had once wanted to destroy. In the third act we get a kind of synthetic restatement of the theme, this time in a Christian context, with the Abbot begging Manfred to "reconcile thyself with thy own soul, / And thy own soul with heaven" (3. 1. 99–100). This is the final redoubling of the psychological and metaphysical, the dovetailing of inside-and-outside patterns.

Once we understand the metaphysical pattern that Byron has woven from these three religions, we soon realize that Manfred is caught in the Hobson's choice of being damned if he acts and damned if he doesn't. He wants the sublimation that will give him release, yet he does not want to give up control. By the very nature of the cosmos that Byron has erected around Manfred, and by the very nature of the dualism he has created within him, Manfred is powerfully powerless. Condemned by his birth to be "half dust," condemned by his theurgistic power to be "half deity," Manfred will be conscious of, but never able to reconcile, the ideal and the real, the fire and the clay.

Manfred's achievement of this awareness is the result of a central romantic "rite of passage": it is the acceptance of being "betwixt and between." It is not a happy place to be; in fact, it is positively dangerous to be there for long since the protagonist is suspended in an unsupportable limbo. Again Hartman explains (using *liminal* where *subliminal* might have better expressed the notion of marginality):

> During this *liminal* or *marginal* phase the candidate is segregated and exposed to spirit-powers directly, without forms or mediations available to men in society. He discovers in this way both his individuality and his isolation, both selfhood and the meaning of society.
>
> If we reflect that marginality is dangerous not because it is empty but because the absence of conventional social structuring allows room for an irruption of energies society has not integrated, then we see how similar this state is to the "chaos of forms" which art explores. The artist is surely the liminal or threshold person par excellence, while art provides society with a 'chaos of roles' strengthening the individual's sense of unstructured community yet offering him ideal parts to try.[26]

In a sense Manfred is indeed this romantic artist attempting to resolve the "chaos of forms" into sense, except that he has finally run out of "parts to try."

In this context it is especially interesting to look at Martin's watercolor illustrations of *Manfred*, for Martin understood that Byron's central concern was to picture man at the margin, or as Harold Bloom has asserted, at the edge of a "purgation through sublimation."[27] Manfred wants release, oblivion, transcendence, a life "beyond" the self—call it what you will, the point is that he wants psychological transport on his own terms. But his terms cannot be met, at least not in this world. Hence Manfred is trapped on the border, at the brink, on the threshold, unable to transcend the clay, unwilling to be consumed by the fire. This is precisely what he becomes in Martin's two illustrations: pinnacled brightly on the mountaintop about to jump into oblivion, or at the edge of the mountain pond almost enticed across the margin of nature by the Witch of the Alps.

26. Geoffrey H. Hartman, "History-Writing as Answerable Style," p. 80.
27. Harold Bloom, *The Visionary Company: A Reading of English Romantic Poetry*, p. 242.

John Martin, *Manfred and the Witch of the Alps*, 1837. The Whitworth Art Gallery, University of Manchester.

Martin's forms are as carefully constructed as Byron's cosmos. In the more famous *Manfred on the Jungfrau*, Manfred is poised, arms uplifted, supplicating release. By his side is the Chamois Hunter, in a sense personifying that part of Manfred that is the clay, the human, trying to restrain that part of Manfred that is superhuman, the theurgistic. The scene is vast, with all nature seeming to whirl down into the valley floor below, almost as if all the trees, snow, shrubs are to be swept from the mountainsides. Only two huge birds to the right side of Manfred are exempt from this suction. By and large Martin portrayed the sublimity of the scene by reconstructing Byron's verbal images into visual ones; in fact he even glossed his image with Manfred's own words (2. 2. 74–80, 103–11). Admittedly Martin filled in the gaps with his own imagery, but this painting could justifiably be called an explication de texte.

Manfred and the Witch of the Alps, however, could not. Here we find Manfred at the center of the vortex, so to speak, no longer on the Jungfrau but now beside that meltwater stream on the valley floor: it is almost as if he has been swept down into the center. The whole scene is bisected by the gapped rock slabs that open out onto an iridescent glacial flow and behind that by the snowy peaks. No longer is Manfred in the middle distance, off to the side—now he is right before us, stage center. Everything else, however, is the same: same posture of supplication, same magician's robe, same "at the brink" location; in fact even the same two-person arrangement, except that now the Chamois Hunter has been replaced by a ghost image of Manfred himself.

Why this extra self that is so clearly not in the play? I would like to think it is because Martin perceived the duality of Manfred's life, split between fire and clay, psyche and soma, theurgy and humanity. So here Manfred is literally split: the magical part off to the right in ghost outline; the mortal part to the left. Across the waters, under the rainbow, is the Witch of the Alps promising sublimation through submission, release through obedience.

It is all simultaneously wonderful and aweful: the colors of the rainbow so bright and appealing, the bluish glacier and cloud-frosted Alpine peaks so otherworldly. It is the world "across the river," the promised land over the threshold. Manfred, however, is in this world, the world of these spiny trees, these hard brown slabs of rock. There is almost a straight horizontal line across the lower third of the painting, almost a second horizon: all above surreal, all below harsh and natural.

The unresolved tension between these two worlds is the pressure we feel throughout *Manfred*, and it is this sense of tension that Martin knew so well how to portray. He had plenty of practice, for he had painted this same scene five years earlier in *The Last Man*: same solitary, supplicating figure, same chasm, same vastness, same central light at the horizon, so reminiscent as well of his *Demosthenes Haranguing the Waves*. In fact, this is The Romantic Scene made by Martin, as well as by Byron, into the image of man's place in the world: pinnacled, isolated, alone in nature, enticed by the imagination to reach beyond, but condemned by the flesh to remain.

Hence the central paradox of the romantic quest for elevated consciousness is still unresolved. Wordsworth knew something must be sacrificed if he was to stay long in the yew bower, the Ancient Mariner never quite reconciled what he imagined with what he experienced, and Manfred is here likewise caught at the edge of transport to new awareness. Clearly one must give up the illusion of self for the sublime experience. We will now see two possible resolutions to this dilemma: the passive resignation of Keats's Endymion (helped to a considerable extent by authorial fiat), and the heroic disinterestedness of Shelley's Prometheus. Once again we will find the psychological complexities of sublimation played out for us in the daemonic self-reflexive structures above the protagonists as well as in the lower sky paintings of Alexander Cozens and John Constable.

5

Keats and Cozens:
The Systematic Sublime

I am certain of nothing but of the holiness of the Heart's affections and the truth of Imagination—What the imagination seizes as Beauty must be truth—whether it existed before or not—for I have the same Idea of all our Passions as of Love they are all in their sublime, creative of essential Beauty. In a Word, you may know my favorite Speculation by my first Book [*Endymion*] and the little song I sent in my last—which is a representation from the fancy of the probable mode of operating in these Matters. The Imagination may be compared to Adam's dream—he awoke and found it truth.—
John Keats, "Letter to Benjamin Bailey," 22 November 1817

So far I have tried to choose works that are not only successful by themselves but also important in the history of art. Now I should like to discuss two works that are neither: John Keats's *Endymion* and Alexander Cozens's *The Cloud*. These are both relatively desultory attempts to depict sublimity, interesting in retrospect not for what they achieve but for what they attempt. What they attempt is a systematic method of prescription, the creation of paradigm by which the sublime experience can be first induced and then later reproduced. I am interested in them, in large part, for what they *assume*, not for what they produce. They assume that sublimity is not a privileged or sacramental experience but one that can be predicted, decoded, and appreciated by the sensitive observer of nature. For Cozens this confidence can be seen in his system of "blotting," while for Keats the conviction resulted in a regular rising of the imagination through discrete levels of consciousness into the liminal. What is extraordinary about these attempts is that the descriptions are so pro-

saic, so artificial, so unsublime in the rhetorical sense: Cozens
detailed his in *A New Method of Assisting the Invention in Drawing Original Composition of Landscape* (1785), while Keats almost literally graphed his in the "pleasure thermometer" passage
of *Endymion*, book 1. A look at their models will, I hope, give
some indication of the importance of the sublime to the romantic
artist.

Keats's critics generally agree that, as a work of art, *Endymion*
is a wonderful failure. Where critics usually are content to show
how a poem hits the mark, *Endymion*'s critics spend their time
detailing how the poem goes so far afield. No other romantic
poem that I can think of has had so much written on where it goes
wrong, and so little on where it goes right. Yet, until recently, the
whole criticism of *Endymion* as a faltering masterpiece might be
summarized in a sentence: *Endymion* falters because Keats was
writing a piece of Platonic speculation, a philosophical allegory,
when he knew little of allegory and less of Platonism; or because
he was writing an erotic daydream about ideal love when he
knew little of sex and less of love. These two camps, the allegorists and the anti-allegorists, have monopolized *Endymion* criticism for the last fifty years, and they are now at a standoff.[1]

I think the question of organization and intention may be partially resolved if we place *Endymion* in the context of the romantic quest for sublimity, except that Keats is, initially at least, more
interested in codifying procedure than in displaying results. In
Endymion we witness a youthful poet's travelogue to the horizon
complete with wrong turns, culs-de-sac, and detours. That he
does not succeed is usually attributed to his not understanding
the route, but it is precisely this misunderstanding that becomes
important. In matters of the sublime, missed paths are often
more interesting (and certainly more understandable) than completed rites of passage.

I must say that I think the same is also true of Alexander
Cozens. Both artists sought to find "methods" to stretch the
imagination upward to the horizon: Cozens sought to simplify
what William Vaughan has called "transcendent landscape,"

1. A concise summary of this critical impasse can be found in Stuart M. Sperry,
Keats the Poet, p. 92, n. 2.

while Keats sought to address elevated states of consciousness.[2]
Theirs was a feckless task, of course; the sublime is not to be
achieved "by the numbers"; it is the result of both happenstance
and preparation, a miracle of half-unexpected delight. But their
shortcuts, resulting from high seriousness as well as from a touch
of youthful impetuosity, are well worth considering if for no other
reason than that they show a curiously romantic concern for map-
ping and charting states of transport.

I must be candid and say now that a reading of *Endymion* as a
map to sublimity will not make it any less of a wonderful failure,
for as a map it hardly adheres to a consistent scale. But such a
reading may explain such organizational problems as the Glaucus
episode, the Cave of Quietude passages, or Endymion's often
frantic quest for Cynthia. In fact, such a reading may even explain Cynthia herself, who has been prodded and poked by both
allegorists and anti-allegorists without much success: she remains, for the critics as well as for Endymion, just out of reach,
just over the edge. Quite simply, as I hope to show, the awkward-
ness of *Endymion* lies not so much in the dramatic form Keats
chose, nor in the secondhand cosmic systems he borrowed from
the Neoplatonists, but in the chaotic psychic state of the ephebic
hero, in the difficulty an immature poet faced in trying to write
about an immature protagonist. Although Keats knew his hero
had a problem, he did not have the depth of understanding necessary to unfold and elevate the consciousness of his "brain sick
shepherd prince" in such a way as to cause us to "suspend dis-
belief." In projecting the inner states of Endymion outward,
Keats constructed a highly disjointed structure, at times an in-
comprehensibly confusing map to sublimity and Beyond, and
most readers have been left almost hopelessly confused.

The plot of *Endymion* is rather like a Wagnerian opera: it starts
simply enough, rises to a wonderful crescendo of confusion, and
then ends all too abruptly. Briefly, this is the story. On the side of
Mount Latmos the handsome shepherd Endymion has a beatific
vision ("a thing of beauty," we are told, in the most famous and

2. William Vaughan, *Romantic Art*, chap. 5.

misleading lines of the poem, "is a joy forever") of a beautiful goddess and announces to his sister Poena that he will dedicate himself to finding this dream woman. He does not realize that this dream woman is really Cynthia, the Goddess of the Moon, and so he starts his search by descending into the depths of the Earth. This is the standard subterranean trip of heroes since Homer; here Endymion encounters the requisite characters from classical mythology (Venus, Alpheus, Arethusa) but, alas, not his dream woman. So he turns upward to "the giant sea above his head," and there, picking his way across the littered floor of the ocean, he finds Glaucus, a man who has been cursed to live forever without his love, Scylla. Endymion breaks the curse, unites the lovers, and in so doing receives Venus's promise of safe passage to higher realms. Endymion faints with joy and is returned to Earth. All this has taken approximately three thousand lines, and our hero is right back where he started—on Earth without his dream woman, without the sublime.

As book 4 opens we expect that Endymion will indeed take Venus's kind offer and cross the "mortal bar" to higher spiritual realms. But just as he is set to win "the immortality of passion," he meets an Indian Maid whose fresh-faced beauty and doleful "Song of Sorrow" tempt him to abandon his quest. They fall into a lovers' swoon and together rise above the horizon into the heavens. This altitude-gaining journey is, as Northrop Frye has contended, a revolutionary aspect of romanticism, for it articulates movement across the sacred boundaries of the Christian world view. It violates the sense of "proper place," giving a mortal access to realms of divinity.[3] Admittedly, to make this upward journey Endymion must be prepared; he must first seek out success in the nether world and then be magically anesthetized out of normal consciousness, but he does indeed cross that "fragile bar / That keeps us from our homes ethereal." Amazingly, he makes it literally across the horizon. When he wakes in the heavens to find his dream woman, Cynthia, leaning over him, it is an irreligious scene, as Wordsworth knew when he called it a "pretty

3. Northrop Frye, *A Study of English Romanticism*, pp. 3–51.

piece of paganism." It is also rather difficult to believe. Keats
could not sustain this scene for long, and Cynthia soon disappears
by authorial fiat. Endymion rapidly loses altitude, recrosses the
horizon, and enters what has puzzled critics since the nineteenth
century—a strange deep sleep in what is called the Cave of Solitude. When he wakes he finds, lo and behold, the Indian Maid
beside him once again, and this time, to ensure her continued
presence, he proposes a life together; he promises to forget
Cynthia, to abandon his quest for the sublime, and to live forever
with the Indian Maid. Strangely, the Indian Maid refuses, and
Endymion morbidly decides to be a hermit, contemplating sim-
pler pleasures. But he soon has second thoughts, realizes that he
cannot live without the Maid, runs to her, embraces her, and mi-
raculously she now is transformed into the goddess of his dreams.
She becomes Cynthia. All this is most confusing, and we are as
amazed as Poena, who is also witnessing this metamorphosis. But
no matter, we may be a little bewildered—Endymion is not. He
has his dream woman in the flesh and disappears off into the
woods, presumably to live happily ever after.

No critic has ever really understood this plot; it is as Keats himself admitted rather "green," but I would like to venture an interpretation in terms of romantic sublimation. To do this I need
first to detail the various levels of consciousness in the poem—
subconsciousness, "normal" consciousness, sublime consciousness, and liminal transcendence, then to tell where in the cosmos
these thresholds are located, what "projected" characters inhabit
them, and why. In this admittedly reductionistic reading I am
continually indebted to Northrop Frye's "schema of four levels of
imagery: heaven, the innocent world, the ordinary world and
hell," which are the physical counterparts of inner psychological
states. In his chapter on "Endymion: The Romantic Epiphanic,"
Frye attempts to "factor out" the schematic part of the romantic
myth of transport, but even Frye has to admit that Keats's allegory of consciousness is finally confusing, for there is really no
orderly progression up and down through the various states.[4]
What I should like to do, then, is set up the levels in a far more

4. Ibid., pp. 125–67.

rigid way than Frye (let alone Keats) ever intended because I think that although these levels will not fit precisely, we can see Keats developing what could have been a coherent system.

Keats, like traditional Western mythmakers, arranged his system so that activities occurring below the earth tended to be representative of subconscious experience, while activities occurring above the earth reflected supraconscious or enlarged experience. The lowest and hence most self-constricting of these psychological levels is the Cave of Quietude:

> There lies a den,
> Beyond the seeming confines of the space
> Made for the soul to wander in and trace
> Its own existence, of remotest glooms.
> Dark regions are around it, where the tombs
> Of buried griefs the spirit sees, but scarce
> One hour doth linger weeping, for the pierce
> Of new-born woe it feels more inly smart:
> And in these regions many a venom'd dart
> At random flies; they are the proper home
> Of every ill: the man is yet to come
> Who hath not journeyed in this native hell.
> But few have ever felt how calm and well
> Sleep may be had in that deep den of all.
> There anguish does not sting; nor pleasure pall:
> Woe-hurricanes beat ever at the gate,
> Yet all is still within and desolate. (4. 512–28)

Here in this deep cave Endymion feels he can be at peace with himself. But it is a peace paid for by loss of any comprehensive consciousness; it is a drugged peace—it is in fact the anti-sublime, the self at its most constricted:

> Happy gloom!
> Dark Paradise! where pale becomes the bloom
> Of health by due; where silence dreariest
> Is most articulate; where hopes infest;
> Where those eyes are the brightest far that keep
> Their lids shut longest in a dreamless sleep.
> O happy spirit-home! O wondrous soul!
> Pregnant with such a den to save the whole
> In thine own depth. (4. 537–45)

The Cave of Quietude is a condition of the spirit so traumatic that the "soul" (psyche, self) not only accepts angst but takes refuge in it. This is the world inhabited by Blake's "cold earth wanderers." As Dugald Stewart, one of the most influential commentators on the sublime in the early nineteenth century, wrote, "the opposite to the *sublime* is not the *profound*, but the *humble*, the *low*, or the *puerile*."[5] Nevertheless, it is a level of consciousness, a level of just barely being conscious, a childish level of feeling sorry for the self which, carried to the extreme, can become withdrawal or regression, even suicide.[6]

Higher than the Cave of Quietude on an awareness continuum is the consciousness achieved in the "realm of Flora and old Pan." Here man is integrated with nature; here Endymion will finally ascend his rightful throne as "pastoral prince" and vegetation king. This "green world" is explained in the "Hymn to Pan":

> O thou, whose mighty palace roof doth hang
> From jagged trunks, and overshadoweth
> Eternal whispers, glooms, the birth, life, death
> Of unseen flowers in heavy peacefulness;
> Who lov'st to see the hamadryads dress
> Their ruffled locks where meeting hazels darken;
> And through whole solemn hours dost sit, and hearken
> The dreary melody of bedded reeds—
> In desolate places, where dank moisture breeds
> The pipy hemlock to strange overgrowth;
> Bethinking thee, how melancholy loth
> Thou wast to lose fair Syrinx—do thou now,
> By thy love's milky brow!

5. Dugald Stewart, *Philosophical Essays*, 3d ed., p. 390.
6. In this context it is interesting to note that, with few exceptions, when Endymion goes under the Earth he becomes selfish, but when he goes above the Earth he becomes selfless. In both directions his identity as a human being, as an individual, is denied. In "A Cartography of the Ecstatic and Meditative States," Ronald Fischer makes the point that there is a mutually exclusive relationship between ergotropic and trophotropic states of perception. Although one state may be achieved through meditation and the other through hallucination, they both remove the "self" from any normal focus. So too in *Endymion* both intense introspection and ecstatic rapture cause the protagonist to cross distinct boundaries of consciousness represented topographically as subterranean and superterranean worlds.

By all the trembling mazes that she ran,
Hear us, great Pan! (l. 232–46)

Here is another kind of peacefulness, not the self-annihilating ennui of the Cave of Solitude, but one very much like the vegetable quiet world of Keats's own *To Autumn*.[7] Here is the stillness of the ever-renewing cycle, the "soul-soothing quiet" of birth, life, death, and rebirth. This pastoral level extends upward from the earth "to the very bourne of Heaven," stopping just before the levels of sublimity begin. In this stratum there is only the "leven" (l. 296) that allows rising into the "element filling the space beyond" (l. 302); there is just a "touch ethereal" (l. 297), not the ether itself. The ether is part of the next higher level: it is at the edge of the sublime.

Before proceeding further up the pathway of Keatsean transcendence, it may be helpful to pause to see exactly how familiar Keats was with the concept of the sublime. As we have seen in Wordsworth, Coleridge, and Byron, and as we shall see in Shelley, the sublime was in no manner a rigid aesthetic. By the turn of the century, the speculations of Burke, Addison, Gerard, Knight, Alison, and so on, had been so assimilated that no one, certainly not the romantic artists, seriously questioned the verifiability of the experiences. In fact, by the first part of the century, codifiers like Thomas Reid, Abraham Tucker, and Dugald Stewart had been almost forgotten by the new generation. In *From Classic in Romantic*, Walter Jackson Bate showed how quickly the sublime became a "given" in romantic theories of sensation, and we get an inkling of its assimilation not just by its application in the sister arts but also by the way theories of the sublime are influenced by wholly separate disciplines.[8]

7. The movement from the "still vegetable world" of nature into the sublime is thought by Jack Stillinger to be one of the major organizing patterns of the Odes; see his introduction to *Twentieth Century Interpretations of Keats' Odes*.
8. Walter Jackson Bate, *From Classic to Romantic: Premises of Taste in Eighteenth Century England*. The acceptance and assimilation of sublimity as a state of consciousness as well as an aesthetic principle is the stated conclusion of Samuel Holt Monk's *The Sublime: A Study of Critical Theories in Eighteenth-Century England* and the implied premise of Stuart Ende's Freudian interpretation, in *Keats and the Sublime*.

In this context Keats is especially interesting, for his knowledge of sublimity is clearly more informed by science than by
aesthetics or psychology. As an apprentice apothecary-surgeon
he had more than a passing knowledge of chemistry, so it is not
by happenstance that we find words like *abstract*, *essential, intense, empyreal, ethereal*, as well as *sublime*, playing an important role in his poetic vocabulary. George Bornstein, Bernard
Blackstone, and Stuart Sperry have already shown that these
pseudo-scientific terms are not casual references but specific detailing of chemical processes Keats had studied or observed.[9] In
chemistry, *sublimation* was allied to *distillation*, which occurs
"when evaporation is performed in vessels either perfectly or
nearly closed, so that the volatile parts which are raised in one
part of the apparatus, may be received and condensed in the
other part." Sublimation "is founded on the same principles as
distillation, and its rules are the same, [in fact] it is nothing but a
dry distillation."[10] Essentially both operations require the seal-
ing off of a fluid, the application of heat, and the "elevation" of a
spirit or essence. It is not surprising, then, that the distillation
process became a central analogy in Keats's metapsychology, for
here indeed is a trope to explain how the imagination "sublimes"
experience.[11] In fact, in most of the twenty or so appearances of
sublime in Keats's poetry, the word refers either to the process of
elevation or to the separation of a desirable quality ("essence")
from dross.[12]

With this in mind, returning to *Endymion* we witness the almost chemical terms in which the process of the youthful protagonist becoming "full alchemized and free of space" is described. To achieve the "sublime," Endymion must seal himself
off from matter, must let the imagination alone distill received

9. George Bornstein, "Keats' Concept of *The Ethereal*"; Bernard Blackstone,
The Consecrated Urn: An Interpretation of Keats in Terms of Growth and Form,
pp. 101, 112–13, 149–50 and Sperry, *Keats the Poet*, pp. 30–72.
10. William Nicholson, *First Principles of Chemistry*, 2d ed., pp. 34–35.
11. One finds this same process explained in Keats's letters, as in the famous
letter to Bailey (22 November 1817), "I have the same Idea of all our Passions as of
Love. They are all in their *sublime*, creative of *essential* Beauty."
12. William Price Albrecht, *The Sublime Pleasures of Tragedy: A Study of
Critical Theory from Dennis to Keats*, pp. 136, 187.

beauty into "essence." To enter these higher levels of consciousness, Endymion must forsake the outer world of Pan and try to
"cross the fragile bar / That keeps us from our homes ethereal."
He must be careful, however, lest he settle for a false sublime, or,
as Keats called it in reference to Wordsworth, the "egotistical
sublime."[13] He must not "merge" with nature; he must transcend
"normal consciousness," not through nature, but around it. So at
the beginning of his journey across states of consciousness he
pays no attention to the celebrations of Nature and sings no
praises to the "completions of the actual world." In terms of the
romantic rite of passage, when he refuses to pay heed to Pan,
"Dread opener of the mysterious doors / Leading to universal
knowledge" (1. 288–89), he becomes the budding solipsist taking
the journey inside the self.

This brings us to the central crux in *Endymion*. If Endymion is
not to pass through the doors opened by Pan (as explained to the
nineteenth century by Wordsworth), if nature is not to provide
the path, then how is he to find his way to the "ethereal home,"
to higher consciousness, to the sublime, let alone to the liminal?
Keats actually drew a map of the way in one of the most famous
passages in the poem—the passage that he called the "pleasure
thermometer." I have provided a rough paraphrase to the right:

Wherein lies happiness? In
   that which becks
Our ready minds to
   fellowship divine,   How can we elevate
A fellowship with essence;   our consciousness until
   till we shine,   we are free from the
Full alchemiz'd and free of   constraints of self?
   space. Behold
The clear religion of heaven!
   Fold

13. Keats's dislike for the dogmatic in art, for "poetry that has a palpable design
on us" ("Letter to Reynolds," 3 February 1814), is especially directed against poets
like Wordsworth and Hunt who can describe their "travels to the very bourne of
Heaven" only in terms of their own personal moralizing. What Keats wants in the
sublime is just the opposite, negative capability, the unobtrusive and the undog-
matic search for truth.

A rose leaf round thy finger's
    taperness,
And sooth thy lips: hist,
    when the airy stress
Of music's kiss impregnates
    the free winds,
And with a sympathetic
    touch unbinds
Eolian magic from their lucid
    wombs:
Then old songs waken from
    enclouded tombs;
Old ditties sigh above their
    father's grave;
Ghosts of melodious
    prophecyings rave
Round every spot where trod
    Apollo's foot;
Bronze clarions awake, and
    faintly bruit,
Where long ago a giant battle
    was;
And, from the turf, a lullaby
    doth pass
In every place where infant
    Orpheus slept.
Feel we these things?—that
    moment have we stept
Into a sort of oneness, and
    our state
Is like a floating spirit's. But
    there are
Richer entanglements,
    enthralments far
More self-destroying,
    leading, by degrees,
To the chief intensity: the
    crown of these
Is made of love and
    friendship, and sits high

The first step is to
immerse the self in
Nature . . .

then realize that in
doing this you have
connected yourself to
the history and art of
all men.

And if you are able to
do this and to free
yourself into nature,
then elevated
consciousness will
come.

Upon the forehead of
humanity.
All its more ponderous and
bulky worth
Is friendship, whence there
ever issues forth
A steady splendour; but at
the tip-top,
There hangs by unseen film,
an orbed drop
Of light, and that is love: its
influence,
Thrown in our eyes, genders
a novel sense,
At which we start and fret; til
in the end,
Melting into its radiance, we
blend,
Mingle, and so become a
part of it.

The self will begin to
disappear; love and
friendship will follow
until finally you will
lose consciousness and
and achieve the mystic
oneness, the liminal.

(l. 776–811)

What we have here is a heuristic primer of transcendence, a
map of elevating consciousness, a plan for the psychojourney to
(and past) the sublime. The first step in this process is the intense
realization of the beauties of nature and the distillation of these
beauties into what Keats called "essences." This initially occurs
in the level of Pan. The next step is the imaginative reconstruction of these natural phenomena into images and metaphors that
reflect higher spiritual truths. This mythic or daemonic transformation is annoyingly vague, to us as it was to Keats's contemporary readers. But next come "richer entanglements . . . more
self-destroying" (emphasis mine), in which man links his destiny
with others outside himself. In psychological terms, Keats is here
talking about "other-directed" sympathies, merging one's self
with others. Finally at the top is the ultimate spiritual union in
which Each melts into the All and All is "stained by the radiance
of Heaven." Here at the tiptop is the divine white light of complete selflessness; the sublime experience becomes liminal, language at last useless, art in vain.

Understandably, much critical commentary has been devoted to these lines, for they are the key summary of the poem. On one side are the critics imbued with Neoplatonism, who point out the similarities to the *scala perfection*, the ladderlike ascension to unity with the One. They are quick to see that the layers of emanations leading down from the One into nature are very much like those proposed by Plotinus, Porphyry, Iamblichus, and so on. On the other side are the critics who mistrust this kind of mechanical reading, who point out that Keats added this topmost layer as an afterthought in January 1818, ostensibly to make the poem Neoplatonic, and that the rest of the poem repudiates the topmost level, for Endymion finds happiness not in a spiritual love but in a physical one.[14]

Viewing *Endymion* as a map to sublimity (and beyond) may be of some help. When the upper levels are added above the subconscious and "normal" levels, we have a structure that looks like this:

Pleasure Thermometer	Major Characters or Place	Cosmic Levels
Liminal Consciousness (1. 779–81; 805–11)	The One "Fellowship with essence" "Very bourne of heaven"	Empyreal level
Sublime Consciousness (1. 796–804)	Cynthia/Phoebe/Diana "Fragile bar" in *Endymion*	Ethereal (daemonic) level
	NATURAL HORIZON	
"Normal" Consciousness (1. 781–86)	"Mortal bar" in *I Stood Tiptoe* Poena, Indian Maid "Realm of Flora and old Pan"	Natural level
Subconsciousness	Cave of Quietude	Subterranean level

In the left column are the levels of consciousness as depicted on the "pleasure thermometer," in the middle column are the main characters, or locales, which often act as projections of Endy-

14. This discussion of the pleasure thermometer is best set forward by comparing Claude E. Finney, *The Evolution of Keats' Poetry*, pp. 298–302, with Newell F. Ford, "The Meaning of 'Fellowship with Essence' in *Endymion*."

mion's consciousness, and finally, in the right column, is the actual cosmic level on which the activity occurs. In this "map of consciousness," Endymion as a character is not involved, since the paradigm is simply a projection of his own psychological states.

I have already discussed the subconscious world reflected in the subterranean Cave of Quietude, which forms the lowest stratum. Above is the natural world, the "green world," the conscious world, the world Endymion begins and ends in. This is the level explained in lines 781–86 of the pleasure thermometer and populated by Poena and other mortals. Between the conscious and the subconscious levels is a level that might be called Analogical Consciousness. I did not include it in the chart because it is not really a projection of Endymion; it is, however, the level referred to in lines 786–96: This level acts as a kind of reflective consciousness, for it explains characters who mimic Endymion's own attempts to gain higher consciousness. Here especially is Glaucus, who, like Endymion, has attempted to scale the heights of awareness. In terms of an allegory of consciousness, both have tried to leave ordinary awareness to find a more exciting and heightened consciousness. However, Glaucus has found out what Endymion does not yet know: this search may lead to self-isolation, for Glaucus has not been liberated, but imprisoned.[15]

15. When Glaucus tells his story we may well get the feeling that "this is where we came in," as he repeats Endymion's experience almost step by step, emotion by emotion. As a young man, Glaucus "began / To feel distemper'd longings" (3. 374–75) for Scylla, whom he loved "to the very white of truth." Endymion also began to feel longings for Cynthia, whom he pursued "to the very bourne of heaven." Glaucus, cursed by his "ambitious magic," has spurned the "tempering coolness of his native home" to pursue Scylla. And like Endymion the inner part of this pursuit, the psychological part, leads Glaucus through a labyrinth of projected feeling, until finally in desperation he realizes that heightened consciousness cannot be sustained for long. He then does what Endymion has not yet done—he calls on Circe for aid.

Here the stories break apart. Endymion has not come this far; he has not been so totally possessed. But he sees, or he should see, that if he continues to pursue Cynthia, Glaucus's fate will also be his. Given enough time, a Cynthia will become a Circe.

In exchange for giving his self up to Circe, Glaucus has been given a new consciousness, a "balmy consciousness" that obliterates the natural world. Stuck in

Many critics have been uneasy discussing Glaucus's role in the poem, but when he is viewed as a mythic or analogical duplication of Endymion's own self, his role may be seen as having an organic, if not textual, necessity. Glaucus shows Endymion and the reader what may happen in the search for elevated consciousness. Keats was probably unsure how well he had mirrored Endymion in Glaucus, so he repeated the doppelgänger motif in the other mythic stories. Venus's position in the Venus-Adonis episode is much like Endymion's position with Cynthia, except that things are backward, for Venus is an immortal, pining away for the love of a mortal. The other equally intense relationship that parallels Endymion's is the love of Arethusa for Alpheus. In this mythic interlude Arethusa is counterpointed with Endymion in that both of them are torn between common and ethereal desires. All these characters—Glaucus, Venus, Arethusa—have blinded themselves to "natural reality" to engage in a Daedalean pursuit of self-ful-ness. They have withdrawn from others to become priests of the self. They have mistaken "fellowship with essence" for "fellowship with self."

So far we have witnessed two readily understandable levels of consciousness: the anti-sublime retreat into selfishness and the finding of self through others in the human world. The next higher level represents a drastic change in consciousness, for Keats now takes us into worlds of the sublime. Above the "natural level," just across the "fragile bar that separates us from our home ethereal," is the first supraconscious level, a kind of daemonic level. Here are the wisplike creatures who seem to

---

Circe's bower of bliss, he is little more than a sleeper and feeder. Lost forever is Scylla. Eventually this "balmy consciousness" turns to suffering, just as it did for Lycius in *Lamia* and for the Knight in *La Belle Dame*; but Glaucus is finally saved. He has gone through a process Endymion will eventually start in book 4, a process of "spiritualization through humanization"; Glaucus begins to "feel out of himself," to return to "human consciousness." In the moment he decides to warn the sailors of Circe, he learns he will be released from the constriction of self. Endymion, who now recognizes the reflection of his self in Glaucus, immediately cries out: "We are twin brothers in this destiny!" (712) and then, like Prospero in *The Tempest*, dons the magician's cloak, waves the wand nine times, repeats the magic "signatures," and Glaucus is freed.

lead Endymion about; here are, as Keats first described them in *I Stood Tiptoe*, the

> Shapes from the invisible world, unearthly singing
> From out the middle air, from flowery nests,
> And from the pillowy silkiness that rests
> Full in the speculation of the stars. (186–89)

Charles I. Patterson actually calls this "the daemonic level, believing that it acts as

> a metaphor for the particular area of activity of the human consciousness; for, of course, Keats did not literally believe in daemons but used the idea of a daemonic world as an objective correlative to an inner proclivity within man. The term denotes trance-like states of mind like some of those which psychologists and psychiatrists now discuss. The daemonic state in Keats's poetry is a sharply focused trance in which a person still perceives specific objects and situations vividly and concretely.[16]

But Patterson makes no attempt to see this level as only one of a series, for this level is just below the threshold of the liminal. Keats's alchemical term for the "stuff" in this "wondrous region" is *ether*, and George Bornstein has shown that *ethereal* in *Endymion* represents not only a cosmic level but also the penultimate "elevation of [a] psychological process."[17] The ether is probably the most complex stratum in *Endymion*, if only because here the chameleon Cynthia and her fellow spirits live. It is the sum and substance of the sublime, the very stuff Cozens was attempting to "blot in" at the edge of his mountain silhouette.

A number of interesting things about Cynthia have been overlooked, usually because she has been passed off as a goddess causing, not reacting to, changes in Endymion. In the psychological schemata she is, of course, a projection of Endymion, and so her chameleon shapes are a reflection of changes within him. She is neither allegorical nor divine: rather, she is the "outering" of his consciousness. If Cynthia is a symbol, and that is certainly

16. Charles I. Patterson, *The Daemonic in the Poetry of John Keats*, p. 11.
17. Bornstein, "Keats' Concept of the Ethereal," p. 99.

open to question, then she is a symbol of a state of awareness
rather than of an actual quality or person. If *Endymion* is an allegory, as many have contended, then it is an allegory of what happens to "a mortal man who bent / His appetite beyond his natural
sphere" by desiring annihilation of the self through sublimation.

I quite agree with Stuart Ende, who contends in *Keats and the
Sublime* that Cynthia "dramatizes the ambivalence of the sublime" and that the "sublime experience with Cynthia is much
like the moment of vision in other romantic poems," but I find it
heady going when Ende couples this assertion with Freudian
psychology. Ende starts simply enough with the intriguing suggestion that "The quite genuine desire for the repression that is
the sublime calls forth or rather expresses a subtle but insidious
form of self-hatred: to desire the repressive power of otherness
over the self is to turn against the self." However, I am befuddled
when this is applied to the characters. For ultimately Ende
identifies

> the Indian Maiden with self-acceptance and Cynthia with self-
> repression: but this cannot be the whole story, or what incentive
> would there be for Endymion to have begun by seeking Cynthia?
> Initial narcissism, Freud says, is broken by two radical departures,
> the formation of relationships and the rise of an ego ideal. Later
> self-hatred, which to his dismay Freud found increases with time,
> results from the ego ideal's rejection of the ego, which I take as a
> parallel to the muse's possible rejection of the ego, which I take as a
> parallel to the muse's possible rejection of the poet, in an outward
> version of the inner struggle. The poet's acceptance of his own bro-
> kenness, his own sorrow, defuses, as it were, the threat of the
> muse—he has already acknowledged the brokenness that she partly
> has caused. This last point may seem a radical addition to our para-
> digm, but it is entirely consistent with both Freud and the narrative
> of *Endymion*. Endymion's "fall" begins his quest for Cynthia, the
> muse who he hopes will heal the rift he experiences.[18]

Although it may well be that Cynthia is indeed the "muse," I
have trouble understanding her in the context of "self-hatred" resulting from "the ego ideal's rejection of the ego."

18. Ende, *Keats and the Sublime*, pp. 63, 67, 82–83.

Above the ethereal level of Cynthia is indeed the "pure serene," the transcendent. I suspect that Keats originally intended
to have Endymion arrive at the highest level, at empyreal transport, thereby making book 4 into a nineteenth-century *Paradiso*,
but that he finally backed away from having his hero "ensky'd"
because he was unsure how to sustain the image of the highest
level on the pleasure thermometer (in fact he seems to have
found out it was indescribable) and because final transcendence
would have meant totally forsaking the natural world, the world
of "Flora and Old Pan."

Once these various levels of consciousness (liminal, sublime,
"normal," and subconscious) are schematized and placed in their
corresponding physical levels (empyreal, ethereal, natural, subterranean), the enigmatic pleasure thermometer passage is less
confusing. Or so I hope. Indeed, what Keats did was to construct
a map of consciousness by which we can chart the psychological
awareness of his protagonist. By using this structure, Keats implied an answer to Endymion's early question, "Wherein is peace
of the mind?" Is it in the first level, the realm of nature, where
we enter into a participation with organic change? Or is it in subconscious levels where awareness is contracted self-centered-
ness? Or perhaps peace is found just above the natural level,
where there are "richer entanglements, enthralments far / More
self-destroying"—in other words, a life transformed through sublimation, in which the metaphorical Cynthia and her manifold
forms are treated as real. Or, finally, is happiness found in the
mystical moment, in the tiptop drop of light in which we become
selfless, melting into radiance?

I suspect the youthful Keats was never quite sure, and this
may account for the two different endings. If the second ending
of the poem (in which Cynthia enters the Natural level as the Indian Maid) is taken as Keats's last word, then the Natural level is
the chosen place. But if the Cave of Solitude is taken as Keats's
last word, then he is ambivalent, choosing each level in moderation, none in excess. The obvious question is that if the climax of
the poem occurs in the Cave of Solitude, and if the denouement
follows in the scene with the Indian Maid, then why does the

poem continue? Why does Endymion not just grab the Indian
Maid and run? Although many recent critics would agree with
Harold Bloom that the "ending" of *Endymion* is "mechanical"
and in places "desperate," even the most sympathetic reader will
at least admit that the conclusion is overly abrupt.[19] Every critic
has his own explanation for the lack of closure; my own is that I
suspect it was because Keats was becoming unsure about his own
pleasure thermometer. He really did not know how to make
things finally fit. The rest of the answer may be annoyingly simple—Keats still had five hundred lines to write so that book 4
would have a thousand lines, so that the poem would have four
thousand lines, so that his original bargain with Benjamin Bailey
(to write an epic romance with four books of a thousand lines
each) would be met. This seems too simple, but it is probably
true—for the rest of the poem does nothing but show the long
and tortured vacillation within Endymion's mind, a vacillation
that we have already had for more than three thousand lines.

   In psychological terms, this second ending of *Endymion* (the
union with the Indian Maid) is, I think, much too easy. No sooner
has Keats shown Endymion to be alone than he takes the very
phantoms that his protagonist had learned to be unreal and
makes them real. Having shown psychological changes mirrored
through natural changes, having welcomed Endymion back into
the realm of "Flora and old Pan," Keats then sends him back up
through the daemonic realm on a trip that we now realize is potentially self-annihilating. This is a kind of desperate attempt on
Keats's part to achieve the topmost scale on the pleasure thermometer—"fellowship with essence," the mystic experience,
and the attempt fails (as it must) to endure. In a deus ex machina
scene, Endymion is lowered back to Earth, Cynthia and the Indian Maid become one, and the lovers run off together.

   As an exasperated John Middleton Murry has said about this
tacked-on ending, "Why drag in truth?" In terms of psychology,
it is just as ridiculous that Endymion should run off with the Indian Maid as it would have been had he become truly "ensky'd."
But Keats was finally a poet, not a psychologist. He needed an

---

19. Harold Bloom, *Yeats*, pp. 18, 92.

ending, and poems of this type do not end unless the protagonist accepts irresolution and a lack of closure (Wordsworth in *Yew Trees*), drastically changes consciousness (Coleridge's Ancient Mariner), dies out of consciousness (Byron's Manfred), or is transported beyond consciousness (Shelley's Prometheus). This is probably why there is so little conviction at the end, and so much conclusion, for the kind of unity that insures that every Jack shall have his Jill is the unity and consistency demanded by drama, not psychology.

Still, with the exception of the ending, which is disjointed, we have seen Keats work out an organization that is systematic, if not finally coherent. Rather than mechanically show the growth of the poet's adolescent mind, Keats has attempted to show the actual process, the continuous expansion and contraction of Endymion's consciousness. This systolic rhythm of awareness, the changing levels of consciousness from ergotropic to trophotropic states to normalcy, is the main organizing pattern of the poem. It is this psychological process, more than the personal allegory, the theme, or the plot, that connects all the disparate parts of the poem.

Granted, *Endymion* is not a great success, but in retrospect it is unfortunate that Keats turned away from cataloging states of consciousness, if only because he was becoming tantalizingly "modern." However, I believe that this turn away from "picturing the sublime" represents not a lessening of faith in the poetic imagination, as Glen O. Allen has asserted, but rather Keats's realization that attempts to prescribe sublimity were destined to prove futile.[20] Metapsychologies like the "pleasure thermometer" tracing the steps to the threshold may well strike us as absurd because we have made the sublime almost synonymous with the mystic, and the mystic experience, we all know, is, by definition, inexplicable. So Keats may well seem to us heedlessly reductionistic, even simpleminded, and indeed many of his own

20. Glen O. Allen, "The Fall of Endymion: A Study of Keats's Intellectual Growth." I do, however, accept his premise that Keats began *Endymion* fully confident that he could be transported to sublimity by "poetic inspiration" (p. 41) but that when it came to finding words to express this, he was significantly disappointed by the results.

contemporaries, especially the critics, said just that. However, Keats's paradigm seems conservative and even pedestrian compared to Alexander Cozens's system of constructing sublime landscapes, as he explained in *A New Method of Assisting the Invention in Drawing Original Landscapes* (1784/1785).[21] Here Cozens, a painter of small renown, but a teacher of considerable influence, laid out a point-by-point plan whereby both apprentice and expert could "facilitate the Invention of Landskips." Once again we will see how the romantic artist's reach for systematic sublimity just exceeds his grasp.

Basically Cozens's system is this. First, the painter should have a general idea of landscape composition; Cozens even lists various kinds to contemplate, the most interesting being:

1. Part of the edge or top of a hill or mountain, seen horizontally, the horizon below the bottom of the view. The horizon is the utmost bounds of the land of a flat country, or the sea, in an uninterrupted view of it to the sky.

2. The tops of hills or mountains, the horizon below the bottom of the view.

11. Objects, or groups of objects, placed alternately on both hands, and gradually retiring from the eye. The horizon above the bottom of the view.

15. A landscape of a moderate extent between the right and left hand, the objects or groups placed irregularly, and no one predominant. The horizon above the bottom of the view.

16. An extensive country, with no predominant part or object. The horizon above the bottom of the view.[22]

Now with one of these in mind, the painter "blots" out in his general form specially mixed globular ink on transparent waxed paper. It helps if the paper is crumpled so as to increase the number of accidental shapes made by the blot. This blot (the technical name is *tachiste*), in Cozens's words, "is a production of chance, with a small degree of design; for in making it, the attention of the performer must be employed on the whole, or the general form of the composition, and upon this only; whilst the

21. Only a few copies of Cozens's *New Method* are extant. The most accessible text is appended to A. P. Oppé, *Alexander and John Robert Cozens*.

22. Cozens, *New Method*, in ibid., pp. 184–85.

subordinate parts are left to the casual motion of the hand and the brush."[23] When dry, the "unmeaning blot" must be tinted, shaded, and washed until the "intended meaning" comes through. It is all rather like having the patient view a Rorschach blot and then paint his vision around it, for the blot is only the rude form that is to be completed by the imagination, or like the spontaneous methods of Zen landscape painters, except that Cozens contends there really is a method involved. He even details how the memory is excited, how the blots are interconnected with "reality," how conscious and unconscious suggestions are involved, but the overriding emphasis is always clear: there is a system to all landscapes that, once mastered, allows the artist to produce sublime effect with regularity.

There is something singularly romantic about Cozens, something so literal-minded as well as hyperbolic about his assumptions concerning the nature of art. Cozens's method is aggressively inductive rather than projective: it is the opposite of sketching; it is passionately based on an a priori faith in spontaneous, not iconic forms. There is no precedent or model for the painter, no internal preconception or external form to delineate. The blot is polysemous, "open" in the semiotic sense to innumerable modifications and meanings by first painter and then spectator. And all interpretations of it are equally "true."

Because many critics have known Cozens's method before viewing his works, most serious interpretations have depended as much on the critic's abilities as on Cozens's adroit "filling in the blanks." In this sense Cozens is not just a romantic painter but also a modern critic, for he demands a rather primitive form of reader-response criticism. Meaning does not inhere in the "text," but rather in the audience. This seeming paradox has not been lost on modern commentators. For instance, in his recent work on *Romantics and Romanticism*, Michel Le Bris even went so far as to claim:

> Nature is never virgin because our eyes are never "innocent." Nature only becomes landscape for us when we project on to it our own inner spaces. We find the strongest expression of the "natural

23. Ibid., p. 169.

sublime" not so much in the landscape painters, who were still too subject to the temptations of the picturesque, as in the painful aspiration towards infinity that is seen . . . above all [in] the fantastic patches of the strange Alexander Cozens, inventor of "blot drawings." [Cozens] attained the point of hallucinatory tension between sleeping and waking where the formless mysteriously takes on meaning, where chance and intention seem at last to merge. In such an enterprise, is the artist creator or created, a blank page written upon Nature, or a dreaming Prometheus summoning up with his inks our own dark powers? So, in the name of Nature, Cozens embarked on the great quest for the landscape of the imagination, obstinately tracking down with his racing brush, always poised between hazard and decision, the hallucinatory moment of the genesis of the world.[24]

Cozens was not so kindly understood in his own time. In fact, he was mocked and parodied by many of his contemporaries. William Beckford, his patron as well as pupil and no stranger to eccentricities, described Cozens as "almost as full of systems as the universe," and even his teaching colleague at Eton, a Mr. Angelo, thought Cozens's system farfetched and produced a "scandalous parody."[25] But no matter, Cozens had what he thought was a shortcut, his own "pleasure thermometer," a northwest passage to "transcendent landscapes." Maybe he was just too modern.

His "system" came to him quite by accident. One day he was working with a particularly uninspired student, when he happened on a piece of soiled paper. Quite mindlessly he sketched a landscape around the blotches and was amazed that his composition "did accord with nature." Could he use this method with students? He could; and it worked. One can only imagine his additional satisfaction when he then found that there was historical precedent:

> In the course of prosecuting this scheme, I was informed, that something of the same kind had been mentioned by Leonardo da Vinci, in his Treatise on Painting. It may easily be imagined how eagerly I consulted the book; and from a perusal of the particular

24. Michel Le Bris, *Romantics and Romanticism*, pp. 30–31.
25. Oppé, *Cozens*, pp. 44, 59.

passage which tended to confirm my own opinion, I have now an
authority to urge in its favor; an authority, to which the ingenious
will be disposed to pay some regard.[26]

If Leonardo had been able to transform rude form into design,
Cozens had done him one better—he could actually manufacture
the rude forms to begin with.

His system was not singular; he claimed, as a matter of fact,
that it was operant in all the allied arts. Cozens quoted a Dr.
Brown (perhaps James Brown, author of *Athelston*), who compared blotting to the way a playwright transforms historical fact
into drama, or for that matter, the way a composer can create a
score around certain unconnected notes in nature. If this all
sounds rather like Keats, it should, for both Cozens and Keats
put great faith in the imagination's power to mold design out
of chaos; in Keats's metaphor, "what the imagination seizes as
Beauty must be truth." But as we have seen in the criticism of
Endymion, such shortcuts to inspiration did not go unchal-
lenged. Ruskin, for instance, had only disdain for Cozens's "blot-
tesque method" of generating design, although his own favorite,
Turner, occasionally practiced something quite similar.[27] Perhaps
the only fair way to judge Cozens's prescription is to look at the
results. And the result that is the most startling, I think, is *The
Cloud*.

The first thing one notices is the unusual heaviness and dullness produced by blotting. This quality was not unnoticed by
contemporary critics and needed some explaining. An anonymous student of Cozens's at Eton (perhaps Sir George Beaumont)
attempted just that in a letter to the *London Courant* in 1781.[28] It
is a letter worth quoting, because the ideas are clearly Cozens's,
although they are only implied, not stated, in his *New Method*:

> I have read with great attention the account of the principal paint-
> ings in that of the Royal Academy and was particularly surprised at

26. Cozens, *New Method* in ibid., p. 168.
27. Oppé, *Cozens*, p. 41, n. 3.
28. This suggestion was tentatively made by William T. Whitley, *Artists and
Their Friends in England 1700–1799*, 2:320.

Alexander Cozens, *The Cloud*, circa 1775–1785. The Paul Mellon Centre for Studies in British Art, London.

the comment upon our ingenious friend Mr. Cozens, to whom we have both been so much obliged, and whose happy pencil, you used to say, rather improved than copied Nature. As you left him much younger than I did, it is possible he did not inculcate to you what no doubt everybody will grant, that there are essential distinctions between beauty, greatness, and sublimity and he presumed that tastes admitted the same three degrees of eminence.

You know he attempted, some time ago, to ascertain the characteristic properties of beauty, greatness, and sublimity; among which those relative to sublimity include the article's weight or heaviness, in contradiction to those of beauty—viz., lightness, brightness, cheerfulness.

In consequence of his contemplating the three fore-mentioned principles he has for several years exhibited to the public, pictures of landscapes; attempting to perform them in the third degree of taste, that is the sublime. You cannot have forgotten those delightful specimens of his success in the College at Eton. Those pictures

most justly answer to the epithets, *heaviness, darkness, dullness,*
mentioned by the critic.

But surely he has sufficient authority by reputation to enforce
without any weight of argument to prove, that landscape painting
will admit of sublimity; to which I daresay you, as well as many others who have not had the pleasure of being his immediate scholars,
will most readily subscribe; and lament that any person who has but
a moderate judgment in the art should be so insensible to the merit
of so great a master.[29]

Clearly Cozens (as well as the letter writer) was influenced by
Burke's ideas that sublimity is generated by weight or heaviness,
even darkness and dullness, while beauty is characterized by
lightness, brightness, and cheerfulness. But something more impressive than Burkean heaviness makes *The Cloud* a study in romantic sublimity: it is that the horizon is clearly the focus of the
painting and that the demarcation between earth, cloud, and sky
is the major "event" to contemplate. Our eye goes straight to the
horizon and stays there: it does not return to the foreground simply because there is none.

The Cloud is emphatically not a typical late eighteenth-century Claudean landscape; there is no interest in figures or middle
distance, no coulisse, nor is there real concern with those cumulus clouds rolling in from the left, nor with the black earth, nor
with the open air to the right. The "fetch" of the prospect carries
us to the threshold, and there we remain.[30] Our sight is not
blocked and channeled: there is an unrestricted *veduta* unbroken
by any wall, gap, or arch. There is only one margin, and that is

29. "Unsigned Letter to *London Courant*" as quoted in ibid., 2:319–20.
30. John Barrell, *The Idea of Landscape and the Sense of Place, 1730–1840*,
condenses this aspect of the horizon in continental landscape painting:

> when I was discussing how a landscape by Claude or Poussin was composed,
> I said that the objects in the picture, and the system of planes across it, were
> so arranged as to encourage the direct flight of the eye over the landscape
> and towards the area of light invariably located a little below the level of the
> horizon. In this journey from foreground to horizon the eye passes over the
> objects and the areas of ground intervening, registering about them at most
> only their tonal value, and a rapid diminution in their size. Only after this
> initial journey has been made, I said, does the eye return to examine, at
> leisure, the objects it has passed on its way. (p. 19)

precisely in the middle. Cozens achieves an almost complete collapse of depth. It is as if we are seeing the mountain silhouetted
through a telephoto lens, or in a Japanese woodcut, because all
sense of perspective is lost. With the loss of the depth of field we
sense a still greater imminence of the horizon.

Additionally, our attention is focused not on any event but on a
process: the moving tension of those horizontal lines as they separate the central masses of earth, cloud, and air. And our concentration is especially on the "magnetic area," to the left of center, where we have a sense of developing vortex. These clouds
are the counterpart of that other romantic image, the wave, and
they are rolling in across the foreground plane just as they do in
the paintings of Courbet or Géricault or, better yet, Turner. *The
Cloud* is about margins and thresholds, about the visual lines that
separate, as well as unite, blocks of space. In this important sense
Cozens is, like Keats, concerned with the boundaries ("mortal
bars") that come between earth and ether and the ability of the
imaginative eye to move between them. It is this concern with
the edges of upward space and consciousness that gives Cozens's
work its claim to sublimity, rather than the heaviness of form and
the dullness of shade.

It is clear in *The Cloud* that the earth is only the context above
which the cloud makes its surge and recoil; the earth itself is
without objects of interest. The cloud as well, for all its menacing
potential, is really quite ephemeral: "It has a sense," as A. P.
Oppé has written, "of controlled but burning emotion."[31] It rolls
in across the lower sky, almost compressing light out of the air,
yet for all this activity the upper regions appear almost un-
touched. So the activity of *The Cloud* is only at the horizon; or as
Keats would say, in the ether. The vision of sublimity, the energy
at the threshold, which we have seen stymied in Blake, made
natural in Wordsworth and Wright, set just at and under the edge
in Coleridge and Turner, is here in Keats and Cozens lifted to the
horizon itself. It is now in the unlikely pairing of Shelley and
Constable that we will finally see the earth almost disappear as
the romantic artists momentarily step to the brink to glimpse
into the mist beyond.

31. Oppé, *Cozens*, p. 100.

6

Shelley and Constable: The Empyreal Sublime

I bind the Sun's throne with a burning zone,
        And the Moon's with a girdle of pearl;
The volcanoes are dim, and the stars reel and swim,
        When the whirlwinds my banner unfurl.
From cape to cape, with a bridge-like shape,
        Over a torrent sea,
Sunbeam-proof, I hang like a roof,—
        The mountains its columns be.

                                    —Shelley, *The Cloud*

No two English romantics seem further apart than Shelley and
Constable. Constable was intensive, conservative, rustic, imita-
tive, and provincial, while Shelley was expansive, revolutionary,
worldly, experimental, and utopian—or at least according to popular simplifications. So when comparisons are made among the
romantics, Constable is usually paired with Wordsworth, and
Shelley with Turner.[1] These comparisons are appropriate and, indeed, I think, show two important aspects of romantic vision: the
first fixed on the world "out there" and the other on the world
"just beyond." But if there is such a thing as romanticism, and if
this movement represents a shift in temper, a new way of seeing,
then we ought to find even in the extremes represented by

1. The most recent pairings of Constable and Wordsworth are in Kenneth
Clark, *The Romantic Rebellion: Romantic versus Classic Art*, chap. 2, and Karl
Kroeber, *Romantic Landscape Vision: Constable and Wordsworth*, while Shelley
and Turner are compared in John Dixon Hunt, "Wondrous Deep and Dark: Turner and the Sublime," and, especially, R. F. Storch, "Abstract Idealism in English
Romantic Poetry and Painting," in *Images of Romanticism: Verbal and Visual Affinities*, ed. Karl Kroeber and William Walling, pp. 189–210.

Shelley and Constable a few important shared perceptions. I believe such a visual consensus can be found at the horizon, above the mist, so to speak, in the skies. So I would like to compare the middle skies of the poet and the painter, or, more specifically, part of their skies as seen in one of Constable's cloud studies and the conclusion to Shelley's *Prometheus Unbound*. There are certain hazards in comparing a study and an act of a drama out of context, but I hope to show that the affinities are metonymic in relation not just to the artists' other work but to central concerns of romanticism as well. Still, caution is in order because Constable's view is tenative, circumspect, and finally repudiated, while Shelley's is expansive, fantastic, and life-long.

Sometime late in 1820 John Constable began a series of cloud paintings. From what evidence we have, it seems that he spent the autumns of the next two years painting clouds over Hampstead Heath. Now why would a painter who was barely making his reputation painting the world below the horizon take out his easel and paints or pencil and sketchbook almost every day to paint clouds? And why would he do this for two years and then abruptly stop? At this time Constable was not "established"; he needed money, and these were not always sketches or drafts such as the ones he had earlier kept in his notebook; these were often carefully done oils.[2]

Clouds were pleasant enough to the romantic eye, and landscape painters since the seventeenth-century Dutch had painted them, but Constable's "cloudscapes" were hardly schoolboy studies. To understand why Constable painted these clouds is to know why Shelley was so fascinated by describing clouds in verse, even to the slightly embarrassing extreme (to me, at least) of *The Cloud*. To find the answer we need remember first the forbidden allure of clouds in the eighteenth century and then how they were being demythologized by both the romantic imagination and scientific curiosity.

2. I am thinking especially of paintings such as the Hampstead Heath series done in the early 1820s (*Upper Heath, Hampstead Heath, Hampstead Looking West, A View of Hampstead*), landscapes like *Tree and Corner of a House* (1822), as well as pure cloudscapes like *Study of Cirrus Clouds*. For a more complete discussion see Graham Reynolds, *Constable: The Natural Painter*, chap. 5, "The Extended Vista."

Clouds were subjects of increasing interest in the late eighteenth century, for although they were what separated fallen man from divinity, they were clearly part of nature. True, they divided us from the liminal—they were subliminal—hence they were beyond the limits of "proper place," but they were also, thanks to the new advances in meteorology, known to be composed of matter from this world and obedient to the laws of nature. Still, in spite of all the new scientific information, clouds had a literal and figurative aura that could not be easily put aside. The Lord might appear in a pillar of clouds to lead the Jews from Egypt, angels might play harps on the upper sides of clouds, and it was fine if painters wanted to paint them that way; at least they no longer had to paint the skies golden as in medieval times, but neoclassical painters rarely took the liberties with clouds that they were taking with natural forms.

Augustan painters had to be especially cautious about the topside of clouds, which is one reason the "sky dado" is so common in eighteenth-century landscapes. The "sky dado" is a layer of clear sky between the horizon and an upper cloud canopy. It creates the effect of two horizons: one where earth meets sky and the other where sky meets the dark cloud covering. Frequently one sees small clouds painted in this nether sky, but usually they are nothing more than cream-colored streaks. This new sky can be seen in the paintings of Claude and the Poussin brothers, and it represents, I think, a nascent romantic concern with upper atmosphere that was both literal and metaphoric, for it enabled the painter to obscure special boundaries without disturbing the solid planes of earth and sky.

By the turn of the nineteenth century clouds had suddenly become demythologized as religious images, thus becoming fit subjects for poets and painters. The middle air became a "common sky." This opening of the air was the result partly of the theological breakdown of the Christian world view and partly of the buildup of scientific curiosity and skepticism. What makes Constable and Shelley so extraordinary is that they bridge both developments, and we can see this in one simple way: Constable was the first to paint clouds from the topside down, and Shelley was the first to describe them from that point of view. In other words, their backs are often at the heavens as they look down to earth. It is more than a bird's-eye view (Claude had attempted that); it is an angel's-eye view. About half of Constable's cloud studies in the early 1820s are from this vantage point, and doubtless if he had been aware of how much liberty he was taking with his "station," he would have been even more private with these works. Shelley, however, knew exactly what he was doing and, as Desmond King-Hele has pointed out, almost flaunted this vantage for the sacrilege it implied.[3]

While Shelley's empyreal elevation is predictable (after all it represents the logical aspiration of the poet in *Mont Blanc*), this height is perplexing to see in Constable because he was elsewhere so dutifully humble. For instance, in the large canal pictures, painted just prior to his cloudscapes, Constable is always at ground level, or even below ground level looking up. In paintings such as *The White Horse, Stratford Mill, View on the Stour*, and *The Hay Wain* the painter's feet are resolutely planted in this world: in fact, in each painting a river is actually flowing, or backing water, near the painter's feet, almost to remind us where we are. We are in the anti-sublime world, in the literal slush. In each of these paintings the horizon is almost exactly two-thirds of the way up the painting, putting the perspective at the eye level of a person six feet tall (as well as giving the proper "visuality" if hung "on line" at the Royal Academy). Constable was so conservative with point of view in the large paintings, so very conscious of his audience (he was at this time very eager to be elected to the Academy), that when he did experiment, it was so subtle that we may not even be aware that he was taking chances. In *The Leaping Horse* he actually lowered the vantage so that the viewer is below the waterline looking "up" to see the horse and barge and "back" to see the horizon. It produces a most dynamic effect as the energy of the leaping horse and the dammed-up water seems to come falling out toward us—in fact it produces an effect oddly like Turner's vortex, in which energy seems to swirl out toward the viewer, almost sucking us in, except that here we are going to

3. Desmond King-Hele, *Shelley: His Thought and Work*, pp. 219–27.

be sucked into the quagmire of this world, not into the horizon of the next.

I mention all this because given such a conservative purview one wonders how conscious Constable was of the sublime possibilities of his cloudscapes. It is almost as if he were craving to be released from the three-mile radius of his plot of artistic ground, as if he had had enough of what he called "my limited and restricted art found under every hedge." I think a case can be made that like the atheist who converts to Catholicism and then complains that the service is too liberal, or like the rowdy adolescent who becomes an overly pious elder, Constable for a while in the early 1820s became fascinated by doing the opposite of what he was accustomed to do. For a very short time he attempted to paint an unrestricted *veduta*, a view unbroken by wall, gap, bridge, bushes, or any block. He crept out from under the hedge, so to speak, to become concerned with the possibility of painting distance without the defining lines and elevation, without the context of earth.

In the 1950s E. H. Gombrich found a series of sketches at the Courtauld Institute of Art that Constable had done just after the turn of the century imitating scenes by Alexander Cozens. Cozens's sketches are highly schematic, even accompanied with scientific descriptions penned on the bottom, and Constable's copies even included the gloss. As Gombrich contends in *Art and Illusion*, Cozens taught Constable "not what clouds look like, but a series of possibilities, of schemata, which could increase his awareness."[4] Clouds clearly fascinated Constable for a time, but after these studies he rather abruptly dropped his eyes, lowered his point of view, and concentrated again on earthly matters. In fact, by the time he traveled to the Lakes in 1826 his interest in "skying" was secondary to his concern with subjects on the ground. He was clearly interested in the relationship of clouds to earth, in "weather skies," in the orographic effects of clouds, but his clouds became ways to accentuate and highlight earthly mat-

4. Ernst Hans Gombrich, *Art and Illusion: A Study in the Psychology of Pictorial Representation*, p. 178.

ters.[5] Perhaps this is because he felt confident in his mastery of cloud painting, or perhaps because he sensed his proper place was below the mist.

Constable's short-lived fascination with seeing clouds from above may have some biographical background as well. In 1819 he had moved into London. His new wife was in delicate health: she was a fragile woman from the start, and the city air exacerbated her respiratory problems. So they moved temporarily to Hampstead, which proved a propitious choice, for not only was it far enough from city pollution for her breathing to improve, but it was also high enough to furnish Constable a new point of view. Hampstead was five hundred feet above London, and for the first time Constable could, nay, had to, look down on mist and fog. I think this must have had a profound effect on a painter whose earlier visual experiences in East Anglia had been confined to flat land well below the sky. Here at Hampstead he was forced to look on the landscape from above. He still kept the sketchbook that he had had in Suffolk, except that now he kept a running account of cloud activity; and it was from this sketchbook that he constructed his masterful views of Hampstead Heath which, I think, rival any of his Stour Valley paintings for scope and composition. Indeed, in the first half of the twentieth century they were some of his most popular works. They are full panoramas of browns and greens, reminiscent of the Dedham Vale paintings, but much more studied and composed around middle ground motifs. When you look at the clouds of these early 1820 paintings like *Hampstead Heath* and *Upper Heath, Hampstead* and compare them to, say, the earlier clouds of *View of Dedham Vale* (1809), the results of Constable's "skying" (as he called it) are evident. Here for the first time we see that Constable has changed his skies—these are truly interesting clouds that do not so much obscure spatial boundaries as lead our eye out from, and over, the natural forms.

Kurt Badt, in *John Constable's Clouds*, attributes this change in elevation and concentration to Constable's interest in the new

5. L. W. C. Bonacina, "John Constable's Centenary: His Position as a Painter of Weather."

science of meteorology, and Badt's thesis makes considerable biographical sense, for Constable had from early in his life shown interest in "natural philosophy," especially in geology and botany.[6] By the 1820s there was a general excitement in the scientific observation of the skies, excitement made systematic by the researches of John Dalton and made acceptable by the establishment of the Royal Meteorological Society. Badt further contends that two works especially influenced Constable: Thomas Forster's *Researches about Atmospheric Phenomena* (1812, 1815, 1823) and, more importantly, Luke Howard's *The Climate of London* (1820). These are practical books; they attempt, really for the first time, to be scientific about description (*cumulus, stratus, nimbus*, and so on, are used for the first time) as well as about prediction. Constable, as son of a windmiller, would have been interested if for no other reason than that clouds and weather must have been a subject of family concern and interest.

This influence seems clear enough, but I wonder about Badt's single-minded explanation:

> The change in the treatment of sky and clouds which occurred in Constable's painting can hardly be understood as the result of his own efforts. The change came about too quickly for that. And why, if Constable derived the necessary insight from his own resources, did he have to do so much work in order to make a practical certainty of it? No, only an external stimulus can explain why Constable suddenly felt an urge to paint a mass of cloud studies all at once. He did not arrive at this point in his career by the simple process of painting his way to it, but was guided to it *intellectually* from outside; that is why he had to try the new idea out in practice to see whether it would stand the test of being transferred to the medium of painting. Once this is admitted, it is obvious that the stimulus can only have come from Luke Howard.[7]

I think a more complete explanation may be had by remembering Constable's meticulous copies of Cozens and by considering Constable part of the general romantic turn toward experimenting with picture planes, which was, after all, the logical conse-

6. Kurt Badt, *John Constable's Clouds*, pp. 50–61.
7. Ibid., p. 54.

quence of extending picturesque landscapes. One might also listen to Constable himself, for he was quite insightful about the dramatic change in his skies. In a letter to his best friend John Fisher (23 October 1821), he tacitly acknowledged his position between two traditions but clearly chose the more modern:

> The landscape-painter who does not make his skies a very material part of his composition, neglects to avail himself of one of his greatest aids. . . . I have often been advised to consider my sky as "a white sheet drawn behind the objects." Certainly, if the sky is obtrusive, as mine are, it is bad; but if it is evaded, as mine are not, it is worse; it must and always shall with me make an effectual part of the composition. It will be difficult to name a class of landscape in which the sky is not the keynote, the standard of scale and the chief organ of sentiment. You may conceive then, what a "white sheet" would do for me, impressed as I am with these notions, and they cannot be erroneous. The sky is the source of light in nature, and governs everything; even our common observations of the weather of everyday are altogether suggested by it. The difficulty of skies in painting is very great, both as to composition and execution, because with all their brilliancy they ought not to come forward, or, indeed, to be thought of any more than extreme distances are; but this does not apply to phenomena or accidental effects of the sky because they always particularly attract. I know very well what I am about, and that my skies have not been neglected, though they have often failed in execution, no doubt from an over-anxiety about them, which will alone destroy that easy appearance which nature always has in all her movements.[8]

This letter, written at the height of Constable's interest in "sky-ing," is especially important for one key phrase: the sky is the "chief organ of sentiment" in a landscape. That certainly had not been the case with Constable before 1820, while after 1825 it was never the exception. Perhaps Kenneth Clark said it most succinctly when he made the necessary compromise between meteorological and psychological interpretations, concluding that Constable's clouds do indeed represent the "romantic conjunctions of science and ecstasy."[9]

8. As quoted, but not glossed in ibid., p. 55.
9. Clark, *Romantic Rebellion*, p. 275.

John Constable, *Study of Clouds and Trees*, 1821. Royal Academy of Arts, London.

If we look carefully at *Study of Clouds and Trees* (1821), we may be able to "see" hints of this "ecstasy" in the making. First we must notice that the vantage point is extremely high for Constable; we are looking down and out, not up and sideways, which had been the earlier view. Second, what has happened to the landscape? Not only has it been shunted down to the side, but it is imprecise, even amorphous. It is impressionistic—there is no interest in outline, division of color, or verisimilitude. It is a side-long and slanting view. I mention this because Constable did many cloud paintings that totally excluded the earth; they were, I suppose, clearly aides-mémoire, but here Constable included the earth only to exclude it. It is there paradoxically to show that it is really not there.

This is an aggressively out-of-balance composition, and again not at all what we expect from Constable. The sky is so buoyant and mobile that we feel that some change, a drastic change, is imminent. There is a vague but growing sense that some release is in the offing. We have been painted "up to the threshold" of explosion; soon those murky trees will be swaying, those hazy leaves will be shaking. Yet there are no stormclouds in sight, no cumulo-cirrostratus or nimbus clouds (which Constable could paint so well, as we can see in his paintings at the Victoria and Albert Museum); these are the clouds that come before the rain and are full not so much of vapor as of promise. These are the "luminous" clouds Coleridge describes in *Dejection: An Ode*, "foretelling / The coming-on of rain and squally blast."

Look especially at the clouds across the center. These are cumulus clouds, yet they are not the puffy "lamb-backs" usually seen near Hampstead; rather they are piled up on each other like a snowy range of mountains. In fact, if one sets aside "meaning" for a moment and just thinks in terms of form, it seems as if the horizon runs along the tops of these clouds as if they were the rounded summits of snow-topped hills. This horizon is most unstable, almost trembling with change. Other clouds underneath are moving toward us, and there is a still higher canopy of undifferentiated clouds that gives a sense of compression. This is not, as Kurt Badt would contend, primarily a scientific study—if so why the patch of landscape and the overly active cloudscape— rather it is alive with potentialities. Constable's *Clouds* is almost as mythopoetic as Shelley's ever-changing poetic cloud. True, when we read Constable's own inscription on the back we see that his interest is meteorological:

Hampstead,
Sept. 11, 1821.
10 to 11 Morning under the sun
Clouds silvery grey on warm ground
Sultry. Light wind to the S.W. fine all day—but rain in the
night following.

But this gloss was written after the fact, probably long after the time when Constable was putting the cloud paintings together.[10]

10. For more on the chronology of Constable's cloudscapes see Frederick Cummings and Allen Stacey, *Romantic Art in Britain: Paintings and Drawings*

Still he remembered the importance, the release from the sultry heat—the "rain in the night following." It seems to me that Constable was as interested in the lighting of the clouds, in the way that their luminosity forebodes things to come, as in their presence as objects in space. He attempted to give a sense of tension, of contraction before explosion, of the sublime moment. What Constable learned in the 1820s about the sublimity of clouds he never forgot. They became the "chief organ of sentiment" for the rest of his career; in his later works the sky invariably creates the mood of the landscape below. Constable formed in clouds the metaphor of his own disposition: they became the upper register of psychological states. In fact, by 1823 he put so much emphasis on the cloud cover in *Salisbury Cathedral from the Bishop's Grounds* that his good friend and patron Bishop Fisher asked him to please lighten it. The sky was brooding and edgy, as if it would funnel down to earth and draw up even the large cathedral. Constable repainted the scene, giving a light-skied version, full of sunshine, to the bishop's daughter as a wedding present and giving a darker, but full-skied, version to the bishop. He kept the darkest one, the most dynamic, the most glorious, for himself.[11]

By the mid-1820s Constable had ventured to his furthest extent in picturing sublimity through clouds. In *Seascape Study with Rain Clouds* (1824–1828) he painted a most Turneresque and frightening sky-explosion in black. The horizon is low and cracked, the sea is pitch black, and the sky is wildly twisting downward. Off to the sides, patches of yellow and blue and white seem to appear momentarily and then are gone. It is almost as if Constable needed to "play out" his vision in the early 1820s, almost as if he needed to once and for all endow the sky with all the power of transport before returning to earth.

Constable did finally return to what he knew best and felt safest with—the landscape. He had, however, changed: his clouds became darker and more dour. They were no longer full of the

1760–1860 (Philadelphia: Philadelphia Museum of Art, 1968), pp. 201–2 as well as Badt, *Constable's Clouds*, chap. 5.

11. Reynolds, *Constable: Natural Painter*, p. 78.

nebulous promise of relief; now they were plunging down from above in torrents of rain. Constable's later paintings are not just damp, they are waterlogged. According to a wonderful story, he had become so concerned with falling rain that Henry Fuseli took to wearing his mackintosh and unfurling his umbrella before he walked into a Constable exhibition. But however wet they became, Constable's skies were never again as potentially dynamic. They carried light and rain down to earthly subjects rather than being the effervescent subject matter of the skies. In the late 1820s Constable returned from Turner to Ruisdael, from Shelley to Thomson; his vision became more particular and confined. He returned to subjects "under the hedge," so to speak, but now with a knowledge of what lay beyond.

As I mentioned earlier, the literary counterpart for Constable's earthly vision is best found in the poetry of Wordsworth. But I think Constable's cloud studies are Shelleyan, especially those with the 1821 point of view. No other romantic poet but Shelley attempted what Constable, in this short hiatus, attempted; only Shelley so single-mindedly sought to describe the world beyond "the painted veil," above the clouds, in such a systematic way.

This interest in picturing sublimity runs through much of Shelley's poetry from *The Daemon of the World* to *The Triumph of Life*. It is the object of the Alastor-poet's quest; it is the central event of *Mont Blanc*:

> Dizzy Ravine! and when I gaze on thee
> I seem as in a trance sublime and strange
> To muse on my own separate fantasy,
> My own, my human mind, which passively
> Now renders and receives fast influencings,
> Holding an unremitting interchange
> With the clear universe of things around. (34–40)

It is the "frail spell" in *Hymn to Intellectual Beauty*:

> No voice from some sublimer world hath ever
>   To sage or poet these responses given
>   Therefore the names of Demon, Ghost, and Heaven,
> Remain the records of their vain endeavour,
> Frail spells. (25–29)

It is the momentary epiphany in *Lines Written among the Euganean Hills*, or what seems lost in *Stanzas: Written in Dejection, Near Naples*—such a catalog could go on and on. But I am especially interested in what happened when Shelley attempted to describe this experience using the clouds as the sub-limen, the threshold.

Like Constable, Shelley's interest in clouds was part scientific and part poetic. He too had been influenced by Luke Howard's *Essay on Clouds*, and he too had sought to make these empirical studies part of a metaphor for states of consciousness. Clouds appear over and over in Shelley's poetic skies, often with an intensity of meaning far exceeding our expectations, or even those of his contemporaries. For Shelley, clouds became the ethereal, vaporous filament that separated us from the Beyond. They also became, as Donald Reiman has argued, "an analogue of the human mind."[12] However, unlike Constable, whose clouds only imply sublimity, Shelley repeatedly attempted to pierce the cloud cover and picture the empyrean. His *Prometheus Unbound*, finished at almost the same time Constable was starting his cloud studies, is his most extended and self-conscious attempt to take us "up to the margin" and then just beyond. If, as many critics have contended, this work marks the end of the first phase of romanticism, it is because after act 4 of *Prometheus Unbound* there was really nowhere left to go.

Act 4 of *Prometheus Unbound* has posed a peculiar kind of critical problem, one that was especially upsetting both to Shelley's supporters and to his detractors in the nineteenth century, and that still exists today. For those who liked Shelley, the fourth act was an ethereal celebration of love's apocalypse and a wonderfully wrought choric song of joy, a "sublime afterthought." For those less impressed, it was a melee of songs reminiscent of the policemen's chorus from *The Pirates of Penzance*, or "the most amazing piece of surplusage in literature," or even "mere excrescence on the play."[13] But neither defenders nor detractors have

12. Donald H. Reiman, *Percy Bysshe Shelley*, p. 116–17.
13. Act 4 of *Prometheus Unbound* elicited some of the most emotional responses in all literary criticism, espcially in the nineteenth century. For these par-

been able to marshal any real dramatic need, let alone any cohe-
sive plan, for what seemed so obviously an appendage, although
for many a wonderfully wrought one. We know now that Shelley
waited almost half a year after completing act 3 before adding
these strange antiphonal hosannas, and it is logical that by this
time—so imply the detractors—he may have forgotten the tune.
Shelley aficionados answer that teleologically act 4 does belong, perhaps not in, but with, the play. It is indeed a celebration
of what the drama is all about, and it does have some dramatic
function aside from providing the obvious spiritual crescendo.
Usually, and quite possibly wisely, this is all that is said.[14] The
"dramatic function" is left for the reader to determine. What
has been overlooked, I think, is that the fourth act is a well-
organized denouement of the romantic vision, demonstrating
how, at the instant when sublimity is momentarily achieved, the
hierarchies of the mind and cosmos come to be rearranged into
the millennial levels and language ceases to transport image. In a
sense, this is the opposite of Blake's *Mental Traveller*, in which,
instead of folding into itself, the mind folds out to a new level.
Act 4 presents the ultimate unity of reality and actuality, of mind
and matter. It is the temporary end to the romantic quest over
the clouds and out of the self—there are no characters (Prometheus himself never appears), just mind and myth. The horizon,
if we are to trust our wispy informers, is at last breached.

---

ticular quotations, first pro, then con, see *The Poetical Works of Percy Bysshe
Shelley*, ed. Edward Dowden, 2:298; Sidney Lanier, "The English Novel, Lec-
ture V," in *Works*, ed. Clarence Gohdes and Kemp Malone, 4:91, and J. Slater,
"Shelley and *Prometheus Unbound*," p. 193.
    14. *Prometheus Unbound* is finally coming into its own in criticism, although
the last act has still been relatively neglected. The following is just a brief sum-
mary of what I think are the most germane recent comments: Harold Bloom,
Shelley's Mythmaking; David J. Hughes, "Potentiality in *Prometheus Unbound*";
Earl Wasserman, *Shelley: A Critical Reading*, pt. 3; Richard Harter Fogle,
"Image and Imagelessness: A Limited Reading of *Prometheus Unbound*," in *The
Permanent Pleasure: Essays on Classics of Romanticism*, pp. 87–100; I. A. Richards, *Beyond*, pp. 179–201; Stuart Curran, *Shelley's Annus Mirabilis: The Maturing of an Epic Vision*, chap. 2; Charles E. Robinson, *Shelley and Byron: The
Snake and Eagle Wreathed in Flight*, chap. 6; Leonard Neufeldt, "Poetry as Subversion: The Unbinding of Shelley's Prometheus"; and V. A. De Luca, "The Style
of Millennial Announcement in *Prometheus Unbound*."

In the first three acts Shelley has shown us an artfully per-
verted cosmos, where all the usual cosmic structures are reversed. The Christian hierarchies are rearranged so that Lucifer-
Jupiter is above, Christ-Prometheus is still in the middle, and
Demogorgon-God is far below. Thus the Spirit of the Earth calls
up (not down, as in *Manfred*) the spirits of the elements. Gods
and phantoms do not exist up in the heavens, but down near
Demogorgon's cave. Above Prometheus, in the hierarchy that
extends upward to Jupiter, are creatures that have always been
considered subterranean: the Furies, Geryon, Gorgon, and Chi-
maera. What happens in the Promethean mind of act 4 is the re-
structuring of these hierarchies along Christian millennial lines.
Both the Spirits of the Mind and the Spirits of the Elements are
free to "dive, soar or run," and, like liquids of different weights
that have been shaken together, Mind and Matter float up and
down through each other until they reach proper balance. As the
spirits float up from captivity, some continue out beyond the
clouds of heaven into what was once the realm of Jupiter, while
others remain "enchantments of the earth" (4. 161–65). Tunnel-
ing through the middle of this new horizon is a constant train of
dark Forms and Shadows that seem to gleam and vanish and then
gleam again as they "bear time to his Tomb in Eternity." As this is
happening, the Spirits of the Earth and Air draw back the "fig-
ured curtains of sleep," letting the multitude of life-giving essences flow back into the cosmos. Spirits of the Human Mind
clothed in sounds move out of the flux back into the various levels of eternal thought, celebrating the release of repressed energy. We are, at last, above the clouds.

These Spirits of the Mind are, incidentally, the same spirits
who consoled Prometheus after the torturing of the Furies. They
are "emblems of the human mind first, under the old order, repressed and tortured, but now, in the new order, free to control
not only the earth but planets beyond the earth."[15] This change

15. How strangely reminiscent this is of Platonic versions of creation, in which
a universe is formed from some primordial flux or chaos by a creative intelligence.
But also how typical this is of Shelley, for as Carl Grabo, *Prometheus Unbound:
An Interpretation*, has pointed out:

in the role of the Spirits of the Mind is a crux in understanding
the play as a vision of expanding consciousness. Phenomena that
had previously been attributed to the individual mind have now
become part of the cosmic Mind, part of the One, and in so doing
have elevated consciousness across the threshold. The liberated
Spirits of the Mind sing:

> We come from the mind
> Of human kind
> Which was late so dusk, and obscene, and blind;
> Now 'tis an ocean
> Of clear emotion,
> A heaven of serene and mighty motion
>
> From that deep abyss
> Of wonder and bliss,
> Whose caverns are crystal palaces;
> From those skiey towers
> Where Thought's crowned powers
> Sit watching your dance, ye happy Hours! (4. 93–104)

And this union is bonded again as the Spirits of the Mind and
the Hours join:

> Then weave the web of the mystic measure;
> From the depths of the sky and the ends of the earth,
> Come, swift Spirits of might and of pleasure,
> Fill the dance and the music of mirth,

Shelley goes somewhat beyond Platonism in his belief that all creation is
alive, that earth, air, fire and water house each its suitable form of being. In
Platonism the heavenly bodies are divine intelligences, as are earth and
moon in *Prometheus Unbound*. There are, too, in its mythology, gods,
daemons, and others, members of a hierarchy similar to that of the angels
and seraphs in the Christian heaven. But matter as Plotinus conceives it is
the least real of all created things, at the farthest remove from the central
and life-giving One. Matter in his conception is the plastic stuff in which the
creative intelligence of a deity manifests itself, materializes itself, by shaping
in it the forms of its thought. It is of the nature of things, in the philosophy
of Plotinus, for thought so to materialize itself. Shelley's acceptance of this
belief, as far as it goes, is evident in *Prometheus Unbound*. (pp. 172–73)

A continuation of this argument can be found in John J. Lavelle, "Shelley's Py-
thagorean Daemons," in *The Evidence of the Imagination: Studies of Interactions
between Life and Art in English Romantic Literature*, ed. Donald H. Reiman
et al., pp. 264–84.

As the waves of a thousand streams rush by
To an ocean of splendour and harmony! (4. 129–34)

Now completely united, the animating spirits of Mind and Matter spin round the earth, flying in and out of the earth's shadow ("the pyramid of night"), then passing either out into the cosmos or back closer to the earth. Just below heaven, a new kind of gravitational field is pulling together a new planet Earth that will be ruled by the Spirit of Wisdom, not by the repressive Jupiter.

Although Shelley would have us believe that this ideal world, what *he* would consider the apocalyptic liminal consciousness, is beyond the confines of time and space, we can see that the procrustean demands of language forced him to fix it in imaginable space. And the space he chose is right on the edge of fantasy, in the skies at the horizon, in the luminescence of Constable's clouds.

During all this activity in the clouds above the earth, other spirits of the mind are still floating and flying to their appointed stations, some of the more imperialistic even going "into the hoar deep to colonize: Death, Chaos, and Night." They are presumably going into the liminal, into the world beyond our ken, beyond our language. As they travel along, they sing:

SEMICHORUS I
We, beyond heaven, are driven along:
SEMICHORUS II
Us the enchantments of earth retain:
SEMICHORUS I
Ceaseless, and rapid, and fierce, and free,
With the Spririts which build a new earth and sea,
And a heaven where yet heaven could never be.
SEMICHORUS II
Solemn, and slow, and serene, and bright,
Leading the Day and outspeeding the Night,
With the powers of a world of perfect light.
SEMICHORUS I
We whirl, singing loud, round the gathering sphere,
Till the trees, and the beasts, and the clouds appear
From its chaos made calm by love, not fear.

SEMICHORUS II
We encircle the oceans and mountains of earth,
And the happy forms of its death and birth
Change to the music of our sweet mirth. (4. 161–74)

Already the spirits are being centrifuged so that each different group is whirling into its own circular orbit, but the only ones we can comprehend are those still gathered at the horizon. The traditional layers of up and down are still firmly in place. By the time Panthea and Ione describe "the circle and the orb," all the inner spaces between them have become

Peopled with unimaginable shapes,
Such as ghosts dream dwell in the lampless deep,
Yet each inter-transpicuous, and they whirl
Over each other with a thousand motions,
Upon a thousand sightless axles spinning. (4. 244–48)

Panthea's vision also includes a sight of the lowest terranean level—the "black deep" where the evil genii, demons, and "anatomies of unknown things" that once flew the commands of Jupiter are now "jammed in" together, one on top of another. In terms of the psychodrama, thoughts that once "actualized" evil in the universe have returned to the subconscious levels. But they have not vanished: they have simply sunk out of consciousness. Evil is still possible as long as the mind exists, man can still "think" it into being.

The animated Moon and Earth now celebrate the coming cosmic equilibrium of "Man, one harmonious soul of many a soul, / Whose nature is its own divine control, / Where all things flow to all, as rivers to the sea" (4. 400–402). By the time Demogorgon has risen from his cave, all the spirits have settled into their millennial positions. As Carl Grabo has written in *Prometheus Unbound: An Interpretation*, "The liberated mind of man has become the creator of its own universe, molding love and unity from discord and anarchy," but the universe is still layered; it is still confined to up and down; it is still stratiform.[16] Although Panthea claims the boundaries are "intertranspicuous," we can

16. Grabo, *Prometheus Unbound*, p. 133.

see that they are still in place. Demogorgon addresses the reani-
mated and restructured cosmos:

> Ye Kings of suns and stars, Daemons and Gods,
> Aetherial Dominations, who possess
> Elysian, windless, fortunate abodes
> Beyond Heaven's constellated wilderness.

A VOICE *from above*
Our great Republic hears, we are blest, and bless.

DEMOGORGON
> Ye happy Dead, whom beams of brightest verse
> Are clouds to hide, not colours to portray,
> Whether your nature is that universe
> Which once ye saw and suffered—

A VOICE *from beneath*
> Or as they
> Whom we have left, we change and pass away.

DEMOGORGON
> Ye elemental Genii, who have homes
> From man's high mind even to the central stone
> Of sullen lead, from heaven's star-fretted domes
> To the dull weed some sea-worm battens on:

A *confused* VOICE
We hear: thy words waken Oblivion.

DEMOGORGON
> Spirits, whose homes are flesh: ye beast and birds,
> Ye worms, and fish—ye living leaves and buds,
> Lightning and wind; and ye untameable herds,
> Meteors and mists, which throng air's solitudes:—

A VOICE
Thy voice to us is wind among still woods.
                                        (4. 529–48)

In Shelley's final vision everything has its place and is in it.
The gods and daemons are above, and the grateful dead are below, reincorporated into the system. Evil is under control. The
animating spirits have permeated nature and the mind of man,
keeping the new hierarchies in order, and all the other spirits are

in place, keeping the world of sensual music in tune with the cosmos. The most specific charge that is usually leveled against this act is that the main characters never appear. But unlike *Endymion*, in *Prometheus Unbound* it is of singular importance that Asia and Prometheus should *not* appear: their symbolic roles have ended. They have, we assume, been merged into the spirit voices that finally drown out the interpretive songs of Panthea and Ione.

The final picture, a remarkably Platonic one, looks something like this:

LIMINAL	The One	Empyreal level above the Clouds
SUBLIMINAL {	"Daemons and Gods, Aetherial Dominations" Spirits of Mind Spirits of Elements "elemental genii" Forms / Shadows [Phantasm of Jupiter] [Furies]	 Daemonic Level in the Clouds
CONSCIOUS {	The Earth, Ocean, Mercury, Apollo Asia, Panthea, Ione Fauns, Echoes	Mythic level "Actual" level on the Earth
SUBCONSCIOUS {	"Happy Dead" Chimaera Geryon [Jupiter]	"Black Deep" below the Earth

Perhaps it is now easier to see why Shelley could not have ended his drama with the closing of the third act:

> The loathsome mask has fallen, the man remains
> Sceptreless, free, uncircumscribed, but man
> Equal, unclassed, tribeless, and nationless,
> Exempt from awe, worship, degree, the king
> Over himself; just, gentle, wise: but man
> Passionless?—no, yet free from guilt or pain,
> Which were, for his will made or suffered them,
> Not yet exempt, though ruling them like slaves,
> From chance, and death, and mutability,

The clogs of that which else might oversoar
The loftiest star of unascended heaven,
Pinnacled dim in the intense inane. (3. 193–204)

Act 4 shows us what act 3 tells us: it is the framing of the sublime. Like any good Platonist, Shelley bases this frame on a rather rigid hierarchy of Intelligence, yet when all is said and done, his concern is with his vision, not with apparatus.

In a way, however, the formation of the layered hierarchy in the fourth act is what the dramatic action in the first three acts has been preparing us for. There really are only two acts of *Prometheus Unbound*: act 1, the downfall of Jupiter, and Prometheus's reunion with Asia; and act 2, the creation of the Promethean mind. Critics of a generation ago such as W. P. Ker, who believed that Shelley "in prudence ought to have stopped when he had finished" at the end of act 3, and Olwen Campbell, who remarked that Shelley "spoiled his dramatic poem . . . by giving us this wonderful rhapsody," have overlooked the most important part of the play and an important aspect of romanticism as well.[17] *Prometheus Unbound* is not about Prometheus; it is about the unbinding of Prometheus and the liberation of that mind and universe: it is about the picturing of consciousness unfolding at the threshold. The dramatic action is the bursting of mind into new form, the growth of an expanded consciousness. It is the movement of all the animating parts of the cosmic mind toward the patterns of perfection.

When *Prometheus Unbound* is seen as the continuation of an interest in sublimity, it fits both a poetic and a historical context. It is not sui generis. Shelley is taking the romantic vision about as far as it can go, almost to the vanishing point. The play starts, as do *Endymion*, *Manfred*, and *The Rime of the Ancient Mariner*, with a distinct "daemonic realm"—the *genii loci*—above and within the protagonist. Then, as in the earlier poems, the realms are made one through the creative powers of the protagonist's imagination. But what makes *Prometheus* distinct is that this romantic "rite of passage" ends in an epiphany of sorts when the

17. William Paton Ker, "Shelley," in *The Art of Poetry*, p. 47; and Olwen Campbell, *Shelley and the Unromantics*, p. 202.

no-longer-untested poet sees in the heavens what is really within himself. Shelley's fourth act goes farther than its predecessors by showing how the individual psyche, complete with its own animating daemons, merges into the Universal Mind. In this way the fourth act is like Endymion's dream-within-a-dream, a vision-within-a-vision, except that in *Prometheus* the mind and cosmos of the individual man are transferred into collective Mind and Cosmos. Each has become All, and All has become One.

At the end, Shelley's vision is just on the near side of the utterly fantastic, while Constable's is just on the far side of the picturesque mundane. The imagery of Shelley's *Prometheus Unbound* ends without closure, without any sense of upper limit, while Constable's later landscapes are nothing if not finally well defined and limited. Yet, for all their dissimilarities, both artists were drawn to the upper edge of landscapes, one to turn back and the other to go beyond. That their shared sight took them quite literally into the clouds was certainly the result of scientific curiosity, but it was also an indication of the new willingness to reform, or at least experiment with, the received dividing lines and spatial boundaries.

A few decades after Constable and Shelley, John Ruskin rhapsodized about clouds in English landscape paintings; in fact, one of the most interesting aspects of *Modern Painters* is that Ruskin spends so much time discussing clouds. Ironically, he disparaged Constable for painting all-too-lowly subjects while Constable was really a foremost cloud painter, almost as impressive as Ruskin's favorite, Turner. But this may have been because Ruskin never saw Constable's cloud studies, since they were never exhibited until the twentieth century. But Kenneth Clark, who has seen what Ruskin never saw, concluded that Constable, in his own quiet way, was "every bit as revolutionary as Goya."[18] I might add that he was even as revolutionary as Shelley. To see how far that revolution has extended, we need to turn away from the nineteenth century and examine our own.

18. Clark, *Romantic Rebellion*, p. 272.

Conclusion

'the sublime' / In the old sense. Wrong from the start
—Ezra Pound, *Hugh Selwyn Mauberley* (1920)

So far my argument has been that the raising of the ground level, or, if you prefer, the lowering of the skyline, was one of the more important rearrangements of signs that occurred at the end of the Renaissance and was one of the more observable consequences of the dissolution of Christian metaphysics. This shift can be best seen in poetic cosmologies and transcendent landscapes of the early nineteenth century, as the distinction between earth and sky became blurred by a literal and figurative mist. A new fog, so to speak, rolled in across the horizon. I should now like to contend that this blurring of planes still inheres in modern art, more in modern painting than in modern poetry, and that it still has profound implications concerning Western culture.

But first, to reiterate the obvious: man has always looked to the horizon with awe, and clearly how he interprets its awesomeness is a barometer of the longings, if not expectations, of his culture. The luminous world at the edge is so rich in potentialities that the painter who fills it with cherubs is telling us as much about his culture as the painter who shoves this world up to the top of his canvas as if to forget it, or the painter who lowers it to eye level as if to make it a part not only of his world but of ours as well. This last painter can make us more than detached spectators; he can make us part of the scene. In the artist's barely conscious decisions concerning what to paint and where to stand to paint it reside many of the unarticulated beliefs of his culture, for he is every bit as bound up in the social codes as is his audience.

As interesting as what the individual artist does by himself is what happens when a generation of artists work out similar perceptions in different media. Such similarities are essentially the

185

basis for periodization in the arts, and although inter-art analogies have come in for their share of contemporary critical scorn, they are still, as critics like Werner Hofmann, E. H. Gombrich, Mario Praz, or Wylie Sypher have shown, a potentially valuable method of understanding the past. I am particularly interested in the affinities of sublime skyscapes because I believe that here was one of those unnoticed correspondences in both visual and verbal media that mark a shift in the language of images that we used to call *Romanticism* but now, in part to show our suspicion of periodization, we call *romanticism.*

No one has ever denied the importance of the English poets in the history of romanticism; in fact, I daresay they have been lionized out of proportion, certainly in the nineteenth century and probably still today. But you rarely hear mention of the English landscape painters, even though their innovations were important and, in some cases, profound. I grant that in the last decade matters have been rapidly changing, but if you look at any survey of art history, or any collection of romantic painting published prior to the 1970s, you will see that if the English are mentioned at all, it is only to show how important the French really were. To be sure, Turner is considered central to the Western tradition, but he was the exception, and the way he was treated in his own time by his own countrymen supposedly shows how unenlightened the English really were. That they could have preferred John Martin to Turner, let alone to Constable, for most of the century says more than enough. In fact, very few English painters aside from Turner and Constable ever had a European following; painters like George Stubbs, George Romney, John Flaxman, and Benjamin Robert Haydon were known, but not well, and certainly they were never considered of lasting importance. To make matters worse, most of the other painters whom we currently appreciate, like Samuel Palmer and Henry Fuseli, were usually grouped with the English eccentrics from Blake to Dadd and passed off as painters of "personal vision."

You can still ask almost anyone who has stayed awake in an art appreciation class who the great romantic painters were and he will tell you that they were French (Delacroix, Géricault, Ingres, Manet, Degas, Cezanne, Van Gogh) and that the major movements (Impressionism, post-Impressionism, Expressionism) were French as well. In most art history of the nineteenth century, as we have learned it, if a painter did not keep to the French timetable he simply could not be considered first-rank. This characterization may be simpleminded, but it is not altogether unfair, for the French were indeed important in experimenting with technique, color, outline (or lack of it), subject matter, theme, style, anxieties, and the rest of what we loosely call romanticism.

Additionally, there is another rather cynical reason the French are still considered so important, and that simply has to do with the politics of art in general and the writing of art history in particular. Someone once said that it is not history that repeats itself but historians who repeat each other. Art historians are especially susceptible. Until recently, art historians have seemed almost enthralled by a belief in the apostolic succession of Great Painters. In fact, since Vasari there has been a mild obsession with the image of a single thread unspooling from the center of culture, winding its way past first one, then another Italian or French painter, and finally weaving them all into one unbroken pattern to make the fabric of Western civilization. This interpretation, which has first Florence and then Paris as the central locale, first Baroque and then Impressionistic art as the central concern, has only very recently been challenged. In fact, until Werner Hofmann wrote *Art in the Nineteenth Century* in the 1960s, there had been almost no attempt to isolate iconographies and trace them through the sister arts created by "minor" figures in non-European cultures, or for that matter, even Northern European cultures.

We are now realizing that there are many other European traditions as well, other threads, so to speak, that unraveled in the nineteenth century and are still interwoven in the modern fabric. It may be that some of them will prove of more lasting importance than the recognized traditions. One of these other traditions, a Northern Protestant tradition as opposed to the more accepted Southern Catholic one, found its chief inspiration in a kind of secular mysticism, in what first Carlyle and now M. H. Abrams have called Natural Supernaturalism. The temperament that animated this tradition is essentially the other half of the Ex-

pressionistic mind, the Teutonic half, the half still concerned
with sunrises, angels shining through clouds, ice floes, ship
masts, gnarled tree roots, and supernal mountaintops. This is the
half that wrote no manifestos, made no public statements, held
no thematic exhibitions; this, in a sense, was the conservative
half, the half that "stayed at home," the half that was still high on
religious passion, but low on accepting Christian context in
which to express it. In contradistinction to the French, these
painters were unconsciously iconoclastic in imagery and technique. They were more complex than the usual label *picturesque*
implies; they had other less pictorial interests, interests that still
influence us. In fact, this alternate tradition may well account for
the rather startling occurrence in this century of what is blood-
lessly called Abstract Expressionism. It is into this tradition that
I think the English landscapists of the early nineteenth century
will finally be fitted.

From the vantage of the 1980s looking backward to the Northern European landscapists, the great innovator was not Claude,
Rosa, Poussin, or the Dutch landscapists, but Caspar David
Friedrich (1774–1840). What is startling about this assertion is
that while Friedrich seems to us to have been such a force, he
was virtually unknown outside Germany in his own time. His
position in the pantheon of Great Painters is now so secure that
Anatole Broyard reviewing coffee-table books on romantic painting in *The New York Times* (17 October 1981) even complained
that Friedrich seems to be taking over the nineteenth century.
Clearly, Friedrich's influence can be seen more in the temper of
the times, in the once academically popular concept of Zeitgeist,
than in any direct form. For, remarkably, the first major retro-
spective exhibition of Friedrich's work was held at the Tate Gallery in 1972, followed a few years later by a much larger showing
mounted jointly by the museums of West Germany's Hamburg
and East Germany's Dresden (which together own most of his
works). In our past neglect of Friedrich's oeuvre we may also see
the inadvertent tyranny of museum administrators, for without
exhibitions there can be no real cultural currency, and without
scholarly access and approbation there can be no assimilation.
Indeed, it may well be that Friedrich's depictions of landscape

Caspar David Friedrich, *Monk by the Sea*, 1809. Verwaltung der Staatlichen Schlösser und Gärten, Berlin.

sublimities, rather than the Southern European tradition of the picturesque, will provide the context in which to discuss what was happening not only in English painting but in American art as well.

One can so easily see in Friedrich's work the nascent German expressionism, that eerie sense of imminence at the horizon, that omnipresent luminous void hovering in the middle distance that almost compresses the viewer out of the picture, out of nature. In so many of Friedrich's paintings the literal human standpoint is reduced to the absolute minimum, as if to make the towering expanses all the more overwhelming. This sense of dissembling, which can be seen in Friedrich's *Monk by the Sea*, is, after all, part of the central shock of the sublime.

The configuration of forms we see here is not at all unlike what we have seen developing in English romantic landscape painting from controlled Wright to exuberant Turner. The force that somehow inheres in these massive interpenetrating forms also generates the frisson that we can feel while looking at the almost self-conscious English contrivances of James Ward's *Gordale Scar* (1811–1815), Philip James de Loutherbourg's *The Falls of the Rine at Schaffhausen*, or even Samuel Palmer's *Moonlit Landscape* (1829–1830). We can sense this force again in the lighting and structuring of the massive forms of earth and sky in works of American landscapists like Frederic Church, Albert Bierstadt, FitzHugh Lane, Martin Johnson Heade, and others who now travel under the appropriate tag of *Luminists*.

By far the most influential critic and exponent of this reinterpretation of romantic art has been Robert Rosenblum, who, in *Modern Painting and the Northern Romantic Tradition*, argues that beneath these landscapes lurk the religious energies that animated one of the most important impulses in the modern temper: the desire to be free of the dross of nature. These images, very often expressed in vast horizontal planes, are not so much of the eternal world as they are the new iconographies of natural religion—the texts, so to speak, of the new pantheism. In his introduction to the Slade Lectures at Oxford, Rosenblum asserted that they form the basis of

> an important, alternate reading of the history of modern art which might well supplement the orthodox one that has as its almost exclusive locus Paris, from David and Delacroix to Matisse and Picasso. My own reading is based not on formal values alone—if such things can really exist in a vacuum—but rather on the impact of certain problems of modern cultural history, and most particularly the religious dilemmas posed in the Romantic movement, upon the combination of subject, feeling, and structure shared by a long tradition of artists working mainly in Northern Europe and the United States. Such a view is by no means intended to minimize the glories of the French tradition of modern art, which hardly needs support. It is meant rather to suggest another, counter-French tradition in modern art, which may help us to understand better the ambitions and the achievements of such great artists as Friedrich, Van Gogh, Mondrian, and Rothko by viewing them not, so to speak through Parisian lenses, but rather through the context of a long Northern Romantic tradition whose troubled faith in the functions of art they all share.[1]

1. Robert Rosenblum, *Modern Painting and the Northern Romantic Tradition: Friedrich to Rothko*, p. 7–8.

In the lectures that follow, Rosenblum articulates an impressive, although occasionally hard-pressed, case that the sublimities of Friedrich form one of the spools from which the thread of modern art will unwind.[2]

The transvaluation of the Christian experience of awe and epiphany, the development of this new vocabulary of signs centering on the horizon, continued through the nineteenth century into our own, being re-formed and recast and finally abstracted into the colors and forms of Abstract Expressionism. The accompanying illustrations present a visual summary of the process.

What we see in retrospect is the transformation of a once privileged sacramental experience—the sublime—into a repeatable pattern of forms. Ruskin in *Modern Painters* may have disparaged the attibution of holy sentience to landscapes, to those "blue mountains," for in a way it is the pathetic fallacy carried to the nth degree, but he knew well that it was exactly this imputation that was enlivening English and European art. In a sense, the abstracted forms of this scene were once again transformed in our own day into the emblematic structures of Abstract Expressionism, which sought to make the enduring horizontal lines into almost a hieroglyph of the human condition in nature.

These changes were not wrought without resistance, for they

2. Writing specifically of *Monk by the Sea*, Rosenblum claims we are in the presence of a revolutionary visionary who so intuitively knew the power of his forms that he tinkered with the world at the horizon until he finally "got it right," until he made the earth and sea and sky into almost primordial forces, until he made them objects of awe:

> Yet within this Northern Baroque tradition of sea painting, the tradition most accessible to and compatible with Friedrich, the *Monk by the Sea* strikes an alien, melancholic note, strange not only in the presence of so dense, so haunting, and so uninterrupted an expanse of somber, blue-gray light above a low horizon, but in the disturbing absence of any of the expected components of conventional marine painting. . . . Just how daring this emptiness was may even be traced in evolutionary terms, for it has recently been disclosed in X-rays that originally Friedrich had painted several boats on the sea, one extending above the horizon, but that then, in what must have been an act of artistic courage and personal compulsion, he removed them, leaving the monk on the brink of an abyss unprecedented in the history of painting but one that would have such disquieting progeny as Turner's own 'pictures of nothing' and the boundless voids of Barnett Newman. (Ibid., pp. 12–13)

Vincent van Gogh, *The Starry Night*, 1889. Collection, The Museum of Modern Art, New York. Acquired through the Lillie P. Bliss Bequest.

Edvard Munch, *Coast at Aasgaard*, 1907. Bildarchiv Preussischer Kulturbesitz, Berlin.

Lyonel Feininger, *Bird Cloud*, 1926. Busch-Reisinger Museum, Harvard University, Cambridge, Massachusetts.

Ralph Albert Blakelock, *The Sun, Serene, Sinks into the Slumberous Sea*, 1880s. Museum of Fine Arts, Springfield, Massachusetts. The Horace P. Wright Collection, W13.34.

Piet Mondrian, *Dune Landscape*, circa 1911. Collection Haags Gemeentemuseum, The Hague.

emptied one sacred text of its mysteries in order to fill up another. We are as stymied before some of the canvases of Rothko, Newman, or Still as we are before the mountainscapes of Friedrich or the awesome celestial ceilings of Renaissance churches. The impulse remains; the context has been re-formed. These modern transformations initially had to be effected in the Protestant North where the religious impulse was still strong but the ecclesiastical forms weak. Indeed, Rosenblum traces the results of this reattribution of sublimity not only as it pertained to how the horizon was painted, but also as to how it led artists like Carstens, Runge, or Palmer to re-form such mundane images as tree roots and church spires into metaphors of spiritual yearning. By the time Van Gogh painted his landscapes, the two traditions of North and South had momentarily meshed, and so we see in works like *The Sower* (1888) how the now-iconic luminescence at the horizon floods the natural world with its literal glory or, better yet, in the deservedly famous *Starry Night* (1889) how the very heavens pinwheel their magical aura from the celestial world above into our world below. At the horizon we make the

Mark Rothko, *Green on Blue*, 1956. University of Arizona Museum of Art, Tucson. Gift of Edward J. Gallagher.

transition not up into the dark and mysterious, but into the exhilarating and wonderful.

That landscape should have become by the late nineteenth century a storehouse of religious symbols is not surprising. What we overlook, however, is that the English landscapists, still so often considered to be working their tiny plots of ground, as Constable so often said of his own work, were also caught up in the same evangelical excitement. What we have witnessed in the specific works of Wright, Turner, Martin, Cozens, and Constable was not isolated but, as we so readily recognize with Wordsworth, Coleridge, Shelley, Byron, and Keats, part of a central shift in literal standpoint, a profound rearrangement of point of view, a willingness to look beyond.

Romantic landscape paintings represent not so much the fading of faith as simply its reattribution, a change in perspective. One need only look at Munch's landscapes, and especially his seascapes, to see the Scandinavian restatement of this concentration on the holy brink. In *Coast at Aasgaard* (1906–1907), for instance, we see the forms of sky and shore as they are interlocked by a bolt of sunlight. The same brink is in Holder's Swiss mountainscapes, which he himself labeled "paysages planétaires" (planetary landscapes) to give the sense of a supernatural cosmology lingering at the horizon, a joyous mystery just above the rift. The same numinous edge can be seen in northern German landscapists like Emil Nolde (*Before Sunrise*, circa 1894) and Franz Mark (*Tyrol*, 1913–1914) or even in the works of Russian Vasily Kandinsky (*Mountain Landscape with Church*, 1910), except that in Kandinsky there has been a gradual abstracting of forms until only the geometric surfaces remain. Lyonel Feininger's *Bird Cloud* of 1926 shows these new forms almost aflutter, worlds beyond now dipping down into this world, our world. "Above" and "below" are no longer opposites; "this" world and "that" world are not exclusive: they are part of one whole.

Erwin Panofsky once coined the term *pseudomorphosis* to describe the appearance at different times of certain visual signs that tempt the critic to suppose they are all part of the same cultural process when in truth they share no structure deeper than their surfaces. The temptation on the critic's part is, of course, to assume that similar structure mandates similar meaning, and consequently the critic neglects what novelists and all story-tellers have known: coincidence is a central constituent of reality. It may be foolhardy to contend that without seeing each other's works landscape artists all over Europe were re-forming the way we look out on the world around us in a similar way, but such does seem to me to be the case. Is it any stranger that calculus was developed by at least three different mathematicians, all un-known to each other, in the same generation, or that the DNA was understood by different scientists in almost the same month? It is only when you look at German or Scandinavian painted vis-tas that the English ones seem to coalesce into a pattern. I would not argue, as does Rosenblum, that there has to be a central source (Caspar David Friedrich), or even any conscious inheri-tance, but only that the similarities are striking, probably too nu-merous to be accidental, and, most importantly, derive from the same demythologizing of the Western heavens and the same longings of Western man.

Just for the argument's sake, let us briefly look at what was happening in nineteenth-century American painting. Ever since John Baur coined the term *luminism* in the early 1950s, there has been a steadily growing interest in examining the textures and tonalities of light in American nineteenth-century landscapes. It is almost as if critics needed the nomenclature before they could categorize the almost phosphorescent phenomena that glowed on the horizons of painters like Frederic Church, Albert Bierstadt, Martin Johnson Heade, William Bradford, FitzHugh Lane, John Frederick Kensett, and Ralph Albert Blakelock. These atmo-spheric effects, achieved by the flooding of brilliant light across a mountaintop or over a bay, give the viewer an eerie sense of still-ness, silence, and solitude. The sensation is religious: nature has become the cathedral and the artist her priest. One need only pause before the ice floes, volcanoes, waterfalls, and twilights created by Church, the Yosemite Valley scenes of Bierstadt, the thunderstorm and Marshfield Meadow vistas of Heade, or the coastlines of Kensett to see the external world of American na-ture becoming an elaborate analogue of holiness, just as it was for the English and the Northern Europeans. It is oddly appropriate that one of the earliest Luminists, Thomas Cole, should have painted *Expulsion from the Garden of Eden* (1824) in which the proto-Americans, the Adam and Eve of the new world, are being exiled from an Eden through a freestanding cathedral arch into a veritable jungle of awesome sublimities. Little wonder that the American landscapists should have found sermons in stones, altars in oaks, spires in mountains, and the glory of God at the horizon, for the book of American nature lay as open before them as the scriptures.

Barbara Novak, Earl A. Powell, and John Wilmerding, among other interpreters of American art, have reasserted with visual proof what literary critics from Perry Miller on have concluded: if there was ever a climate ripe for secular sublimities it was that of nineteenth-century America.[3] Not only was there an evangelical fervor alive in the land, a fervor first inculcated by the Puritans with their sense of a promised land and then carried into the mid-nineteenth century by the millennial movements of the Great Awakening, but there was also the intellectual tradition of New England Transcendentalism, which made such passions respectable. There is no better description of the romantic sublime than Emerson's famous passage on the world beyond the slush:

> Crossing a bare common, in snow puddles, at twilight, under a clouded sky, without having in my thoughts any occurrence of special good fortune, I have enjoyed a perfect exhilaration. I am glad to the brink of fear. In the woods too, a man casts off his years, as the snake his slough, and at what period so ever of life, is always a child. In the woods is perpetual youth. Within these plantations of God a decorum and sanctity reign, a perennial festival is dressed, and the guest sees not how he should tire of them in a thousand years. In the woods, we return to reason and faith. There I feel that nothing can befall me in life,—no disgrace, no calamity (leaving me my eyes), which nature cannot repair. Standing on the bare ground,— my head bathed by the blithe air, and uplifted space,—all mean

3. Barbara Novak, "American Landscape: Changing Concepts of the Sublime," as well as her *Nature and Culture: American Landscape and Painting, 1825–1875*; Earl A. Powell, "Luminism and the American Sublime," in John Wilmerding, *American Light: The Luminist Movement, 1850–1875*, pp. 69–95, and Wilmerding, "The Luminist Movement: Some Reflections," in *American Light*, pp. 97–155.

egotism vanishes. I become a transparent eyeball; I am nothing; I see all; the currents of the Universal Being circulate through me; I am part and parcel of God.[4]

Or Thoreau meditating on the inner and outer landscapes as consciousness crosses the horizon between in here and out there:

> If with closed ears and eyes I consult consciousness for a moment, immediately are all walls and barriers dissipated, earth rolls from under me, and I float, by the impetus derived from the earth and the system, a subjective, heavily laden thought, in the midst of an unknown and infinite sea, or else heave and swell like a vast ocean of thought, without rock or headland, where all riddles solved, all straight lines making there their two ends to meet, eternity and space gambolling familiarly through my depths. I am from the beginning, knowing no end, no aim. No sun illumines me, for I dissolve all lesser lights in my own intenser and steadier light. I am a restful kernel in the magazine of the Universe.[5]

Whitman, as well, understood that sublimity need not depend on hugeness or terror as Burke had suggested, but rather on the intuitive sense that a passage to elevated consciousness could be found through the ordinary forms of this natural world. In a passage reminiscent of Wordsworth's "On the Sublime and the Beautiful," he remarked:

> While I know the standard claim is that Yosemite, Niagara Falls, the upper Yellowstone and the like afford the greatest natural shows, I am not so sure but the prairies and the plains, while less stunning at first sight, last longer, fill the esthetic sense fuller, precede all the rest, and make North America's characteristic landscape. Indeed, through the whole of this journey, what most impressed me, and will longest remain with me, are these same prairies. Day after day, and night after night, to my eyes, to all my senses—the esthetic one most of all—they silently and broadly unfolded. Even their simplest statistics are sublime.[6]

The fascination with the horizon is as hard to overlook in Transcendentalist prose as it is in Luminist painting. Again and again

4. *The Complete Works of Ralph Waldo Emerson*, ed. Edward Waldo Emerson, 1:9–10.
5. Henry David Thoreau, journal entry of "August 13, 1858."
6. Walt Whitman, *Specimen Days*, p. 94.

the American painters returned to those landscape scenes not just bisected by coruscating light but linked by it. Again and again we see not just in their choice of subjects, but also in the literal standpoint of observation, the tilt of their heads, how concentrated they were on the point where earthline, or, better yet, waterline and skyline meet. In their paintings of Narragansett Bay, Niagara Falls, ice packs, or mountain lakes we are forced to the joint between the natural world and the one beyond. It is Frederic Church more than any other who made the horizon almost an architectonic device to generate a flux between these worlds. The intrusions of supernal light that characterize such masterpieces as *Twilight in the Wilderness* (1860) and *Aurora Borealis* (1865) are the logical extensions of what we first see in Church's Central American volcano pictures painted during the Civil War. In one of these Martinesque landscapes, titled *Cotopaxi,* he has the horizon literally breaking apart with a volcano erupting in the background while right before our eyes an eerie waterfall is eroding a canyon out from beneath our feet. But this is clearly done for shock; later Church learns the implications of a cleft horizon. Equally disturbing in the sense of rearranging our notions of secure place are Bierstadt's sunrises and sunsets in Yosemite, which, like Church's paintings of celestial lights, show an intense distillation of light entering the natural scene from the side, from *behind,* not from above, mountain forms. In these paintings the horizontal band has been breached by the vertical, giving the impression that there is a pathway into this holy light right here in this world.

In Ralph Albert Blakelock's *The Sun, Serene, Sinks into the Slumberous Sea* we see a scene that may lack the measured texture of other Luminist works but certainly captures the atmosphere of the American transcendental spirit. Under the title's sibilant alliteration is a becalmed seascape, rather like a Turner horizon at rest; what is particularly striking is that while all the parts are balanced—even the clouds—the axis of sunlight breaks the horizon in such a way as to provide an almost eye-level view into the Beyond. Looking at this painting is almost like sighting the aura on cross hairs. The skyline has been so lowered that we sense ourselves almost at the brink. This is surely not the Claudian organization of distant vision: foreground coulisse, middleground pool of reflecting water, distant mountain, and, finally, at the very top, almost beyond sight and certainly beyond comprehension, the horizon. Such an unaffected, but not unstudied, view as this almost intimates the configuration of massive interdependent forms that we have seen again and again and come to associate with an important strain of modern art.

It is in the struggle to get free from the dross of the physical world, in the desire to get to the edge of something more profound than reflection of observable forms, that we see the romantic landscape made quintessentially modern. For instance, in Piet Mondrian's *Dune Landscape* (circa 1911) the geometrical patterns hold earth and sea and sky together as if they were part of one continuous interlocking grid. Mondrian carried these geometries still further in paintings like *The Sea* (1912) and *Composition No. 10 Pier and Ocean* (1915), in which only the reticulated lines remain to inform us of the once-recognizable forms. You could argue that this is symbolism and only inadvertently naturalism, but I suspect Mondrian was consciously continuing a tradition of romantic landscaping, only that here the Cubist, so to speak, has emptied the accepted traditional forms, leaving only the outlines behind.

The logical conclusion of such a process is that when the lines themselves are removed only the colors will remain and that, if they are properly configured, the blocks of colors alone will continue to excite our primordial aspirations. In a sense, one of the developments of modern art is that painters overthrew the "text" of Friedrich's *Monk by the Sea*, exiling the internal spectator and compressing the visible forms until only the colors remained to separate the masses. That such concision was achieved in America under the aegis of Abstract Expressionism testifies not only to the shifting center of the art world but also to the fulfillment of the American traditions of Transcendentalism in literature and of Luminism in the arts. It also represents the continuation of the more general romantic quest by artists like Clyfford Still, Mark Rothko, and Barnett Newman, who candidly admit that their visions are first sacramental, then aesthetic.

Although it may still be hard to appreciate, much less to inter-

pret, the abruptness of so much of their work, when the Abstract
Expressionists are seen as continuing the ongoing tradition of romantic anxiety and aspiration it may make their works seem less
distant and severe. In fact, Barnett Newman's 1948 essay "The
Sublime Is Now" makes the case that he, at least, wishes to be
placed in the context of the mid-eighteenth-century theorizing
about the sublime rather than to be seen as an aggressive revolutionary. Newman claims artistic ancestry not from the forefathers
of Paris, but from some deeper instinct within mankind:

> I believe that here in America, some of us, free from the weight
> of European culture, are finding the answer, by completely denying
> that art has any concern with the problem of beauty and where to
> find it. The question that now arises is how, if we are living in a time
> without a legend or mythos that can be called sublime, if we refuse
> to admit any exaltation in pure relations, if we refuse to live in the
> Abstract, how can we be creating a sublime art?
>
> We are reasserting man's natural desire for the exalted, for a con-
> cern with our relationship to the absolute emotions. We do not
> need the obsolete props of an outmoded and antiquated legend. We
> are creating images whose reality is self-evident and which are de-
> void of the props and crutches that evoke associations with out-
> moded images, both sublime and beautiful. We are freeing our-
> selves of the impediments of memory, association, nostalgia, legend,
> myth, or what have you, that have been the devices of Western Eu-
> ropean painting. Instead of making cathedrals out of Christ, man, or
> "life," we are making it out of ourselves, out of our own feelings.
> The image we produce is the self-evident one of revelation, real and
> concrete, that can be understood by anyone who will look at it with-
> out the nostalgic glasses of history.[7]

Newman may protest too much about his own independence.
Works of a pictorial art are still, like any language, mediations
between "events"; they are visual metaphors and as such have a
history. The modern painter is still working with the same decod-
ing devices—painted images on canvas—and far from severing
all his links with the past, he is instead enmeshed in a tradition of
the landscape sublime. Newman is taking the iconography of the
sublime, however, as far as it can go—for many critics, too far.

7. Barnett Newman, "The Sublime Is Now," p. 53.

But Newman is by no means alone in ambition or design. Perhaps a still better example can be found in the works of Mark Rothko. Rothko not only provides us huge abstractions of earlier horizontal forms, but he also in his masterwork, the so-called Rothko chapel in Houston, reminds us of the religious context from which this tradition first sprang. In the chapel, which houses half a dozen wall-size canvases, we witness the pre-Adamite separations of earth, sea, and sky, the cleaving of this palpable world and the ineffable one beyond, and we feel the sensation of this momentary fusion.

The idea of a chapel in the secular world of modern art may well seem contradictory, but the subliming process has always been a meditative experience, and, before the nineteenth century, the physical church provided the setting. As with Newman, the sublime for Rothko is in no way embedded in dogma, received text, or ceremonies; it is instead simply an elevating passion. He explains:

> I am not interested in relationships of color or form or anything else . . . I am interested only in expressing the basic human emotions—tragedy, ecstasy, doom, and so on—and the fact that lots of people break down and cry when confronted with my pictures shows that I communicate with those basic human emotions. The people who weep before my pictures are having the same religious experience I had when I painted them. And if you, as you say, are moved only by their color relationships, then you miss the point.[8]

This same belief in the inspirational power of abstract forms is echoed by Clyfford Still, who also attempted to envision the sublime:

> THE SUBLIME? A paramount consideration in my studies and work from my earliest student days. In essence, it is most elusive of capture or definition—only surely found least in the lives and works of those who babble of it the most. The dictator types have made a cliché of "sublime" concepts throughout the centuries to impress and subjugate the ignorant and desperate.[9]

8. Mark Rothko, as quoted in Selden Rodman, *Conversations with Artists*, pp. 93–94.
9. Clyfford Still as quoted by Ti-Grace Sharpless in Still, *Catalogue of Exhibition*, n.p.

Presumably, Still is railing against the expropriation of secular revelation by the ecclesiastical "dictators," and he is joined by his colleagues in resenting this. It is no happenstance, for instance, that Barnett Newman gave many of his color-field paintings titles that are redolent with religious overtones: *Covenant, Day One,* or *Primordial Light,* for what he would like us to see when we look at his huge canvases of raw color bisected by a single line is a spiritual expression.[10]

It may be straining credulity to see slabs of color placed horizontally—as, say, in Rothko's *Green on Blue* (1956)—as emblematic of a tradition stretching back to the early nineteenth century, or to see them as the modern counterpart of ancient human aspirations, but I think the case can be tantalizing if not wholly convincing. There is no doubt that such speculation wears the intentional fallacy ragged, for the critic scans the visual "text" for influence and mindfulness, rather than just looking at the painting. Had there not been a concurrent shifting of tempers in the sister arts—think, for instance, of Mahler's *Resurrection Symphony* or Delius's *Mass of Life* or what we know about transcendent aspiration both articulated and denied in modern literature, especially poetry—we might well think that the nineteenth-century secularization of the sublime was a minor peripheral movement in Western culture, or that these similar forms were an example of pseudomorphosis.

Very often the best place to see the force of new currents in the cultural stream is in the rock-hard resistance to them. No one needs to be reminded of the rush of opprobrium in the 1950s and 1960s to the profanities of Abstract Expressionism, because it still exists. As I mentioned in the Introduction, the conservative hesitancy to tamper with this particular human aspiration has been a constant in modern life. In fact, returning briefly to the literary context and jumping back a hundred years, it is interesting to juxtapose a poem like Arnold's *Empedocles on Etna* with the earlier romantic poems, for *Empedocles* contains all the elements of

10. Barnett Newman even claimed that all artistic activity mimics God's original creative act, see "The First Man Was an Artist."

its predecessors, except for the self-reflecting realms at the margin. Here is a yearning protagonist who, like Manfred and Endymion, suffers considerable internal turmoil and seeks escape from an empty life by climbing to the topmost part of the natural world. He struggles to be sublimed, to be transported to the horizon. He aches for entry into the daemonic world of his romantic forebears, and we almost expect to see him break into the subliminal world. But Arnold places Empedocles just below the edge, where natural imagery is only about to become supernatural; he never lets him go beyond. So instead of calling down the daemons of his own psychic universe, Empedocles lectures on the futility of life and the hopelessness of making it whole. Then he leaps headlong *down* into a volcano, crying, "receive me, hide me, quench me, take me home!" (2. 36).

Arnold removed *Empedocles* from the 1853 edition of his *Poems*, saying that "it adds nothing to our knowledge of any kind," that it is "indeterminate and faint, instead of being particular, precise and firm," and that it is "too modern." He then concluded by saying *Empedocles* is too concerned with "the dialogue of the mind itself." This is of course precisely what the other romantic poems—*Yew Trees, The Rime of the Ancient Mariner, Manfred, Endymion*, and *Prometheus Unbound*—are all about. Arnold may have wanted to create an Endymion or an Ancient Mariner or a Manfred, but he did not want to give him access to the reflexive universe, presumably because it would be sacrilegious. So where the romantic poet had shown his "hero of consciousness" transcending the ordinary, Arnold showed him being consumed by it. There is no sublimation here, only submission.

One finds this same conservative response to the romantic sublime echoed a decade later in Tennyson's *The Higher Pantheism* (1869). There is no better example of the sublime remythologized and set back into Christian context than these lines:

> The sun, the moon, the stars, the seas, the hills and the plains,—
> Are not these, O Soul, the Vision of Him who reigns?
> Is not the Vision He, tho' He be not that which He seems?
> Dreams are true while they last, and do we not live in dreams?

Earth, these solid stars, this weight of body and limb,
Are they not sign and symbol of thy division from Him?
Dark is the world to thee; thyself are the reason why,
For is He not all but thou, that hast power to feel "I am I"?
Glory about thee, without thee; and thou fulfillest thy doom,
Making Him broken gleams and a stifled splendor and gloom.
Speak to Him, thou, for He hears, and Spirit with Spirit can
    meet—
Closer is He than breathing, and nearer than hands and feet.
God is law, say the wise; O Soul, and let us rejoice,
For if He thunder by law the thunder is yet His voice.
Law is God, say some; no God at all, says the fool,
For all we have power to see is a straight staff bent in a pool;
And the ear of man cannot hear, and the eye of man cannot see;
But if we could see and hear, this Vision—were it not He?

By the time Hardy, Hopkins, or even Swinburne came to address this interest there was room only for cynical denial (*Shelley's Skylark*), complete self-effacement (*God's Grandeur*), or riotous parody (*The Higher Pantheism in a Nutshell*). The sublime experience had once more turned institutional, and the poet was again consigned to his "proper place" well below the horizon.

I daresay one might make the same case with the English painters. In a sense I think Turner had an influence on landscape painters rather like what Shelley had on later poets. He had simply gone too far. So the pre-Raphaelites swerved back to "numbering the streaks of the tulip," to painting nature as pastoral, picturesque, or beautiful. Look at the skies above the horizons in the paintings of Hunt, Millais, Burchett, Rossetti, Hughes, and others and you will see that they are singularly without borders, without thresholds, without an "upper register." The pre-Raphaelite horizon is either way off in the corner, sunk out of sight, or made rigid. The Victorian landscapists left it for the Northern Europeans and Americans to continue the interest in picturing the sublime.

Clearly, the impulse endured in the verbal text as it had in the visual. One need only recall any number of Emerson's prose works (*The Divinity School Address, Nature, Experience*), many passages in Thoreau's *Walden*, the last parts of Whitman's *Leaves of Grass* (especially after section 31), or Yeats's *A Vision* as well as the lyrical plays to realize that reaction was limited.[11] And almost a century later, as the threshold was being re-imaged by the Abstract Expressionists until only the essential forms remained, so too modernist poets like Pound and Jeffers were attempting to re-create the sensation in words. Because the experience is initially visual, they had a more complicated task. But Wallace Stevens in poems like *The Auroras of Autumn* or *The Sail of Ulysses* or even *An Ordinary Evening in New Haven* attempted to give expression to what is so condensed in his lyrical *The American Sublime* (1935):

> How does one stand
> To behold the sublime
> But how does one feel?
> One grows used to the weather,
> The landscape and that;
> And the sublime comes down
> To the spirit itself,
>
> The spirit and space,
> The empty spirit
> In vacant space.

Thus the romantic attempts to envision the sublime, growing from the secular interests of eighteenth-century aesthetics and then being crowded out by religious concerns of the mid-nineteenth, only to reappear in our own time, do make, I think, a case for an important modern artistic impulse. While literary criticism has acknowledged this impulse in the romantic poetry, art criticism has been slow to recognize how such aspiration was translated to canvas. Recently, however, such interpretations have begun appearing with some regularity. There was a major exhibition titled *Romantic Art in Britain* at the Philadelphia Museum of Art and the Detroit Institute of Art in 1958, which for the first time overtly attempted to tie English art into the Northern

11. For a dense, but interesting, treatment of Emerson, Whitman, and Yeats in this context see Harold Bloom, *Poetry and Repression*, chaps. 8–10, as well as his *Agon: Towards a Theory of Revisionism*, while for Yeats and Stevens see Helen Regueiro, *The Limits of Imagination: Wordsworth, Yeats, and Stevens*.

Protestant tradition (Rosenblum wrote one of the introductory essays to the catalogue and clearly had a hand in the selections). There was also a major exhibition of American landscape art at the Museum of Modern Art in 1976 appropriately entitled *The Natural Paradise: Painting in America, 1800–1950*. If an exhibition can be called provocative, this was it; its clear bias was to tie the Abstract Expressionists to the tradition of American Luminism. John Wilmerding wrote one of the explanatory essays, "Fire and Ice in American Art: Polarities from Luminism to Abstract Expressionism," and Kynaston McShine and Robert Rosenblum contributed articles on the "Abstract Sublime" linking the American vision with its European counterparts. This rising critical interest in attempting to compare nineteenth- and twentieth-century American sublime landscapes was also the subject of an entire issue of *Art in America* (January-February 1976) and finally resulted in an internationally important exhibition of Luminism at the National Gallery in 1981 entitled *American Light: The Luminist Movement, 1850–1875*. This show once and for all set the American landscape in the wider context of romanticism and showed the strong sense of abstract formal design that continued into twentieth-century American art.[12]

There have been smaller and more specific exhibitions that also testify to our changing sensibilities. While in the 1970s the Tate Gallery and the Yale Center for British Art held a number of exhibitions of English landscape art, in 1981 the British Museum, the Yale Center, and the Art Gallery of Ontario mounted a showing of Turner entitled *Turner and the Sublime*, and later that year the Fitzwilliam Museum in Cambridge showed a potpourri of English landscapes between 1750 and 1850, *Beauty, Horror and Immensity*, which emphasized what the compiler, Peter Bicknell, called the "topographical sublime." Thanks to the publication of

12. Here are the important catalogs: *Romantic Art in Britain: Paintings and Drawings, 1760–1860*, essays by Robert Rosenblum, Frederich Cummings, and Allen Staley (Philadelphia: Philadelphia Museum of Art, 1968); *The Natural Paradise: Painting in America, 1800–1950*, essays by Barbara Novak, Robert Rosenblum, and John Wilmerding (New York: The Museum of Modern Art, 1976), and *American Light: The Luminist Movement*, ed. John Wilmerding (New York: Harper and Row, 1981).

the descriptive catalogues to these shows, the dissemination of this new pan-European interpretation of English romantic art promises to influence general art history.[13]

In the last year (1982) we have seen the publication of two massive coffee-table editions of romantic art by French critics, Michel Le Bris, *Romantics and Romanticism*, and Jean Clay, *Romanticism*, which clearly emphasize the Northern Protestant tradition at the expense of the Paris tradition. And both books pay conspicuous homage to the English achievement from Cozens and Palmer to Constable and Turner. One expects such chancy reconsiderations in academic articles and books, but when the critics are French and the books cost over sixty dollars, you know the interpretive adjustments are starting to take form. The art history textbooks may well be next.

What has not fully occurred, however, and what I hope my work will also aid, is a growing awareness that the sister arts are not so easily separated as books with chapters on romantic architecture, sculpture, literature, painting, and music would have us believe. Changes in consciousness, so often initially witnessed simply as changes in standpoint, are far more pervasive in different media than is usually acknowledged. True, inter-art comparisons may often have the inappropriateness of comparisons between apples and oranges, but they may also be one of the few ways to understand such unwieldy concepts as neoclassicism, mannerism, gothicism, baroque, and even romanticism. I think that diachronic comparisons can be especially rewarding with nineteenth-century sublime landscapes because the "pictorializing" of nature, the reading of "the book of nature," was so clearly the intent of both verbal and visual artists. Robert Browning may have overstated the closeness of correspondences ("Does he paint? He fain would write a poem— / Does he write? He fain would paint a picture"), but the affinities, I think, are clear. Al-

13. Andrew Wilton, *Turner and the Sublime*, and Peter Bicknell, *Beauty, Horror, and Immensity: Picturesque Landscape in Britain*. In 1980 the Yale Center exhibited British landscapes titled, *Presences of Nature: British Landscape, 1780–1830*. The descriptive catalog by Louis Hawes includes a discussion of various sublime scenes and landscapes categorized by geographic place.

though we may not be able to argue *ut pictura poesis*, we can, I hope, admit some interactive relationships between visual and verbal modes in English romanticism, relationships that still continue to excite the imagination and provide possible explanations for our current perceptions.

Works Cited

Unless otherwise noted, all poetry citations are from David Perkins's *English Romantic Writers* (New York: Harcourt, Brace, 1967).

Abrams, M.H. *The Mirror and the Lamp: Romantic Theory and the Critical Tradition.* New York: W. W. Norton, 1953.

————. *Natural Supernaturalism: Tradition and Revolution in Romantic Literature.* New York: W. W. Norton, 1971.

Adams, Hazard. *William Blake: A Reading of the Shorter Poems.* Seattle: University of Washington Press, 1963.

Albrecht, William Price. *The Sublime Pleasures of Tragedy: A Study of Critical Theory from Dennis to Keats.* Lawrence: The University Press of Kansas, 1975.

Allen, Glen O. "The Fall of Endymion: A Study of Keats' Intellectual Growth." *Keats-Shelley Journal* 6 (1957): 37–57.

Appleton, Jay. *The Experience of Landscape.* New York: John Wiley, 1957.

Auden, W. H. *The Enchafed Flood: Three Essays on the Romantic Spirit.* New York: Random House, 1967.

Badt, Kurt. *John Constable's Clouds.* London: Routledge and Kegan Paul, 1950.

Barrell, John. *The Idea of Landscape and the Sense of Place, 1730–1840.* Cambridge: Cambridge University Press, 1972.

Bate, Walter Jackson. *From Classic to Romantic: Premises of Taste in Eighteenth Century England.* Cambridge, Mass.: Harvard University Press, 1946.

Beer, John. *Blake's Visionary Universe.* Manchester, England: Manchester University Press, 1969.

————. *Coleridge, the Visionary.* 1959. Reprint. New York: Collier Books, 1962.

Berenson, Bernard. *Sketch for a Self-Portrait.* New York: Pantheon, 1949.

Bicknell, Peter. *Beauty, Horror and Immensity: Picturesque Landscape in Britain.* Cambridge: Cambridge University Press, 1981.

Blackstone, Bernard. *The Consecrated Urn: An Interpretation of Keats in Terms of Growth and Form.* London: Longmans, Green, 1959.

Bloom, Harold. *Agon: Towards a Theory of Revisionism.* New York: Oxford University Press, 1982.

————. *Blake's Apocalypse: A Study in Poetic Argument.* Garden City, N.Y.: Doubleday, 1963.

————. *Poetry and Repression.* New Haven: Yale University Press, 1976.

————. *Shelley's Mythmaking.* New Haven: Yale University Press, 1959.

————. *The Visionary Company: A Reading of English Romantic Poetry.* Garden City, N.Y.: Doubleday, 1961.

————. *Yeats.* New York: Oxford University Press, 1970.

Bloom, Harold, ed. *Romanticism and Consciousness: Essays in Criticism.* New York: W. W. Norton, 1970.

Boase, T. S. R. "Shipwrecks in English Romantic Painting." *Journal of the Warburg and Courtauld Institute* 22 (1959): 332–46.

Bonacina, L. W. C. "John Constable's Centenary: His Position as a Painter of Weather." *Quarterly Journal of the Royal Meteorological Society* 68 (1937): 483–90.

Bornstein, George. "Keats' Concept of *The Ethereal.*" *Keats-Shelley Journal* 18 (1969): 97–106.

Bradley, A. C. *Oxford Lectures on Poetry.* London: Macmillan, 1909.

Brisman, Leslie. *Romantic Origins.* Ithaca: Cornell University Press, 1978.

Brooks, Cleanth, and Warren, Robert Penn. *Understanding Poetry.* 3d ed. New York: Holt, Rinehart and Winston, 1960.

Brown, Wallace. "Byron and the English Interest in the Near East." *Studies in Philology* 34 (1937): 55–64.

Burke, Edmund. *A Philosophical Enquiry into the Origin of Our Ideas of the Sublime and Beautiful.* Edited by J. T. Boulton. 1857. Reprint. London: Routledge and Kegan Paul, 1958.

Butler, Eliza M. *Byron and Goethe.* London: Bowes and Bowes, 1956.

Byron, Lord (George Gordon). *The Poetical Works of Lord Byron.* Edited by E. H. Coleridge. London: John Murray, 1905.

————. *The Poetic and Dramatic Works of Lord Byron.* Edited by John Nicholas and J. C. Jeaffreson. Philadelphia: E. Claxton and Co., 1883.

————. *The Works of Lord Byron.* Edited by Rowland E. Prothero. London: John Murray, 1901.

Cajori, Florian. *A History of Mathematical Notations.* 1929. Reprint. Chicago: University of Chicago Press, 1952.

Campbell, Olwen. *Shelley and the Unromantics.* London: Methuen, 1924.

Clark, Kenneth. *Landscape into Art.* New York: Harper & Row, 1948.

————. *The Romantic Rebellion: Romantic versus Classic Art.* New York: Harper & Row, 1973.

Clay, Jean. *Romanticism.* New York: Vendome, 1981.

Cohn, Jan, and Miles, Thomas M. "The Sublime in Alchemy, Aesthetics and Psychoanalysis." *Modern Philology* 74 (1977): 289–304.

Cole, Thomas. "Essay on American Scenery." *The American Monthly Magazine.* n.s. 1 (1836): 6–14.

Coleridge, Samuel Taylor. *Biographia Literaria.* Edited by John Shawcross. London: Oxford University Press, 1967.

———. *Hints Towards The Formation of a more Comprehensive Theory of Life.* London: John Churchill, 1848.

———. *The Notebooks of Samuel Taylor Coleridge.* Edited by Kathleen Coburn. New York: Pantheon, 1957.

———. "Unpublished Fragments on Aesthetics." Edited by Thomas M. Raysor. *Studies in Philology* 22 (1925): 532–33.

Cozens, Alexander. *A New Method of Assisting the Invention in Drawing Original Compositions of Landscape.* Appended to A. P. Oppé, *Alexander and John Robert Cozens.* Cambridge, Mass.: Harvard University Press, 1954.

Crane, Ronald S. Review of *The Sublime: A Study of Critical Theories in Eighteenth-Century England* by Samuel Holt Monk. *Philological Quarterly* 15 (1935): 165–67.

Cummings, Frederick, and Staley, Allen. *Romantic Art in Britain: Paintings and Drawings, 1760–1860.* Exhibition Catalogue. Philadelphia: Philadelphia Museum of Art, 1968.

Curran, Stuart. *Shelley's Annus Mirabilis: The Maturing of an Epic Vision.* San Marino, Calif.: Huntington Library, 1975.

Curran, Stuart, and Wittreich, Joseph A. eds. *Blake's Sublime Allegory: Essays on "The Four Zoas," "Milton" and "Jerusalem."* Madison: University of Wisconsin Press, 1973.

Curtis, F. B. "Blake and the 'Moment of Time': An Eighteenth Century Controversy in Mathematics." *Philological Quarterly* 51 (1972): 460–70.

Damon, S. Foster. *A Blake Dictionary.* Providence, R.I.: Brown University Press, 1965.

De Luca, V. A. "The Style of Millennial Announcement in *Prometheus Unbound.*" *Keats-Shelley Journal* 28 (1979): 78–101.

Digby, George Wingfield. *Symbol and Image in William Blake.* Oxford: Oxford University Press, 1957.

Durr, R. A. *Poetic Vision and the Psychedelic Experience.* Syracuse, N.Y.: Syracuse University Press, 1970.

Emerson, Ralph Waldo. *The Complete Works of Ralph Waldo Emerson.* Centenary Edition. Edited by Edward Waldo Emerson. Boston: Houghton Mifflin, 1903–1904.

Empsom, William. *The Structure of Complex Words.* London: Chatto & Windus, 1964.

Ende, Stuart. *Keats and the Sublime.* New Haven: Yale University Press, 1976.

Evans, Frank B. "Thomas Taylor, Platonist of the Romantic Period."

PMLA 55 (1940): 1060–72.

Evert, Walter. *Aesthetic and Myth in the Poetry of Keats.* Princeton: Princeton University Press, 1965.

Feaver, William. *The Art of John Martin.* Oxford: Clarendon Press, 1975.

Ficino, Marcilio. *Opera Omnia.* 1576. Reprint. Torino, Italy: Photo reproduction, 1959.

Finley, Gerald. "The Genesis of Turner's 'Landscape Sublime.'" *Zeitschrift für Kunstgeschichte.* Berlin: Deutscher Kunstverlag, 1979.

Finney, Claude E. *The Evolution of Keats' Poetry.* Cambridge, Mass.: Harvard University Press, 1936.

Fischer, Ronald. "A Cartography of the Ecstatic and Meditative States." *Science* 174 (1971): 897–904.

Fogle, Richard Harter. *The Permanent Pleasure: Essays on Classics of Romanticism.* Athens: University of Georgia Press, 1974.

Ford, Newell F. "The Meaning of 'Fellowship with Essence' in *Endymion.*" *PMLA* 62 (1947): 1061–76.

Freud, Sigmund. *Gesammelte Werke: Chronologische geordnet.* London: Imago Publishing Co., 1940–1968.

———. *The Standard Edition of the Complete Psychological Works of Sigmund Freud.* Translated by James Strachey. London: Hogarth Press, 1955–1964.

Frye, Northrop. *Fearful Symmetry: A Study of William Blake.* Princeton: Princeton University Press, 1947.

———. *A Study of English Romanticism.* New York: Random House, 1968.

Gage, John. *Color in Turner: Poetry and Truth.* New York: Praeger, 1969.

Gaunt, William. *The Great Century of British Painting: Hogarth to Turner.* London: Phaidon, 1971.

———. *The Restless Century: Printing in Britain 1800–1900.* London: Phaidon, 1972.

Gilpin, William. *Observations, relative chiefly to picturesque beauty . . . in Cumberland and Westmoreland.* 1876. Reprint. London: Richmond Publishers, 1973.

Gombrich, Ernst Hans. *Art and Illusion: A Study in the Psychology of Pictorial Representation.* New York: Pantheon, 1960.

Grabo, Carl. *Prometheus Unbound: An Interpretation.* Chapel Hill: University of North Carolina Press, 1935.

Grant, John E. "Redemption Action in Blake's *Arlington Court Picture.*" *Studies in Romanticism* 10 (1971): 21–27.

———. "Studying Blake's Iconography for Guidance in Interpreting the *Arlington Court Picture.*" *Blake Newsletter* 4 (1970): 24–26.

Griggs, Earl Leslie, ed. *Wordsworth and Coleridge: Studies in Honor of*

George McLean Harper. Princeton: Princeton University Press, 1939.

Growing, Lawrence. *Turner: Imagination and Reality*. Garden City, N.Y.: Doubleday, 1966.

Harper, George M. *The Neoplatonism of William Blake*. Chapel Hill: University of North Carolina Press, 1961.

Hartman, Geoffrey H. *Beyond Formalism*. New Haven: Yale University Press, 1970.

———. "History-Writing as Answerable Style." *New Literary History* 2 (1970): 73–83.

———. "The Use and Abuse of Structural Analysis: Riffaterre's Interpretation of Wordsworth's *Yew Trees*." *New Literary History* 7 (1975): 165–89.

———. *Wordsworth's Poetry: 1787–1814*. New Haven: Yale University Press, 1964.

Hartman, Geoffrey H., ed. *New Perspectives on Coleridge and Wordsworth: Selected Papers from the English Institute*. New York: Columbia University Press, 1972.

———. *Psychoanalysis and the Question of the Text: Selected Papers from the English Institute 1976–77*. Baltimore: Johns Hopkins University Press, 1978.

Haughton, Hugh. "Review of Thomas Weiskel's *The Romantic Sublime*." *Times Literary Supplement*, 24 December 1976, p. 619.

Havens, Raymond Dexter. *The Mind of a Poet: A Study of Wordsworth's Thought*. Baltimore: Johns Hopkins University Press, 1941.

Hawes, Louis. *Presences of Nature 1780–1830*. Exhibition Catalogue. New Haven: Yale Center of British Art, 1982.

Haydon, Benjamin Robert. *Diary*. Edited by W. B. Pope. Cambridge, Mass.: Harvard University Press, 1963.

Heffernan, James A. W. "Reflections on Reflections in English Romantic Poetry and Painting." *Bucknell Review* 23 (1978): 15–37.

———. "Wordsworth on the Sublime: The Quest for Interfusion." *Studies in English Literature* 12 (1967): 605–15.

Hipple, Walter John, Jr. *The Beautiful, the Sublime, and the Picturesque in Eighteenth-Century British Aesthetic Theory*. Carbondale: Southern Illinois University Press, 1957.

Hofmann, Werner. *Art in the Nineteenth Century*. Translated by Brian Battershaw. London: Faber and Faber, 1961.

Honour, Hugh. *Romanticism*. New York: Harper and Row, 1979.

Hughes, Daniel J. "Potentiality in *Prometheus Unbound*." *Studies in Romanticism* 2 (1963): 107–26.

Hume, Robert Ernest. *The World's Living Religions*. New York: Scribner's, 1955.

Hungerford, Edward B. *Shores of Darkness*. New York: Columbia University Press, 1941.

Hunt, John Dixon. *The Figure in the Landscape: Poetry, Painting and Gardening in the Eighteenth Century.* Baltimore: Johns Hopkins University Press, 1976.

————. "Wondrous Deep and Dark: Turner and the Sublime." *Georgia Review* 30 (1976): 139–64.

Hussey, Christopher. *The Picturesque: Studies in a Point of View.* 1927. Reprint. Hamden, Conn.: Archon Books, 1967.

Iamblichus. *On the Mysteries of the Egyptians, Chaldeans and Assyrians.* 2d edition. Translated by Thomas Taylor. London: B. Dobell, 1895.

James, William. *Varieties of Religious Experience.* London: Longman, Green and Co., 1929.

Keats, John. *The Letters of John Keats.* Edited by Hyder Rollins. Cambridge, Mass.: Harvard University Press, 1958.

Ker, William Paton. *The Art of Poetry.* Oxford: Clarendon Press, 1923.

King-Hele, Desmond. *Shelley: His Thought and Work.* London: Macmillan, 1960.

Kroeber, Karl. *Romantic Landscape Vision: Constable and Wordsworth.* Madison: University of Wisconsin Press, 1975.

Kroeber, Karl, and Walling, William, eds. *Images of Romanticism: Verbal and Visual Affinities.* New Haven: Yale University Press, 1978.

Kuhn, Albert J. "English Deism and the Development of Romantic Mythological Syncretism." *PMLA* 71 (1956): 1094–1116.

Laing, R. D. *The Politics of Experience.* New York: Pantheon, 1967.

Lamb, Charles. *Works of Charles and Mary Lamb.* Edited by E. V. Lucas. London: Methuen, 1930.

Lanier, Sidney. *Works.* Edited by Clarence Gohdes and Kemp Malone. Baltimore: Johns Hopkins University Press, 1945.

Laski, Marghanita. *Ecstasy: A Study of Some Secular and Religious Experiences.* Bloomington: Indiana University Press, 1962.

————. *Everyday Ecstasy.* London: Thames and Hudson, 1980.

Le Bris, Michel. *Romantics and Romanticism.* New York: Rizzoli, 1980.

Lowes, John Livingston. *The Road to Xanadu: A Study in the Ways of the Imagination.* 1930. Reprint. Boston: Houghton Mifflin, 1964.

McElderry, Bruce R., Jr. "Coleridge's Revision of *The Ancient Mariner.*" *Studies in Philology* 29 (1932): 68–94.

McShine, Kynaston, ed. *The Natural Paradise: Painting in America 1800–1950.* Exhibition Catalogue. New York: The Museum of Modern Art, 1976.

Malins, Edward. *English Landscaping and Literature, 1660–1840.* London: Oxford University Press, 1965.

Manwaring, Elizabeth Wheeler. *Italian Landscape in Eighteenth Century England: A Study Chiefly of the Influence of Claude Lorrain and Salvator Rosa on English Taste, 1700–1800.* 1925. Reprint. London: Oxford University Press, 1965.

Marshall, William H. Notes to *Lord Byron: Selected Poems and Letters.* Boston: Houghton Mifflin, 1968.

Mellor, Anne K. *Blake's Human Form Divine.* Berkeley: University of California Press, 1974.

Mengs, Anton Raphael. *Works.* Translated by Joseph d'Azara. London: R. Faelder, 1796.

Meredith, James Creed. *Kant's "Critiques of Aesthetic Judgement."* Oxford: Clarendon Press, 1911.

Miner, Dorothy, ed. *Studies in Art and Literature for Bella da Costa Greene.* Princeton: Princeton University Press, 1954.

Modiano, Raimonda. "Coleridge and the Sublime." *Wordsworth Circle* 9 (1978): 110–20.

Monk, Samuel Holt. *The Sublime: A Study of Critical Theories in Eighteenth-Century England.* 1935. Reprint. Ann Arbor: University of Michigan Press, 1957.

Moore, George Foot. *History of Religions.* New York: Scribner's, 1922.

Moore, Thomas. *Letters.* Edited by Wilfred S. Dowden. Oxford: Clarendon Press, 1964.

Morris, David B. *The Religious Sublime: Christian Poetry and Critical Traditions in Eighteenth Century.* Lexington: University of Kentucky Press, 1972.

Neufeldt, Leonard. "Poetry as Subversion: The Unbinding of Shelley's Prometheus." *Anglia* 95 (1977): 60–86.

Newman, Barnett. "The First Man Was an Artist." *The Tiger's Eye* I, 1 (1947): 57–60.

———. "The Sublime Is Now." *The Tiger's Eye* I, 6 (1948): 51–53.

Nicholson, Marjorie Hope. *Mountain Gloom and Mountain Glory: The Development of the Aesthetics of the Infinite.* Ithaca: Cornell University Press, 1959.

Nicholson, William. *First Principles of Chemistry.* 2d ed. London: R. Phillips, 1792.

Nicolson, Benedict. *Joseph Wright of Derby: Painter of Light.* New York: Pantheon, 1968.

Novak, Barbara. "American Landscape: Changing Concepts of the Sublime." *The American Art Journal* 4 (1972): 36–42.

———. *Nature and Culture: American Landscape and Painting, 1825–1875.* New York: Oxford University Press, 1980.

Nuttall, A. D. *The Common Sky: Philosophy and the Literary Imagination.* Berkeley: University of California Press, 1974.

Oppé, A. P. *Alexander and John Robert Cozens.* Cambridge, Mass.: Harvard University Press, 1954.

Owen, W. J. B. "The Sublime and the Beautiful in *The Prelude.*" *The Wordsworth Circle* 4 (1973): 67–86.

———. "Wordsworth's Aesthetics of Landscape." *The Wordsworth Circle* 7 (1976): 70–83.

Ower, John. "The Aesthetic Hero: His Innocence, Fall, and Redemption." *Bucknell Review* 23 (1977): 96–115.

Paffard, Michael. *Inglorious Wordsworths: A Study of Some Transcendental Experiences in Childhood and Adolescence.* London: Hodder and Stoughton, 1973.

Paley, Morton. "Tyger of Wrath." *PMLA* 81 (1966): 540–51.

Patterson, Charles I. *The Daemonic in the Poetry of John Keats.* Urbana: University of Illinois Press, 1970.

Paulson, Ronald. *Emblem and Expression: Meaning in English Art of the Eighteenth Century.* Cambridge, Mass.: Harvard University Press, 1975.

———. *Literary Landscape: Turner and Constable.* New Haven: Yale University Press, 1982.

Peckham, Morse. *Romanticism: The Culture of the Nineteenth Century.* New York: George Braziller, 1965.

Pendred, Mary Q. *John Martin, Painter.* New York: E. P. Dutton, 1923.

Peterfreund, Stuart. "Wordsworth and the Sublime of Duration." *Publications of the Arkansas Philological Association* 2 (1976): 41–46.

Price, Martin. "The Sublime Poem: Pictures and Powers." *Yale Review* 58 (1968): 194–213.

Price, Uvedale. *Essays on the Picturesque, as Compared with the Sublime and the Beautiful. . . .* London: J. Mawman, 1810.

Quennell, Peter. *Romantic England: Writing and Printing 1717–1851.* New York: Macmillan, 1970.

Quinlan, Maurice. "Byron's *Manfred* and Zoroastrianism." *Journal of English and Germanic Philology* 57 (1958): 726–38.

Raine, Kathleen. *Blake and Tradition.* Princeton: Princeton University Press, 1969.

Raine, Kathleen, and Harper, George M., eds. *Thomas Taylor the Platonist: Selected Writings.* Princeton: Princeton University Press, 1969.

Raysor, Thomas M. "Unpublished Fragments on Aesthetics by S. T. Coleridge." *Studies in Philology* 22 (1925): 529–37.

Regueiro, Helen. *The Limits of Imagination: Wordsworth, Yeats, and Stevens.* Ithaca: Cornell University Press, 1976.

Reiman, Donald H. *Percy Bysshe Shelley.* New York: Twayne, 1969.

Reiman, Donald H., et al., eds. *The Evidence of the Imagination: Studies of Interactions between Life and Art in English Romantic Literature.* New York: New York University Press, 1978.

Reynolds, Graham. *Constable: The Natural Painter.* New York: McGraw-Hill, 1965.

Reynolds, Joshua. *Discourses on Art.* Edited by Robert Wark. San Marino, Calif.: Huntington Library, 1959.

Richards, I. A. *Beyond.* New York: Harcourt Brace Jovanovich, 1974.

Riffaterre, Michael. "Interpretation and Descriptive Poetry: A Reading of Wordsworth's *Yew Trees.*" *New Literary History* 4 (1973): 230–56.

Robinson, Charles E. *Shelley and Byron: The Snake and Eagle Wreathed in Flight.* Baltimore: Johns Hopkins University Press, 1976.

Robinson, Henry Crabbe. *Diary.* Edited by Derek Hudson. London: Oxford University Press, 1967.

Rodman, Selden. *Conversations with Artists.* New York: Devin-Adair, 1957.

Rosenblum, Robert. "The Abstract Sublime." *Art News* 59 (1961): 39–40, 56–57.

———. *Modern Painting and the Northern Romantic Tradition: Friedrich to Rothko.* New York: Harper and Row, 1975.

Rosenthal, Michael. *British Landscape Painting.* Oxford: Phaidon, 1982.

Ruoff, Gene W. "Wordsworth's *Yew Trees,* and Romantic Perception." *Modern Language Quarterly* 34 (1973): 146–60.

Ruskin, John. *Modern Painters.* New York: Frederick Quimby Co., 1856.

Rutherford, Andrew. *Byron: A Critical Study.* Stanford: Stanford University Press, 1961.

Schiller, Friedrich von. *Essays Aesthetical and Philosophical.* Anonymous Translator. London: G. Bell & Sons, 1882.

Scoggins, James. *Imagination and Fancy: Complementary Modes in the Poetry of Wordsworth.* Lincoln: University of Nebraska Press, 1966.

Shaffer, Elinor S. "Coleridge's Revolution in the Standard of Taste." *Journal of Aesthetics and Art Criticism* 28 (1969): 213–23.

Shelley, Percy Bysshe. *The Poetical Works of Percy Bysshe Shelley.* Edited by Edward Dowden. New York: T. Y. Crowell, 1893.

Simmons, Robert, and Warner, Janet. "Blake's *Arlington Court Picture:* The Moment of Truth." *Studies in Romanticism* 10 (1971): 3–21.

Slater, J. "Shelley and *Prometheus Unbound.*" *Month* 50 (1884): 181–93, 383–95.

Southey, Robert. "Review of Lyrical Ballads." *Critical Review* 24 (1798): 197–204.

Sperry, Stuart M. "Byron and the Meaning of *Manfred.*" *Criticism* 16 (1974): 189–202.

———. *Keats the Poet.* Princeton: Princeton University Press, 1973.

Stewart, Dugald. *Philosophical Essays.* 3d ed. Edinburgh: A. Constable and Co., 1818.

Still, Clyfford. *Catalogue of Exhibition.* Philadelphia: Institute of Contemporary Art, University of Pennsylvania, 1963.

Stillinger, Jack. Introduction to *Twentieth Century Interpretations of Keats' Odes.* Englewood Cliffs, N.J.: Prentice-Hall, 1968.

Sutherland, John H. "Blake's *Mental Traveller.*" *ELH* 22 (1955): 136–47.

Tart, Charles T. *Altered States of Consciousness.* Garden City, N.Y.: Doubleday, 1972.

Taylor, Thomas. Notes to Iamblichus, *On the Mysteries of the Egyptians, Chaldeans and Assyrians.* 2d ed. London: B. Dobell, 1895.

Turner, Victor. *Dramas, Fields and Metaphors: Symbolic Action in Human Society.* Ithaca: Cornell University Press, 1974.

Tuveson, Ernest Lee. *The Imagination as a Means of Grace: Locke and the Aesthetics of Romanticism.* Berkeley: University of California Press, 1960.

Twitchell, James B. "The Metaphysical Pattern of Act IV, *Prometheus Unbound.*" *Keats-Shelley Journal* 24 (1975): 29–48.

———. "The Supernatural Structure of Byron's *Manfred.*" *Studies in English Literature* 15 (1975): 601–15.

———. "The World above the Ancient Mariner." *Texas Studies in Literature and Language* 17 (1975): 103–17.

Van Zandt, Ronald. *The Catskill Mountain House.* New Brunswick, N.J.: Rutgers University Press, 1966.

Vaughan, William. *Romantic Art.* New York: Oxford University Press, 1978.

Walpole, Horace. *Anecdotes of Painting in England . . . to which is added The History of Modern Taste in Gardening.* London: Chatto, 1771.

Warner, Deborah Jean. "The Landscape Mirror and Glass." *Antiques* 105 (1974): 158–59.

Warren, Robert Penn. "A Poem of Pure Imagination: An Experiment in Reading." 1946. Reprinted in *Twentieth Century Interpretations of the Rime of the Ancient Mariner.* Edited by James D. Boulger. Englewood Cliffs, N.J.: Prentice-Hall, 1969.

Wasserman, Earl. *Shelley: A Critical Reading.* Baltimore: Johns Hopkins University Press, 1971.

Waterhouse, John Walters. *Zoroastrianism.* London: The Epworth Press, 1934.

Watson, John Richard. *Picturesque Landscape and English Romantic Poetry.* London: Hutchinson, 1970.

Watts, Alan. *This Is It and Other Essays on Zen.* New York: Pantheon, 1960.

Weiskel, Thomas. *The Romantic Sublime: Studies in the Structure and Psychology of Transcendence.* Baltimore: Johns Hopkins University Press, 1976.

White, John, ed. *The Highest State of Consciousness.* New York: Doubleday, 1972.

Whitley, William T. *Artists and Their Friends in England 1700–1799.* London: The Medici Society, 1928.

Whitman, Walt. *Specimen Days.* 1882. Reprint. Boston: D. R. Godine, 1971.

Wilmerding, John, ed. *American Light: The Luminist Movement.* Exhibition Catalogue. New York: Harper and Row, 1981.

Wilton, Andrew. *Turner and the Sublime.* Exhibition Catalogue. London: British Museum Publications, 1980.

Wlecke, Albert O. *Wordsworth and the Sublime.* Berkeley: University of California Press, 1973.

Wordsworth, Dorothy. *Journals.* Edited by Ernest de Selincourt. London: Macmillan, 1941.

Wordsworth, William. *The Poetical Works of William Wordsworth.* Edited by Ernest de Selincourt. Oxford: Clarendon Press, 1944.

————. *The Prose Works of William Wordsworth.* Edited by W. J. B. Owen and Jane Worthington Smyser. Oxford: Clarendon Press, 1974.

Yeats, William Butler. *Pages from a Diary Written in Nineteen Hundred and Thirty.* Dublin: Cuala Press, 1944.

————. *A Vision.* London: Macmillan, 1925.

Index